4.50

A FIRST COURSE IN BUSINESS ORGANISATION

By the same author

Economics from Square One
(with John Coy)

A First Course in Business Organisation

EDITED BY ALAN DAVIES
B.A.(Admin.), M.A.(Econ.), D.A.S.E., F.C.I.S., F.R.S.A.

WITH CONTRIBUTIONS FROM

Brian Johnson, Distribution Development Manager, Massey-Ferguson (U.K.) Ltd.

John Kelly, B.A.(Econ.), Senior Lecturer in Economic History, Manchester Polytechnic

Norman Matthews, M.Inst.M., Director, Ben Turner Tractors Ltd.

John Swinburne, M.A., M.B.C.S., Principal Lecturer in Computer Studies, Manchester Polytechnic

Norman Thornton, M.A., F.C.W.A., A.M.B.I.M., M.I.O.M., Principal Lecturer in Accountancy, Manchester Polytechnic

Brian Underdown, B.A., M.A., A.C.W.A., Lecturer in Accounting, University of Sheffield

Arthur Williams, B.A.(Econ), M.A.(Manpower), D.P.A., A.C.I.S. Principal, Pembrokeshire Technical College

London
GEORGE ALLEN & UNWIN
Boston   Sydney

First published in 1971
Eighth impression 1981

GEORGE ALLEN & UNWIN LTD
40 Museum Street, London WC1A 1LU

© George Allen & Unwin (Publishers) Ltd, 1971

ISBN 0 04 658036 0 Hardback
     0 04 658037 9 Paperback

Printed in Great Britain
in 10 point Times Roman
by Billing and Sons Ltd, Guildford, Surrey

CONTENTS

PREFACES

TO THE STUDENT

Business Organisation appears under many guises and a variety of names amongst the examinations that young people are required to take at an early stage in their careers. Often, the subject causes difficulty, especially when it comes to written work, because young students do not have much business experience to draw on.

In this book we have tried to present the theory and practice of business enterprise side by side so that the text relates to what is going on now in firms all over the country. Although we have written this book primarily to help students following courses in Business Studies, we have also borne in mind the needs of young students who may use this book as part of a course in General Studies and who need a straightforward account of the main problem areas that managers are employed to deal with.

Whilst you are using this book you will find it useful to maintain a file of clippings from newspapers and journals as a record of current developments in the business field which will provide you with illustrative material for essays. For this purpose we recommend that you should use in particular (either individually, or in groups) *The Financial Times*, *The Sunday Times*, the *Observer*, *The Economist*, and *Management Today*.

At the end of each chapter you will find further reading references and test questions. In the Appendix you will find some hints on examination technique and a further battery of text questions. We hope that what you will learn from this book will help you not only in your examinations but also in your future career, by unravelling some of the complicated relationships that make up a successful business organisation.

TO THE TEACHER

We have attempted, in this book, to provide the framework for a one-year course in Business Organisation. We are mainly concerned with the needs of young students who have either no experience at all of the workings of business enterprise, or whose experience is very limited because they have just started work.

We have tried to do two things: first, to present an intelligible survey of the disciplines which are involved in business to help the student appreciate the inter-relationships that exist between them; second, to fulfil the requirements of examinations at this level.

Most of the examples we have chosen for the purpose of illustration relate to large manufacturing companies in the private sector, because we have found that this context is the most suitable for class discussions and as a basis for written work.

Our contributions in this exercise are made on the basis of personal experience in the specialisms which we have identified, together with the experience of teaching and examining the subject, both in college and in the national professional associations. Our experience as employees in business, as students, teachers and examiners has led us to identify what we feel to be a real need for an introduction to the subject which assumes no previous direct experience of the workings of business, which relates to what the student is likely to find out about the world in general and British business in particular from the press, radio and television and which is orientated towards the needs of a course of study in a technical college or a college of further education.

Each chapter ends with a short reading list and a set of exercises. The Appendix contains a revision programme and a selection of questions set by colleges and various professional associations. The references selected for further reading have been chosen carefully to provide a progression which we hope the student will find stimulating and rewarding and which will enable him to make good use of libraries, an aspect which we consider to be an essential element of any course of study.

This presentation, we feel, will serve particularly the needs of students following courses for the H.N.C. and H.N.D. in Business Studies, courses organised for the N.E.B.S.S. and under the terms of the T.O.P.S. and also those following graduate secretarial courses. We have also kept in mind the needs of students following courses in General Studies and this book may also prove useful as an introductory text in other contexts.

We record our grateful thanks to the Association of Certified Accountants, the Chartered Institute of Secretaries, the Institute of Cost and Management Accountants, the Royal Society of Arts, the Institute of Marketing and the Union of Lancashire and Cheshire

Institutes for permission to reproduce questions from their respective examination papers, to Mrs Joan Clarke, who typed the final manuscript and to Mr Stanley Miller, B.Sc.(Econ.), Lecturer in Economic History at Oldham College of Technology for his help with the drawings.

CHAPTER ONE

First Principles

ALL FORMS of human enterprise have certain basic features in common. The problems that arise in the management of a business undertaking also crop up in the management of social clubs, religious organisations and government undertakings, even though there may be differences in scale. In this book we have chosen to illustrate these problems largely in the context of big public companies, because we have found that this type of business organisation lends itself most easily to an understanding of the subject.

1.1 WHAT IS AN ORGANISATION?

An **organisation** is a set or group of arrangements according to which work is divided up in order to achieve some single objective, or group of objectives. If you are reading this book because you are following a course of study at the end of which you will be required to take examinations in one or more subjects, you will need some method to enable you to divide your time between reading, note taking, writing essays and revision and you may also wish to provide some time for sleep, meals and leisure activities. The method you adopt to use the time at your disposal is an example of organisation; it is a means of allocating resources to some specific end.

The term **business organisation** relates the task of splitting up work to the achievement of specific business objectives, of which the most important is earning profit as a result of producing goods or services. In any incorporated company the objectives of the business and the framework within which the company must operate are set out in documents which are prepared when the company is formed, the **memorandum** and **articles of association** of the company (see page 217). This framework regulates the activities of the **Board of Directors,** who are elected by the **shareholders**. The Board of Directors, in turn, usually appoint a **managing director,** who is the chief executive of the company and who may, or may not, be a member of the Board.

Obviously, in a complicated business enterprise, the Managing

13

Director cannot do everything himself, he may have to depend on the activities of thousands of other people. His first task, therefore, is to find some basis of dividing up work amongst his subordinates and this is achieved through a network of positions called an **executive system**. The activities within this network must be co-ordinated in such a way as to ensure that the the organisation carries out the instructions of the Board of Directors to the satisfaction of the shareholders.

In a large company this is achieved by **departmentalisation**, that is, the grouping together of jobs under different specialisms. These specialisms are co-ordinated by a hierarchy, or **chain of command**, a formal communication structure that enables instructions to be passed downwards and information to be passed upwards to senior management. Figure 1.1 below shows the main departmental divi-

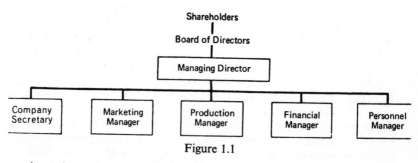

Figure 1.1

sions that are commonly found in manufacturing companies. The boxes represent executive positions, the lines represent the formal channels of communication between them. Each of these specialist areas of management have their own individual characteristics and in each of them there are, in Britain, one or more professional organisations who are concerned with the promotion of the interests of management in these specialised fields by offering qualifications by examination, information on new developments published in their journals, by conferences and by sponsoring programmes of research (e.g. The Association of Certified Accountants, The Chartered Institute of Secretaries, The Institute of Cost and Management Accountants, The Institute of Marketing). The sub-specialisms within these broad divisions are described in the following chapters.

These specialist divisions do not have equal prominence in every type of company. In deciding what departments are essential, management must be guided by the main objectives of the business. Thus, some companies, Imperial Chemical Industries Ltd., for example, are organised on the basis of separate product divisions (see page 21); companies manufacturing electronic components tend to have large and highly specialised research departments; in an iron foundry making castings for a small group of industrial customers the marketing function might well be one of the jobs of the managing director. Organisation is thus a function of the work to be done; in a business enterprise the organisation will reflect the nature of the markets in which the firm is competing.

Characteristics of big organisations

A German sociologist, Max Weber, used the term **bureaucracy** to describe large organisations. A bureaucracy is a large organisation of any kind (e.g. a large manufacturing company, a department in the Civil Service, a large bank, the Roman Catholic Church), which has specific features not found in small organisations. These special features are:

(a) A set of prescribed rules and administrative regulations which provide guidance for the members of the organisation and ensure that uniform standards are maintained.

(b) An arrangement of individual jobs into a hierarchy in which different levels of graded authority are recognised.

(c) A system of written records, which provide precedents to guide actions in the future. The term **bureau** is sometimes used as a synonymn for **office**, the essential features of which are an administrative unit composed of officials plus written records which guide and record their actions as members of an organisation.

(d) A system of positions through which the work of the organisation is carried out, called **executive roles.** A member of an organisation is in his executive role when he is doing his appointed job, and in a large organisation the system of executive roles exists independently of the people who may fill them. If a company changes by expanding into new markets, or developing new techniques of production, the organisational system may have to be changed. New roles may have to be added (e.g. Export Sales Manager, Computer Programmer) and some roles disappear, in which case the roles become redundant.

In large organisations each executive role, from office cleaner to managing director, requires qualifications of some sort which form the basis for the selection of candidates for a particular vacancy.

(e) A system whereby **power** and **authority** are distributed in such a way as to enable the organisation to achieve its objectives. **Power** may be defined as the capacity to change individual or group

15

behaviour; **authority** may be defined as **legalised power** which, in a business enterprise, derives from the owners of the business because they provide the resources to create the company.

An **organisation chart** is a diagrammatic representation of the formal relationships that link the different executive roles in an organisation. **Managerial authority** is the power which the managerial role assumes, power having been *delegated* from some superior source (some higher managerial position), and ultimate authority remaining in the hands of the owners of the business (who are, in a public company, the shareholders).

Each executive role in the organisation is accorded some **status** that is to say, some attributes which enable one position in the organisation to be related to the others. Status is displayed in several different ways, by the use of titles, by the right to a separate office, a company car, by the use of different coloured overalls, by the use of different canteens, etc.

All the features (a)–(e) above are common to all bureaucracies and will be found in every large business organisation in some form or variation.

Business Objectives

The only way in which the efficiency of an organisation can be assessed is by discovering ways of measuring how successful it is in achieving its objectives. A clear statement of objectives is thus a necessary prerequisite to the setting up of an organisation.

All business enterprises have as their primary objective the achievement of a **profit goal,** a rate of earnings yielding an income which is satisfactory to the shareholders. Classical economic theory assumes that the primary objective of the business firm is to *maximise profit*; more recent theories reject this view and they seem to be borne out by the general reluctance of businesses to compete by cutting prices. Businessmen seem to prefer to operate in markets where prices are stable and to confine their competitive activities to other fields, such as to improving the quality of the product, to cutting costs, to improving the effectiveness of advertising and related matters.

Business enterprises may have other objectives as well. They may seek to promote stability and contentment in the labour force (by providing welfare facilities, Christmas parties, works outings), to capture specific markets, to lead in the introduction of new products, to maintain or improve a product's share of the market, but all these objectives are essentially secondary in importance. If all these secondary objectives are achieved and the shareholders, because the rate of return on investment is not satisfactory, become critical, then the organisation will find it increasingly difficult to raise new capital when required and the company may even be taken over by a rival.

There are clear advantages to the company in specifying objectives in terms which leave no room for doubt. By the mere process of recording objectives, apparent contradictions may be illuminated and reconciled and organisational purposes clarified. The recording of objectives makes it possible for subsidiary objectives to be identified and these in turn make it easier to develop criteria against which performance can be measured. For example, within a company's aim of increasing net profit by 10 per cent next year, various subsidiary targets will be set for individual divisions within the company. The Marketing Division may be charged with the task of increasing the sales of one of the products by 10 per cent, in order to provide its individual contribution to the achievement of the overall target. This is an example of the application of **management by objectives,** where key areas in a business are set specific targets and where performance against these targets is measured and reported at regular intervals.

Decision Making, Policy and Administration

So that objectives may be achieved, decisions must be taken at all levels within a company. Decision-making is a process where a choice is made between several possible courses of action; if there are no alternatives, there can be no decision. Decisions produce a pattern according to which scarce resources are allocated and it is possible to categorise decisions according to a time scale. The results of some decisions are apparent very quickly (for instance, the decision to press a button on a conveyor belt which is unattended in a soap factory will soon produce a heap of cartons of soap powder on the shop floor), the results of other decisions may take years to emerge (such as the decision whether or not to develop a new product). Naturally, decisions of the second category are reserved to the higher levels of an organisation.

Members of a business organisation are not completely free to take decisions on the allocation of company resources; the process of decision-making is subject to company policy. **Policy** defines what people in each executive role in the organisation must or must not do and therefore sets boundaries so that the decision-maker (from the charge hand on the shop floor to the managing director) is aware when he may use his own discretion and when he must refer

17

to some superior authority. Policy is, therefore, a guide to decision-making and provides the framework for planning. The term **company policy** describes those guidelines written into the Memorandum and Articles of Association of the company, plus major decisions made by the board of directors and approved by the shareholders. Policy is said to be *imposed* when it derives from legal requirements or from sources outside the organisation, *originated* when it is developed within the organisation. **Policy decisions** are made at all management levels in order to guide the activities of subordinates. Clearly, all policies should reflect and interpret the objectives of the company and preferably they should be written, because there is a danger that policies may be established by custom whenever people work together in groups. For example, it might be company policy to finish the working day at the usual time on Christmas Eve. If, however, for the past three years office parties have broken out spontaneously at lunchtime and no penalties have been incurred by anyone during that time, a new policy has been established by implication!

The following are some examples of decision areas which are normally covered by explicit policy statements:

(a) Identification of the range of products/services which the company offers on the market
(b) Pricing
(c) Methods of selling and distributing the product/service
(d) Whether or not to buy or make raw materials or unfinished goods
.(e) Whether to lease or buy plant and equipment
(f) Methods of raising finance
(g) Methods of selecting and training staff

The following are examples of documents in which policies are normally recorded:

(a) Memorandum and Articles of Association
(b) Internal memoranda
(c) Organisation Manuals
(d) Annual Reports
(e) Employee handbooks
(f) Promotional literature and advertisements

Policies may also be expressed orally in shareholders' meetings, training courses and committee meetings.

Administration is the design, installation and carrying out of procedures in order to implement decisions as economically as possible. **Administrative decisions** are decisions made at every management level to achieve the minimum amount of waste in the execution of company policy. The term **management** is often used in two senses, as a name for a category of leaders in industrial society (we speak, for instance, of 'management' and 'labour'), and as a name for an *activity* another name for the science of directing human activities in such a way as to achieve objectives most economically.

If you call to mind a company with which you are familiar, you will be aware that it consists of three main groups of people: the directors, the managers and the group sometimes referred to as *operatives*, who carry out manual and clerical tasks. The directors are concerned with policy at the highest level: what to produce, how to produce, how to sell, and their decisions are subject to the approval of the shareholders, especially in smaller companies. (In larger companies, if shares are divided between many small shareholders, control over the directors is more remote). The second group, the managers (sometimes called *executives*), are concerned with executing the policy laid down for them by the directors. These executives are themselves organized into a hierarchy of managers, supervisors, section leaders, foremen, chargehands and others, each of whom has an area of discretion defined by his superior. The third group work with limited powers of discretion under the supervision of the managers.

The activity of management has received a great deal of attention since World War I for several reasons. The development of mass production processes created special problems on a scale not encountered previously and, therefore, a search for 'principles' to guide managers in their jobs. Managers were under great pressure to reduce costs during the Depression, and in the period since World War II managers have had to cope with the problems of acute labour shortage, as governments have learnt how to maintain 'full employment'. A decisive influence has been the stimulation by governments of the application of science in industry, first as part of the war effort in World War II and subsequently in massive spending programmes on defence and in the race to conquer space. These huge projects have produced new science-based concerns which have in turn increased the demand for better qualified and experienced managers.

The Functions of the Manager

The basic functions common to managers in every type of enterprise were identified by Henri Fayol (a French mining engineer),

19

whose analysis, based on observing the work of the managing director of an iron and steel corporation in France, was published in 1916. The functions he identified are sometimes rendered into a mnemonic, POSDCORB, and they are as follows:

Planning: Selecting objectives and policies for the future. A separate section is devoted to this subject at the end of this chapter.

Organising: Establishing an organisational structure to do a specific job of work.

Staffing: Developing policies for recruitment, remuneration, promotion, welfare, etc.

Directing: Supervising and helping subordinates to make the maximum contribution to the objectives of the organisation.

Co-ordinating: Identifying deviations from plans, devising means of correcting errors and of taking corrective action to make sure that similar errors do not recur.

Reporting: Ensuring that senior management have sufficient information to enable them to guide the enterprise.

Budgeting: Preparing detailed estimates of expenditure and income to facilitate control and to enable forecasts to be made of future trends.

In carrying out these functions managers are required to be *responsible*. **Responsibility** is an obligation, which arises from the fact that a manager is required to perform certain functions by his superior. It follows that authority must be commensurate with responsibility. Responsibility may not be delegated. If a managerial function is delegated to Manager A and he in turn delegates it to his subordinate, B, and B performs the function incorrectly, perhaps incurring considerable financial loss, it is A who is held to be accountable because he accepted the responsibility in the first place. Managers are required by law to manage in the best interests of the shareholders, but they also have wider responsibilities, to their subordinates, to customers and also to the public at large.

1.2 ORGANISATION THEORY
Management Principles

The principles discussed in this section are derived from the writings of Fayol and Taylor, the originators of the movement in favour of 'scientific management' in the years before World War I, developed to solve the organisational problems which emerged as firms grew rapidly in size because of mergers and changes in production techniques. Taylor and later writers developed up to thirty 'principles' which might be applied to a given management problem. They are not principles in the sense of fundamental truth or general laws, but, in essence, general guidelines which deserve consideration; they are not blue-prints for action and they do not embody a settled doctrine. Some of these principles are identified individually in this section; they all arise from the demands imposed by any system which requires some degree of specialisation.

Specialisation

This provides a basis for efficiency. Output can be increased by breaking down tasks into simple repetitive jobs performed with the help of specialised equipment. As a result, the worker may increase both the quality and the quantity of his output because he is dealing constantly with problems that are closely related. Specialisation, whether in factory, office, school or hospital gives rise to the need for departmentalisation (see page 14) and groupings may be made on the basis of:

(a) *Function:* All companies allow for the grouping of specialists under the main enterprise functions identified in Figure 1.1.

(b) *Territory:* Businesses which serve a wide geographical area usually need some form of regional organisation to maintain contact with local markets.

(c) *Product:* Large and diverse manufacturing companies often divide their activities between product divisions (I.C.I. Ltd has separate divisions for Paints, Alkalis, Dyestuffs, Pharmaceuticals and other products).

(d) *Clientele:* Grouping may be based on categories of customer; as many insurance companies have different departments to deal with accident, fire, motor, life insurance claims, etc.

These groupings are not, of course, mutually exclusive and several different types of grouping may be found within a single company. You may find it helpful to consider what groupings would be appropriate to the task of providing:

Medicinal products for sick children
Machinery repair services to farmers
Transistor radios to teenagers
Surgery for patients with a rare disease
Supersonic aircraft to foreign governments.

Co-ordination

When tasks are divided up into units, some means must be found to ensure that the efforts of each unit are co-ordinated to achieve the objectives of the organisation. Co-ordination is achieved by means of

21

a hierarchy of executive roles, a chain of command. This may be illustrated by means of the organisation chart, Figure 1.2. Each of the boxes in this figure represents an executive role. The activities of Q, R and S are co-ordinated by N; in turn N is responsible to E, E to B and B to A. This is an illustration of the **principle of hierarchy**: each man has only one boss.

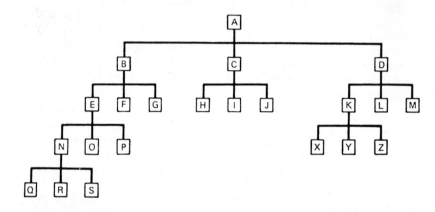

Figure 1.2

The organisation chart records lines of formal authority and responsibility and shows how functions within an organisation are distributed. Most organisation charts take the form of a pyramid of rectangular boxes, which give positions, titles, ranks, names of persons holding each executive role and sometimes a brief description of the responsibilities of each role. Organisation charts are useful as an aid to management for the following reasons:

(a) The task of charting frequently reveals inconsistencies and anomalies and brings them to the attention of management, who might otherwise not have noticed them.

(b) Charts teach how a company is organised and provide a convenient sketch of the entire structure.

(c) Charts help individual members of an organisation to identify themselves with the organisation, provide suggestions as to possible paths of promotion and clarify formal communication channels.

There are, however, important limitations to the use of organisation charts:

(a) A diagram of formal relationships between executive roles is not much use without a systematic attempt to define the components of each executive role in precise terms. An organisation chart should therefore be accompanied by a document which sets out the main tasks to be performed in each role.

(b) An organisation chart can only show the position at a particular point in time. Charts may encourage inflexibility in organisations where the pattern of activity is changing all the time.

(c) An organisation chart can only show *formal* relationships and in any human enterprise *informal* relationships are often equally important. The morale of members of an organisation is sometimes affected adversely because members interpret the charts wrongly, perhaps confusing authority relationships with *status* and being upset by the formal placements given to friends and rivals.

Look again at Figure 1.2. Let us pretend that A is the managing director of a large company and that B, C and D are group managers. The formal lines of authority as they are charted indicate that communications might take the following paths:

(a) If a policy directive is issued by A, Q would receive his instructions via B, and E and N respectively.

(b) If S wished to make a report to the managing director, his report would travel via N, E and B.

What if N has to pass information to Z? The chart appears to lay down a line of communication via A, a long path that looks as if it might involve managers in matters in which they have no interest. In practice the chain of command implies that communications may be transmitted in three possible directions:

(a) *Upwards:* to provide information to senior management to enable them to control the organisation.

(b) *Downwards:* to transmit policy decisions to the lower levels of the organisation.

(c) *Laterally:* or, along the same management level. For example, suppose P controls a unit which receives orders for spare parts and Y is in charge of stock records in the warehouse. If P receives an urgent enquiry for a cylinder block, he will check the stock position with Z, either personally or by telephone and no other levels of the hierarchy need be involved at all.

Co-ordination by committee occurs when some matter is committed to a group rather than to an individual. Committees are used when it is necessary to bring different opinions and specialisms to bear

23

on a particular problem. Committees are useful for the purpose of advice and communication, they provide an opportunity for combined judgement and teamwork. They also have a useful training function, especially in making managers aware of the problems which their colleagues have to deal with. Committees also have important disadvantages. They tie up valuable resources by keeping their members from their normal work and they sometimes tend to produce unsatisfactory decisions, as when members accept compromises and watered down decisions in order to bring meetings to an end. The use of committees also tends to encourage irresponsibility, in the sense that committee decisions are often not attributable to any one individual so that individual committee members can easily shift the blame for decisions that are criticised after the meeting is over.

Delegation

Authority is said to be delegated when it is vested in a subordinate by a superior. Power has already been defined (page 15) as the capacity to change individual or group behaviour. If you pick up this book and wave it over the person nearest to you at this moment and he or she changes into a frog, then you have developed some form of *magic* power! Power in organisations is derived from various sources. The most important source of power is the law which in Britain, for example, confers rights on shareholders entitling them to delegate their powers to directors who, in turn, delegate authority to their staffs. Wealth is an important source of power.

Personality is another significant source of power and often managerial roles are transformed by the personalities of the persons engaged in those roles; consider, for example, the job of the Prime Minister and the differences that have been brought to this managerial role by such personalities as Harold Wilson, Churchill, Lloyd George, Eden and Macmillan. Special skills and knowledge of detailed administrative procedures, 'knowing the ropes', are other sources of power which are relevant to the functioning of organisations.

The process of delegation gives rise to three types of relationship as follows:

(a) **Line relationships,** which arise when the superior's authority is direct and his responsibility is *general*. This preserves the **principle of unity of command** and the scale of direct authority relationships in an organisation is sometimes called the **scalar chain.**

(b) **Staff relationships**, which are *advisory* in nature and do not carry the power to command.

(c) **Functional relationships**, which arise when a manager does not have full authority in matters concerning the organisation under him, as when specific functions are delegated to specialists within the organisation. For example, a manager may not have the power to dismiss a member of his staff without reference to the personnel manager, who is the specialist to whom all personnel problems must be referred.

In practice, because of factors like personality, these functions often overlap. Consider the organisation chart reproduced in Figure 1.3, to which some names have been added for the purpose of

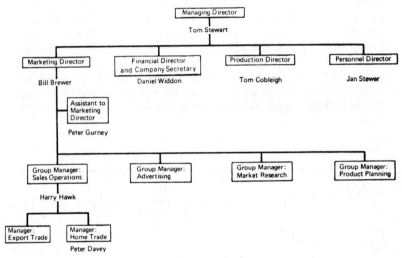

Figure 1.3

discussion here and later in the chapter. The line relationship is expressed in the chain of command, which can be seen to relate Peter Davey to Tom Stewart via Harry Hawk and Bill Brewer. Note that Peter Gurney has no personal authority whatsoever, he is an 'assistant to' Bill Brewer; this is an example of a staff relationship. Jan Stewer is in charge of the specialist personnel function and Daniel Widdon is the financial specialist. Bill Brewer will not take decisions on personnel and financial matters without consulting the specialists concerned; these are examples of functional relationships.

Span of Control is another principle in which the idea is contained

25

that some limit should be applied to the number of subordinates reporting to any single executive. Lyndall F. Urwick, a British management consultant, puts the ideal number of subordinates for a top manager at 5 or 6. The extent to which one person can control the activities of others must largely depend on the nature of the jobs to be controlled. For example, one supervisor could control twenty copy typists engaged in routine work without much difficulty, but one research director could not possibly control in detail the work of twenty highly qualified scientists without some grouping of jobs into a heirarchy.

Note that whenever a decision is made with regard to span of control, the effect is immediately apparent in the number of levels of authority produced in the organisation. In the two organisation charts in Figure 1.4, Chief Executive A, using a span of control with a 'rule of two' (where each supervisor controls two subordinates), controls fifteen people in three separate levels of authrity; Chief Executive B, using a 'rule of four' controls twenty people in only two levels of authority. Span of control therefore produces either a steep or a flat organisational pyramid; the steeper the pyramid, the more levels of authority and the greater the number of levels of authority, the greater the number of possible obstacles to good communications.

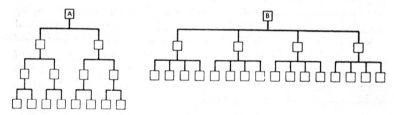

Figure 1.4

Delegation may be achieved by the adoption of the technique of **management by exception,** whereby managers free themselves of day-to-day pressures and concern themselves only with non-routine problems, so that they are able to leave themselves free to consider the application of policy in exceptional circumstances. Many writers have stressed the importance of **decentralization** as a principle for managing very large companies. This allows a high degree of autonomy to individual profit-making units and removes the frustrations which are caused when decisions are delayed because they have to be referred to a remote higher authority. Modern writers emphasise the advantages of decentralised systems, but it is important to remember that such systems may nevertheless be responsive to central control by means of regular reporting systems, efficiency audits, common training programmes, rotation of staff etc.

Delegation is the essential purpose of organisational structure and the way in which delegation is arranged should be an expression of the purpose of the organisation. That is why there can be no *typical* organisational structure and why the application of general management 'principles' may produce answers which are not always consistent because they have to take into account the effects of differences in the quality and quantity of the labour force, production methods, the nature of the market, the availability of finance, Government policy and other variables.

The 'principles' identified in the previous section are derived from the so-called 'classical' school of organisation theory, whose approach is to study organisational problems following an examination of the work to be done in any given context. Organisations, however, have characteristics other than the work to be done. In the first place, organisations are made up of people and anyone who devises a basis for splitting up tasks between a group of people without paying attention to their individual personalities, temperaments and aspirations will soon be faced with the prospect of the organisation breaking down, the first symptoms of which might be frequent quarrels, absenteeism, sickness, or resignations from the group. Furthermore, organisations are not static and are subject to changes in technology, markets, Government policy, etc.

Two schools of organisation theory have emerged since World War I to modify the rather mechanical approach of the 'classical' writers and a brief account of their respective contributions now follows.

The Human Relations School

The first major contributions come from the work of Elton Mayo, who analysed the social factors in productivity at the Hawthorne works of the Western Electric Company between 1927 and 1932. Mayo, and subsequent sociologists and social psychologists, have

27

attempted to define organisations in terms of social environments and have examined the ways in which organisations might be adapted to satisfy the needs of human beings, both as individuals and as members of social groups. This approach is developed at some length in Chapter Five; its significance in one aspect may be noted here by reference back to Figure 1.3. on page 25.

The chart shows lines of formal relationship, the means by which power is distributed and communications are transmitted to achieve the objectives of the company of which Tom Stewart is managing director. But human groups are organised for purposes other than running a business. How would your evaluation of the distribution of power in this organisation change in the light of any of the statements given below and why?

(a) Tom Stewart is Daniel Widdon's brother-in-law.

(b) Harry Hawk is a highly qualified university graduate; the remainder of the managers do not possess formal academic qualifications.

(c) Peter Gurney, Daniel Widdon, Jan Stewer and Harry Hawk play bridge together every Friday night.

This example will give you some inkling of the importance of 'informal' lines of communication in an organisation, sometimes referred to as 'the grapevine'.

The essence of the human relations approach to organisational problems is the attention it devotes to methods of measuring:

(a) Individual needs and wants,

(b) The way in which groups work together,

(c) The way in which individuals and groups respond to different kinds of supervision. Whether a group responds best to close control by an authoritarian boss or to being given the opportunity to contribute to the process of decision making depends partly on the attributes of the group, and partly on the nature of the tasks which the group is given to do. Four classifications of types of management may be recognised in this context:

(i) **Laissez-faire:** the manager does not interfere with the activities of his subordinates.

(ii) **Democratic:** where the manager advises and guides, but where decisions are made by the group as a whole.

(iii) **Benevolent autocracy:** where the group advises, but the manager decides.

(iv) **Dictatorship:** where the manager decides without consultation with the group.

The Social Systems School

This approach was pioneered by Chester Barnard, whose main work, *The Functions of the Executive*, was published in 1938. The approach here is to consider an organisation, not only as a social system in itself, but as part of other 'systems'. Just as the parts of an organisation are linked together, so is the organisation itself linked to other organisations, like a series of cogs in a wheel. A decision made within the department of a single company may affect not only that department but the whole company, perhaps in many years time, and not only may the company be affected but the consequences might well spread to the company's customers, the suppliers of its raw materials, its competitors and perhaps the entire economy of the country.

This approach creates problems of definition. How are boundaries to be set to define the limits of any particular 'system' and how are the characteristics of sub-systems to be identified? Managers are not always successful in predicting the consequences of their actions, yet it is their main task to identify sub-systems and to develop objectives in relation to each. Organisational sub-systems are sometimes called *decision areas* and the 'social systems' approach emphasises two aspects of management in particular:

(a) Communication needs to feed the 'decision areas', that is to say, what information is required, in what detail, with what frequency and by whom. This requirement is discussed in greater detail in Chapter Seven.

(b) Decision making techniques, methods of calculating the payoff for different types of strategy. These are discussed in Chapters Four and Six. The new management sciences which have emerged and developed since World War II. Mathematical Economics, Operational Research, Cybernetics, and many others reflect the approach of the 'social systems' school of organisation theory.

None of the principles identified by the 'classical' writers and developed by the 'human relations' and 'social systems' schools provide a guarantee of success in business. This might lead one to the conclusion that good managers are born, not made. This is not true. What they show is the complexity of human activity and the need for management training to take account of a wide variety of academic disciplines. This need has received a great deal of attention in Britain in the 1960s because of increasing concern about the efficiency of British companies compared with their competitors overseas and has given rise to the establishment of business schools in Manchester and London and the emergence of first degrees in Business Studies at the universities and polytechnics. The academic disciplines generally found in these degree courses are worth recording, because they indicate the qualifications required of the managers of the future: Economics, Mathematics, Statistics, Accountancy, Sociology, Psychology, Politics and Law.

1.3 THE BUSINESS ENVIRONMENT

We consider briefly in this section the environment of a business firm in Britain and the possible relationships that might exist between a single business enterprise and other organisations which are able to exert influence on its policies. The management of an individual company is likely to be required to communicate with the following groups: customers, trade associations, suppliers, distributors, trade unions, financial institutions and governments.

Customers are able to influence policy by refusing to buy a company's product. In some markets customers are able to dictate their requirements in great detail, for instance, large department stores are often able to insist that their suppliers meet very detailed specifications because they are able to purchase in such large quantities. Domestic consumers are able to influence manufacturers through organisations like the *Consumer's Association* and the *Consumer Council*, by means of complaints to officials in Local Government and through letters published in the press.

Trade Associations are associations of firms in a particular industry, who set up a central organisation financed by fees or levies paid by the members. The services performed by the trade association are collection and distribution of information on matters of significance to the industry (as on the likely impact of forthcoming legislation, on current conditions and future prospects in home and export markets), the administration of industrial conferences and training schemes and co-ordination of attempts to develop price and output policies for the industry as a whole. Trade associations sometimes set up **research associations,** which may become centres of collaborative research in the industry (especially where member firms are too small to be able to afford research on an individual basis), and which also provide technical and scientific information services.

Suppliers and distributors are often protected by their own trade associations and may be able to affect a company's policy by refusing to supply its raw materials or to distribute its product.

30

Trade unions engage in collective bargaining and are able to influence wages policies by threatening to withdraw the labour of their members. Companies often have to deal with their labour force at two levels, both local and national, so that agreement at national level will not necessarily prevent a local 'unofficial' strike.

Financial institutions. Besides their own shareholders, managers must deal with such financial institutions as commercial and merchant banks, issuing houses, insurance companies and Government financial agencies, all of whom are able to exercise a decisive influence on management decisions.

Government. In Britain, Government has assumed responsibility for a wide range of services and the impact of government policies to promote and to regulate different parts of the economy is immense. Most industries have a specific government department, which acts as 'sponsor' and is the normal channel of communication between the industry concerned and the Government. Since October 1969, responsibility for most industrial matters has been centralised in the Ministry of Technology.

The functions of Government with regard to business enterprise may be classified as:

(a) *Promotional:* For example, the Board of Trade provides finance for exporters through the Export Credits Guarantee Department. It promotes trade fairs and provides information on conditions in overseas markets. The Ministry of Agriculture, Fisheries and Food administers subsidies for basic products like milk and cereals, and schemes to improve farm and estate management. The Ministry of Technology provides grants and development contracts to stimulate industrial research and development.

(b) *Regulatory:* Business activities are closely regulated by legislation and there has been a substantial increase in the volume of regulations in recent years. The protection offered to investors by the Companies Acts and to members of the work force by the Factory Acts has been extended considerably and the increasing importance of legal departments in many firms is due to the responsibilities imposed on management by the sheer volume of regulations which apply to such matters as pricing policy, pay policy, relations with consumers, health and safety and conditions of employment.

(c) *Direct:* The Government operates certain industries and services itself, as with the nationalised industries, which are run by public corporations. Policies developed by public corporations have a great impact on business firms in the private sector because

31

they control goods and services which are basic to the economy, such as fuel, power, transport, steel.

In addition, the Government is a major consumer of the products of industry and is thus able to exert pressure on its suppliers because of the size of its orders.

Overseas governments, likewise, influence the pattern of trade by such means as changes in tax laws, import controls, regulations on the quality and quantity of goods imported.

Local authorities are another important source of influence on business decisions, because they are large purchasers of goods and services and also because they administer town and country planning regulations and have the power to enforce local by-laws.

1.4 THE PLANNING FUNCTION

The Planning Function is elaborated in the final section of this chapter because it is the most basic of all the management functions and it will help us to relate the main enterprise functions of marketing, producing and financing, described in the following chapters. Also, the importance of planning has received renewed emphasis in Britain since 1962, with the establishment of machinery for economic planning at national and regional levels.

Strategic planning is the process of deciding on objectives, perhaps replacing previous objectives with new ones, of reviewing the resources available to achieve objectives and of manipulating them in order to achieve those objectives. The stages of planning are as follows:

(a) **Forecasting:** which is an attempt to predict what will happen in the future with or without policy changes on the part of the planning organisation. *Implicit forecasts* rely on guesses and intuition, based largely on what has happened in the past; *explicit forecasts* set out clearly the assumptions and methods on which they are based.

(b) **Definition of goals:** goals are defined and related to company policy.

(c) **Programming:** goals must be translated into operational plans for all the constituent elements of the organisation, so that all major strategies are supported by plans and targets for each enterprise function. Firms applying **MbO** (Management by Objectives; see page 17) arrange for individual standards of performance to be agreed with individual managers at this stage.

(d) **Timing and feedback:** programmes must specify not only what action is to be taken by constituent departments, but also *when*, and a system of reporting must be established so that performance may be related to the plan. Many companies use **network analysis** as a means of specifying, in graphical form, the work that has to be carried out in order to complete a given project. Individual **activities** (i.e. jobs in the planning network) are shown as arrows which terminate in circles (called **events**), which are points in time when it is possible to establish that the previous activity has been completed. All tasks are shown in order of precedence and the longest sequence of activities in a network is called the **critical path;** this gives the total time to completion of the project and helps managers by showing where the strongest supervision and the most frequent and detailed reports on progress are needed.

The length of the planning period will be affected by the characteristics of the business and the economic climate, both domestic and world-wide. For example, consider how the market for motor cars and central heating systems is likely to be affected by successive increases in the price of oil and how all businesses are affected by changes in fuel costs.

FURTHER READING

Emery, *Systems Thinking*, Penguin.
Koontz and O'Donnell, *Principles of Management*, McGraw Hill.
O'Shaughnessy, *Business Organisation*, Allen & Unwin.
Pugh and others, *Writers on organisations*, Penguin.
Stewart, *The Reality of Management*, Pan.

QUESTIONS

1. Contrast the 'systems' approach to organisation with the 'classical' approach (A.C.C.A.).
2. Consider how the policies of a limited liability company may be influenced by shareholders, employees and customers (A.C.C.A.).
3. How are the mechanistic concepts of organisation structure modified by the 'human relations' approach? (U.L.C.I.).
4. What is an organisation chart? Explain possible limitations to the usefulness of organisation charts and how these limitations may be overcome (U.L.C.I.).
5. What is meant by the 'policy' of an organisation? How is 'policy' formulated? (A.C.C.A.).

CHAPTER TWO

The Marketing Function

2.1 MARKETING ORGANISATION

The Marketing Concept

THE British Institute of Marketing defines *marketing* as:

'The creative management function which promotes trade and employment by assessing consumer needs and initiating research and development to meet them. It co-ordinates the resources of production and distribution of goods and services, determines and directs the nature and scale of the total effort required to sell profitably the maximum production to the ultimate user.'

This definition is worthy of study, but it may be easier to remember P. F. Drucker's briefer statement that: 'Marketing is looking at the business through the customer's eyes.'

The origins of the **marketing concept** can be traced to the period following the Industrial Revolution when, for the first time, there were indications that the means of production were capable of catching up with the demand for goods. Before the techniques of mass-production came into being there was generally a shortage of manufactured goods. Such virtual absence of competition, by present-day standards, meant that most products and services were assured of an immediate demand.

The productive processes were given further stimulus by two world wars, and despite increasing markets caused by the dramatic rise in world population, by the early 1960s a position has been reached in the more highly developed industrial countries. whereby the flow of manufactured goods was beginning to overtake demand. Companies which had been operating on the basis of a 'we make them, you sell them' policy, began to find that they were no longer able to dispose of their output as profitably as before. The scene was changing from one in which manufacturers had, to a great extent,

34

determined the quantity and the type of goods supplied, to one in which the consumer was beginning to exert a powerful influence upon the manufacturer. As competition became stronger, companies were obliged to undertake some critical appraisal of the fundamental reasons why they were in business.

To the more progressive, it became apparent that, if their business was to be sustained and to grow, research and development could no longer be confined to the field of production, but that it must also be directed towards a study of the needs of the consumer. It is understandable that the United States, with its enormous productive capacity, was one of the first countries to recognise that the very survival of businesses depended upon meeting the needs of the consumer.

Here lies the very essence of the marketing concept: the appreciation that far from being the last link in the business chain, it is the customer who initiates the whole business cycle. It is logical, therefore, that of the three basic business functions with which this book is concerned, we are looking first at marketing. Wealth is produced when goods are sold, not when they are made. Goods are sold when there is a consumer need to be satisfied. It is the first concern of marketing to identify those needs and, having identified them, to devise methods of meeting them at a profit.

Marketing Organisation

Having accepted that the first requirement is to identify consumer needs, the other elements of the marketing concept follow in a logical succession. The process of assessing the consumer's needs involves the techniques of **market research**, the gathering, recording and analysis of all facts and data concerned with answering the questions: what can be sold, in what quantities, at what price, where, how and when? Only when answers to these basic questions are given can the planning of the product be undertaken. There will follow, in all but the simplest of products, a period of research and development before full-scale production can commence. When the goods start to flow from the production line, the appropriate methods of distributing them into the market must be available, and to ensure that consumers are aware of the existence of the product, together with its particular benefits, various promotional techniques will have been developed.

Thus the marketing cycle can be shown in the following diagrammatic form:

Figure 2.1

It will be evident that the marketing function embraces a wide field of sub-functions, each requiring special skills. Before considering each of the sub-functions, we should first consider, in more detail, the roles of the various departments which we would expect to find in the marketing group of a typical manufacturing company:

(a) *Market research*

By the gathering, recording and analysis of relevant data, this department will help to provide answers to the basic questions of what can be sold, in what quantities, where, how and when. It will be concerned with assessing the demand for new products and also with the acceptability of existing products. In both instances, it will study the company's position and that of its competitors.

(b) *Product planning*

Based largely on information provided by the market research department, this section will identify consumer needs in terms of the type of product to be developed and the special features which it should incorporate. Again its research will include comparison with competitive products.

(c) *Product development*

By following a programme of laboratory and field testing in close collaboration with the engineering departments, this team will develop the new product, or product modification, to the point where it can be handed over to the production department for full-scale commercial manufacture.

36

(d) *Distribution*

By planning the methods of transferring the finished goods from the factory to the point of sale and by physically handling the goods, this department is responsible for achieving and maintaining adequate market coverage—by having the right goods in the right place at the right time.

(e) *Sales promotion*

This department is responsible for developing means whereby the consumer is persuaded to buy the product. In most companies the techniques of sales promotion are further sub-divided into specialised departments responsible for advertising and merchandising.

What is a Market?

Originally, the word *market* simply meant a place where people met for the purpose of exchanging goods. Most communities had their own local market place which was the focal centre of social and economic life. Market places, of course, still exist; besides the many street markets which have survived in our towns and cities and the country cattle markets, there are other markets of national importance, such as Smithfield (meat), Covent Garden (fruit, flowers and vegetables) and the Stock Exchange (stocks and shares).

When used in the context of modern marketing, however, the word is taken to mean people or groups of people having in common the need or desire for a particular commodity or service. Thus, when we speak of the confectionery market we are referring to all those who are concerned with buying sweets and chocolates. If it is said that the confectionery market is buoyant, then it means that people are continuing to buy sweets and chocolates at or above previous levels; conversely, if the market is slow or depressed, then people are purchasing less than normal.

Before mentioning some of the ways in which markets are described, let us consider the two broad categories into which markets divide: (a) Industrial and (b) Consumer.

(a) *Industrial*: This is sometimes also referred to as the commercial market. It comprises all those who purchase commodities for use directly or indirectly in pursuit of commercial enterprise.

(b) *Consumer:* This market comprises all those who purchase commodities for their own personal satisfaction.

Marketing managers have a special interest in methods of classi-

37

fying consumers in order to discover differences in taste, spending habits, attitudes, etc., which may be catered for in marketing programmes. **Market segments** are subdivisions of markets which have characteristics that mark them off from other parts of the market for the same product; it may be that the consumers are different in some way, they may buy the product at different times, or for different reasons, or perhaps the product is put to a particular use in a 'segment' which is not general as far as the rest of the market is concerned. You may illustrate this point by considering the market for children's sweets, ladies' underwear, the market for expensive meals in restaurants, in which local and seasonal differences may occur which are not characteristic of the market as a whole. Remember that the person who buys the product is not always the person who uses it; mothers and fathers buy for their families, men buy for women and vice versa and sometimes children buy for their parents!

A convenient way of dividing up a market is according to **social class,** which is a system of classifying individuals and households according to such characteristics as income, occupation, spending habits, education, leisure pursuits, etc.

A system of classifying the population according to occupation is used by the Registrar General in the decennial census; the concept of class, however, goes much further than this. One method of analysis could be to divide the population into three groups: the 'upper' class (about 2 per cent of the population), comprising the aristocracy and large land-owners, the 'working' class, made up of workers in manual jobs and the 'middle' class, a wide intermediate category ranging from qualified members of the professions to the humblest white-collar workers. This grouping, sometimes used in general conversation, is not very helpful because it is not precise enough to distinguish different patterns of behaviour.

Advertisers use a simple lettered scale to classify consumers according to class (families take the grading of the head of the household):

Code	Category	Occupation of head of the household	Percentage of population (1968)
A	Upper middle class	Professional, Senior managerial	4
B	Middle class	Managerial	8
C1	Lower middle class	Supervisory, junior managerial, clerical	22

C2	Skilled working class	Skilled manual	31
D	Working class	Semi-skilled and unskilled manual	26
E		Persons living on pensions and social security	9

This system of classification is used to distinguish groups of consumers, not only by income, but also by such characteristics as cultural interests, leisure activities, education, etc. Of course, these divisions are not hard and fast; hire purchase facilities, for example, help to blur class distinctions but they do not eliminate them. This categorisation is of particular interest to advertisers, who seek to discover which of the advertising media are orientated towards one consumer group more than another. You will realise the significance of this point if you try to classify the following newspapers and periodicals according to what you consider to be their special attraction to AB consumers on the one hand and C1/C2 consumers on the other:

The Observer *The Economist*
Playboy *The Financial Times*
The People *Daily Express*
New Society *Woman*
Tit Bits

The distinction between industrial and consumer markets is of paramount importance, since there is invariably a marked difference in their basic characteristics, such as demand patterns, purchasing motivation, which profoundly affects the techniques employed in serving the needs of each sector. For example methods of advertising, sales promotion and distribution would differ significantly.

It must be remembered, however, that many products are sold to both sectors—washing machines when sold to the housewife are consumer items and when sold to a launderette are industrial. There are, in common use, other broad descriptions of markets such as the export market, the home market, the domestic appliance market, or the agricultural machinery market.

2.2 MARKETING RESEARCH

The objectives of marketing research are implicit in the title; that is, to research and thereby gain knowledge of the market and marketing methods. The practice of marketing research, however, is not so simple.

The Scope of Marketing Research

Marketing, as we have seen, begins with the needs of the consumer. The process of identifying and monitoring these needs forms the basis of marketing research.

There is a tendency to associate marketing research with the introduction of new products, whereas it is equally important in relation to the marketing of existing products. In order to examine the scope and function of marketing research let us consider the information a company marketing research department would supply to management and the methods it would employ to obtain such information.

An enlightened management will usually call for an exhaustive marketing research report prior to committing the large sums of capital often required in connection with the research and development of a product. This report should provide answers to the following questions:

(a) Is there a market for product X?
(b) What is the size of the market?
(c) Is the market growing, saturated or declining?
(d) What are the market characteristics?
(e) Is the market predominantly industrial or consumer?
(f) At what price can product X be sold?

(a) *Is there a market for product X?*

In most cases, common sense coupled to professional experience will provide the answer to this question. For example, if there is already being sold any product which is designed to perform the same function as product X then, regardless of the quantities sold, there is a market. For an entirely new product a survey would be required in order to answer this question.

(b) *What is the size of the market?*

In order to determine the size of the total market (that is, the total number of units which could be sold annually by all manufacturers) it is necessary to examine the relevant data. For example, statistics published by government departments and trade associations give information such as the total number of motor-cars registered in one year and a great range of other data.

In some instances, however, statistics on which to base judgments may not be available. In such cases, one would have to examine the inter-relationship of the subject market and other markets. For example, there may be no published statistics relating to wing mirrors for motor-cars. One would then examine the obvious relationship between wing mirrors and motor-cars, and by conducting a sample survey into the number of motor-cars fitted with wing mirrors and applying the results to the total market for motor-cars, the total markets for wing mirrors could be established.

EXAMPLE:

If a sample survey indicated that 27 out of every 100 motor-cars in use had wing mirrors fitted within the first 12 months–

    and
the total number of motor-cars registed in a year
$= 1,120,000$ approximately–
then
the estimated total market for wing mirrors
$= 27$ per cent of $1,120,000$
$= 302,400 \times 2$ (2 mirrors per car)
TOTAL MARKET
$= 604,800$ units annually.

The above example is, of course, hypothetical, and intended to show only how use can be made of statistics relating to markets which are inter-related.

(c) *Is the market growing, saturated or declining?*
A market may be one of:

    Growth
Saturation (sometimes referred to as *replacement*), or
Decline

In a growth market demand is actually increasing or will increase at some future date; in a saturated market there is no element of growth, demand is governed by the rate at which products are renewed; in a declining market demand for the product is on the wane. An analysis of sales statistics will usually show whether the market is one of growth, saturation or decline.

(d) *What are the market characteristics?*
Market characteristics may well determine the techniques ultimately employed in the marketing of the product. In essence, they are subject to economic, political and sociological considerations.

41

Demand patterns present in a market may be defined as either **elastic** or **inelastic**. Demand is **elastic** when the demand can be increased or decreased by external factors, perhaps political, social or economic. For example, the market for motor-cars tends to be elastic because the demand can be affected by such factors as hire purchase restrictions or purchase tax.

Demand tends to be **inelastic** when it is not subject to variation, as with the market for bread and salt (people do not generally purchase more when their standard of living rises or less should the price increase).

Another important market characteristic is **seasonality**—the tendency for demand to reach a peak at a particular time in the year. Some products, such as milk and bread have no significant seasonality factor. Others like Christmas cards or bedding plants obviously do. The seasonality factor should never be overlooked or presumed not to exist; it is of considerable importance in relation to production schedules, distribution and storage arrangements and is vital in relation to sales.

(e) Is the market predominantly industrial or consumer?

As we saw earlier, many products can be sold to both market sectors. The decision to sell to one or both will be influenced by company policy and will perhaps be made in the light of the company's ability (or inability) to distribute its products to both sectors at once.

The researcher, however, will be expected to quantify the demand emanating from each sector. He will probably submit his report in two parts for example:

> Product X and its application to the Industrial Market.
> Product X and its application to the Consumer Market.

(f) At what price can Product X be sold?

The determination of price is vitally important for two distinct reasons:

(a) The price must be such that costs are covered and profit ensured, and

(b) The price must be acceptable to the market in order to ensure sales.

The consideration of (a) is a costing and financial analysis study whereas (b) is a marketing, and particularly a marketing research, consideration. In practice there would be constant liaison between the two functions within the firm. In considering price in relation to a product the market researcher must:

(a) Determine that the price compares favourably with the prices of other similar products already on the market or

(b) Where there is no similar product on the market ensure that the price is realistic (such that the product will meet with market acceptance).

In relation to products already being marketed the research function takes on the mantle of **market intelligence** (sometimes referred to as **sales or market analysis**). Basically this aspect of marketing research is responsible for the 'feed back' of information to management in connection with: (a) the general market situation and (b) the product and its acceptance relative to competitive products.

This type of information is presented to management in various ways, the most common being the **market intelligence report**. This would include the following information:

(i) Changes, if any, in the general market situation since the introduction of the product.

(ii) The effect on the market of economic measures introduced by the Government.

(iii) An evaluation of competitive activity.

(iv) An analysis of total market sales by manufacturer.

(v) Indications of changes in demand patterns.

Sources of Information

We have examined, in broad terms, the information with which the marketing research function is concerned. We must now consider how this information is collected, interpreted and presented to management.

The first broad division is between: (a) Internal information and (b) External information.

Internal information is obtainable from company records, such as sales statistics, installation returns, and other data; external information is secured from sources other than the company's own records. This information may be broadly categorised by source as follows:

(a) Government Departments; such as Board of Trade returns, and the Annual Abstract of Statistics.

(b) Trade Associations; The Society of Motor Manufacturers and Traders, or The Agricultural Engineers' Association are examples.

43

    (c) Competitive Manufacturers; this information may be obtained as a result of exchange agreements, whereby competitive manufacturers agree to exchange sales or production statistics.

    (d) Individual Customers (the general public); this information is obtained by conducting surveys.

Since (a), (b) and (c) above, require little explanation let us consider what is involved in (d).

Market Surveys

There are four equally important elements in survey work:

Preparation
Research
Analysis
Presentation

In the preparation or planning of the survey it is essential to begin by determining the objectives, that is, what specific information is it essential to derive from the survey. Having determined the objectives the next step is to decide upon the type and scope of the survey. Surveys can be carried out by: (a) Telephone, (b) Post, or (c) Personal Interview.

(a) *The telephone survey*

This would normally be carried out only where the researcher is known to the customer, as with a wholesaler carrying out a survey of the retail outlets which he supplies or a motor manufacturer surveying those firms who distribute his products.

(b) *The postal survey*

This is a most useful method of soliciting individual opinions, especially where the number of candidates to be canvassed is very large and spread geographically. In the preparation of postal surveys, it is of paramount importance to ensure that the questions asked are categoric, where possible calling for an answer in Yes/No terms.

(c) *The personal interview*

This is the most satisfactory form of conducting a survey, provided it is carried out by experienced researchers. It eliminates the uncertainty inherent in the postal questionnaire as to whether the question has been fully understood. This is particularly important where the answer to one question determines what the next question will be.

Surveys may be either:

(a) *total*, usually referred to as **census surveys**, or
(b) *part*, usually referred to as **sample surveys**.

In a total or census survey the total prospective market is examined. In statistical terms the total market would be referred to as **the universe** or the total population. The term is not peculiar to marketing research, but is used by statisticians to indicate entirety: for example, in a survey on motor-cars, say in the U.K., the universe, or total population, would mean *all* motor-car owners in the U.K.

In a sample survey only part of the universe is examined, but the results are taken to be representative of the whole. The technique of the sample survey has been used with great effect by many firms, organisations and government departments. You are, no doubt, aware of the public opinion polls; these are perhaps the best example of sample surveys.

The information collected will fall into one of the following categories:

(a) Quantitative: That is information in numerical form such as the number of motor-cars registered in one year, the number of males earning over £2,000 per annum, etc.
(b) Qualitative: Information of less tangible nature such as the reasons why a person purchased product 'X' in preference to product 'Y'.

Once it has been tabulated, quantitative information can be analysed in a relatively straightforward way. Qualitative information, however, must first be converted into numerical terms.

Sales Forecasting

A forecast is an attempt to predict what will happen in the future. Sales forecasting is an attempt to predict the pattern of sales in some future period in order to provide guidelines for policy decisions. For example, if a forecast, based on current trends, indicates that a company's share of the market will diminish steadily over the next five years, the company (if it wishes to remain in that market), will have to develop policies to reverse the trends identified by the forecast. This is how a *forecast* is used as the basis for developing a *plan*.

45

In a large company, forecasts will be made over the whole range of commercial activity and attempts will be made to identify trends in:

(a) Aspects of activity over which the company has control, such as the size, form, quality, packaging of its products, marketing and production methods, allocation of funds available within the company (undistributed profits, for example).

(b) Aspects which the company cannot control, such as trends of technological change within the industry, the development of new products by competitors, changes in population (by total number, by distribution in terms of age, sex, income), changes in consumer tastes and changes in taxation. The following are some examples of radical socio-economic changes that have taken place in Britain in the last hundred years. See if you can work out your own examples of the impact of these changes on business profits in general and on marketing methods in particular:

The expansion of education
The development of government policies to control inflation
Redistribution of income in favour of lower income groups
The increase in leisure
The emancipation of women
The growth of large cities and suburban areas
Changing attitudes to debt

The most widely used forecasting techniques are:

(a) Projections of the behaviour of sales over some previous period. Internal company records are used for this and the basic assumption is that there is some relationship between demand in the past and demand in the future (as with the relationship between motor-cars sold in 1973 and the demand for spare parts for that model in 1980).

(b) Analysis by correlation. Attempts are made to relate sales to other economic and social variables in order to arrive at a formula for sales in some future period. The following are some examples of key variables often used in this type of analysis: the total level of employment, the rate of growth in national income, changes in population (by total and by distribution in terms of age, sex, income groups), the level of total government spending, trends in demand for the products of other industries, even the weather.

(c) Panels of executive opinion. This is where human judgement and intuition are used to supplement the more formal methods.

This may be through the medium of conferences of senior executives, sales personnel and perhaps distributors and retailers.

Forecasts are usually classified on a time-scale as follows:

(a) *Long term (5–10 years)*: These will consider major changes likely in the external environment, as a result of shifts in population, the development of new towns, or possible changes in overseas markets (for example, estimates of the impact of further increases in the price of oil).

(b) *Short term (2–5 years)*: In this period managers must commit themselves to plan outlines for production, sales campaigns, staff development and other items, and budgets are drawn up which commit the company to allocating scarce resources, although there will be some scope for flexibility.

(c) *Immediate (1–2 years)*: These forecasts comprise detailed production targets, manpower programmes and other areas. Most companies adopt a method of detailed budgeting and reporting at monthly intervals during this period (see page 109).

2.3 PRODUCT PLANNING

The function of product planning is to translate customer needs, as identified by market research, into acceptable products which can be sold at a profit.

People do not buy products merely for what they are, but because of certain needs which they believe will be satisfied by the products. Customers do not buy motor-cars for what they are, but rather for what they provide in terms of convenience and comfort as a means of transport or for deeper reasons of status or self-expression. Manufacturers, therefore, should ask themselves, not: *What products do we make?* but: *What market are we in?* For example, when Kilvert's had captured a quarter of the market in one year with their liquid car polish *Turtle Wax*, and the competition was beginning to fight back, Tom Heywood, their Marketing Director, decided that the market he was competing in was not just the car polish market, but the market for car care products in general. Based on this decision, Heywood's firm bought up the U.K. rights to *Molyslip* oil additives and obtained the U.K. marketing rights for *Dupli-Color*, a comprehensive range of aerosol touch-up paints. These products were then marketed to the same pattern as *Turtle Wax* and similar success resulted. Herein lies the difference between the product-orientated and the marketing-orientated approach not just in selling the product, but in fulfilling the needs of the consumer.

Product planning is concerned with any or all of the following categories:

(a) Completely new products.
(b) Changes to existing products.
(c) Extensions to an existing range of products.
(d) Introducing an established product from another market (as to the export market from the home market or vice-versa).

The first stage in the product planning process will be the identification of a customer need. Market research will establish the nature and extent of the potential market and will evaluate the extent of any competitive activity. If the findings are favourable then a preliminary product specification will be drawn up and, if approved, this will be passed to the research and development section for the production of prototypes for testing. At the same time preliminary costings will be established so that estimates can be made of profit margins.

Tentative advertising and sales plans will be prepared and, depending on the result of product testing and evaluation, a decision will be taken either: (a) to launch the product forthwith, or (b) to carry out more widespread testing (either nationally or in certain test areas), or (c) to discontinue the project altogether. If it is decided to go ahead with the product then a complete marketing plan will be drawn up. This plan will define: (a) the overall objective and, (b) the specific responsibilities of each of the sub-functions involved, such as advertising, sales promotion and distribution.

The length of time required for the whole process will vary from a few months to several years, depending on the type of product. If the product is subject to seasonal demand it may only be possible to test it under realistic conditions during certain periods of the year.

Test Marketing

Before the marketing plan is put into operation, it is usual to subject the product to competitive market conditions in order to test the validity of the assumptions that have been made in the plan. This process, which is normally carried out in carefully controlled areas, is known as **test marketing.**

The purpose of test marketing is to identify all the factors which will contribute to the success of the product. According to the A. C. Nielson Company, a well-known marketing research organisation, at least nine out of ten products launched on the national market on the basis of results obtained from test marketing turn out to be commercially successful.

48

Nielson maintain that the basis of good test marketing practice lies in answering the five questions:

What can be tested?
How big should a test market be?
How many things can be tested at one time?
How long should a test market be kept going?
What are the most common pitfalls in test marketing?

Originally the technique of test marketing was limited to the field of inexpensive consumer goods, such as toothpaste, washing powder, tinned foods, and similar items. Recently, however, there has been a tendency to employ test marketing techniques in relation to such consumer durables as motor-cars, washing-machines, and central-heating systems. With regard to industrial goods it would rarely be practicable to employ such techniques because: (a) one is not dealing with a mass market and, (b) the high cost of producing prototypes. In general the feasibility of test marketing will depend on the cost of the product concerned.

Although it is mainly applicable to a new product, test marketing can also be conducted with new packaging, advertising or any other particular marketing factor.

Product Life Cycles

Just as there are trade cycles of boom and depression and monetary cycles of inflation and deflation so we can identify various phases through which a product passes and which collectively form its life cycle:

(a) *The Development Phase:* during which the majority of investment is incurred and the decision is reached on whether to proceed with the introduction of the product into test areas or with a national launch.

(b) *The Introductory Phase:* the period of test marketing or national launch. Little, if any, profit is likely to be made from the product at this stage. The product will be moving through the distribution channels and making its first appearance to the general public.

(c) *The Growth Phase:* the cumulative effect of advertising, sales promotion and actual selling will be establishing the product firmly on the market. Profitability will reach its highest peak as the market share is increased.

(d) *The Competitive Phase:* the initial advantage gained by product introduction is gradually lost as competitive products appear, perhaps with improved specifications, or at lower prices forcing the manufacturer to intensify his selling effort (and thereby his selling cost) in order to maintain his position in the market. During this period the product usually requires intensified advertising support and promotional schemes.

(e) *The Declining or Revitalising Phase:* when the manufacturer has finally to decide whether to accept that the decline in sales and profitability is such that the product should be discontinued or to implement previously prepared plans to revitalise it in order to prolong its profitable life. He may reduce the price, alter the packaging or select other channels of distribution in order to achieve the required results.

The Importance of New Products

The costs incurred in research and development of a completely new product will frequently be higher than the outlay required to modify an existing product. It can also be expected that the new product will take longer to show a profit return than an improved product. Why then do manufacturers introduce new products?

Despite the greater risks incurred, there are three main reasons:

(a) To provide an effective means of maintaining or increasing market share.
(b) To spread the business risks over a broader product base.
(c) To improve the return on capital employed in the business by fuller utilisation of resources; for example, by ironing out the effect of seasonal variations in production.

Some indication of the importance of new product introductions has been given by Unilever Limited, one of the country's largest industrial concerns, who in 1957 stated that 20 per cent of their sales of detergents, 25 per cent of sales of toilet preparations, and 22 per cent of sales of food products were accounted for by products not on the market six years previously.

Branding and Brand Management

Originally, branding was a means of identifying ownership of property (as with sheep or cattle) or products with their maker (as with silverware or pottery). Within the context of marketing, branding is simply the naming of a product so as to give it added appeal and recognition. For example, a perfume has more appeal to women (and perhaps men) when labelled 'Desire' or 'Irresistible' than if it is simply packed in box marked 'Johnson & Matthews Perfume No. 241/B'.

Branding techniques are used extensively in the marketing of such items as petrol, cigarettes and detergents. In these and many other instances, competition between different brands produced by the same manufacturer is as keen as competition between the manufacturers themselves. For instance, although there are approximately eight well-known brands all competing for a share of the detergent market, only two major manufacturers are involved. Cigarette manufacturers produce different brands for different segments of the market in order to achieve the maximum share of the total market, but they also deliberately market more than one brand aimed at satisfying the same market segment in their efforts to capture the largest share of that particular segment.

The success of branding is dependent upon effective advertising. Branding enables the customer to associate the product on display with the qualities of the product that he has seen advertised, or has sampled on a previous occasion.

The Brand Manager is the co-ordinator of all the factors influencing his product from its inception and throughout its life. Such factors will include: its profitability, specification, packaging, advertising, distribution and relationship to competitive products.

2.4 DISTRIBUTION

The function of distribution is to transfer goods (or services) from the producer to the ultimate consumer. It is the essential link between production and consumption, comprising two main elements, storage and transportation.

We have seen that there can be no mass-production without mass-consumption, similarly there can be no mass-consumption without mass-distribution. The most saleable article is a liability unless it is available to those who wish to purchase it.

The objectives of distribution therefore are to ensure that the right goods in the right quantities are in the right place(s) at the right time(s).

In order to achieve the objectives of distribution, it is essential that the producer chooses the most suitable channel (or channels) of distribution. By channel of distribution we mean a combination of organisation, transportation and storage. Organisation of course involves not only the producer but any firm, or person, who plays a part in the transfer of goods (or services) from producer to consumer.

51

The most common form of organisation involves the transfer of goods from:

PRODUCER

to

WHOLESALER

to

RETAILER

to

CONSUMER

There are variations to this pattern, such as: producer direct to consumer, or producer to retailer to consumer, and so on. The terms wholesaler and retailer are generally understood. However, within these categories there are many different types. At the wholesaler level, for example, there are Brokers or Sole Concessionaires. **Brokers** do not usually become involved in physical distribution (that is, physically handling the goods), but tend to engage in buying and selling. For example, a broker may purchase from a manufacturer his entire production output and then resell to numerous wholesalers, who would be responsible for the physical distribution. In certain circumstances the broker's function is part financier in that he will contract to pay for the goods before they are produced, and thereby provide working capital for the manufacturer. The *sole concessionaire* acts as the manufacturer's representative, usually in relation to imported goods. Sometimes he engages in physical distribution, and sometimes he arranges distribution through conventional wholesalers and/or retailers.

At the retail level there is a broad distinction between what may be termed 'freelance' retailers and 'agents' or 'dealers', the major difference being that agents or dealers usually have binding agreements with their supplier or manufacturer whereas the freelance retailers do not.

There are three basic considerations which influence channel selection:

(a) *Market considerations*

Market characteristics may have an effect upon distribution, and therefore must be examined. For example:

    (i) The channel of distribution chosen to satisfy the 'industrial' sector of the market will usually differ from that chosen for the 'consumer' sector.

    (ii) Where seasonal demand cannot be met by seasonal production, storage facilities may be required for the goods which are accumulating as a result of continuous production. These are sometimes referred to as buffer stocks.

(iii) Variations in purchasing habits between different parts of the country or between different income groups may also have an effect, resulting perhaps, in the selection of two or more channels for the same type of product.

(b) *Product considerations*

The composition, size, weight or technical complexity of the product can all affect channel selection. For example:

(i) Perishable products will require either special transport and storage facilities such as refrigerated containers for rapid distribution to the consumer.

(ii) The actual size and weight of the product can also impose limitations; some products may be shipped partially assembled for final reassembly at the point of sale. This is frequently the practice when distributing to overseas markets.

(iii) Complex products may require installation by qualified technicians and/or after-sales service, including the distribution of spare parts.

(c) *Economic considerations*

In Europe distribution costs account for between 35 per cent and 50 per cent of the retail price of the product. In seeking to distribute his products as economically as possible, a manufacturer will objectively analyse all the alternatives, which will require a decision on the extent to which he himself becomes involved in distribution. For example, capital is often tied up in finished goods. A manufacturer may choose, therefore, a channel of distribution which does not necessitate his holding such an inventory, thus releasing and perhaps even reducing the working capital he requires for his business. In this instance, of course, he will be obliged to give a greater discount to the wholesaler, since the costs of holding inventory will still have to be met. In general terms, distribution costs arise from the storage and handling of goods. Ultimately, the consumer meets these costs in the purchase price of the product.

The discount system has evolved as a convenient method of sharing the gross profit on a particular product between the producer and those involved in distribution and sale of the product. In its simplest form it operates as follows:

Cost of production	=	£100
+Manufacturer's margin of profit	=	£10
Therefore price to wholesaler	=	£110
+Wholesalers profit	=	£5
Therefore price to retailer	=	£115
+Retailers profit	=	£5
Therefore price to consumer	=	£120

In practice, of course, there are many variations involving special discounts, as with volume discount (an additional discount given where large volumes are concerned).

In choosing the channel of distribution, especially in regard to the number of outlets (either wholesale or retail), care will have to be taken to ensure that the total potential business justifies the investment made, thus ensuring an adequate return on capital to those engaged in distribution. Over recent years, increasing costs, especially labour, land and buildings, have resulted in a reduction in the number of firms and outlets engaged in the distributive industry.

In order to safeguard the distribution of their products many manufacturers have adopted a policy of rationalisation. In practice this means that they have selectively reduced the number of outlets for their products with the object of increasing the turnover and profitability of the remainder.

2.5 SALES PROMOTION

Sales promotion might be described as merchandising the product in such a manner that it is self-motivating in attracting the prospective customers and inducing them to buy. This takes a variety of forms, but in all instances it concerns a physical presentation with the sole objective of promoting a sale. For example, point of sale displays are often used by supermarkets and large department stores. Research has shown that the housewife will be more likely to purchase a can of peas if they are loosely assembled in an easily accessible position, rather than being neatly stacked on shelves in a self-service store at a height which causes her to stoop, reach and disturb a neat display. Consequently a sales promotion campaign on cans of peas would be likely to emerge as an eye-level display at a position in the store where shoppers must pass, such as the entrance or exit or cash counter.

There are numerous forms of presentations which involve display, with visual aids to attract the customers and induce them to buy. In addition there are many promotional schemes which are allied to special products; these take the form of incentives such as trading stamps, competitions, dispensers or gifts.

One of the most significant areas of promotional display is on the garage forecourt, where we see exceptional developments in the marketing of spares and accessories, cigarettes and confectionery. Sales promotion is an act of showmanship and persuasion, sometimes subtle, sometimes blatant, but at all times a device to encourage and attract the customer.

Packaging

The emergence of supermarkets, self-service stores, mail order houses, vending machines, the development in spare parts and accessories presentation have all brought the need for a new product characteristic, its package.

The traditional role of packaging, which was largely confined to protection and handling requirements, became subordinate to the increasing need to package for sales promotion, advertising, development of brand image and market penetration in a highly competitive economy.

Not so very long ago, it would have been difficult to visualise the potato, which was sold from a dusty and earthy sack on the forecourt of the greengrocer's shop, being supplied washed and in a bright handy package. It would have been even more difficult for the miner hewing coal in the depths of the earth to visualise that the results of his labour would show up in the market place in neat brown packages, suitable to be placed in the boot of the family car. These examples illustrate the practical applications of this key element in present-day business.

Remember the marketing concept: *Looking at the business through the eyes of the consumer.*

How does the consumer look at the business? The consumer is only interested in the end product.

When a housewife looks at the package on the shelf of the department store, she makes the decision whether to buy it or not to buy. At this point the person on whom the total effort has been concentrated is being influenced—motivated—excited—prejudiced—activated by the package and the message it conveys.

55

Two independent channels have merged together in the final act of giving the consumer what he wants: the function of what it does and the aesthetics of what it looks like. The question of aesthetics versus function in packaging is a continual source of discussion, it might be argued that it is the continual story of packaging.

A package must meet the requirements of aesthetics, creativity and brand image, to uphold the life and future of the product. It must also meet the requirements of protection, handling and distribution. In the final analysis it brings us up to the product image at the crucial point in the chain of marketing events—the point of sale.

Packaging for sales promotion as a specific objective will start at the design and planning stage from a different platform than packaging for long-term identification, protection, brand-image building and selling purposes. The very best example is the seasonal influence of Christmas on many consumer goods.

Promotional packaging is aimed at inducing impulse buying; it has short-term objectives and is subjected to continuous changes. The Christmas season gives special opportunities to stimulate consumer interest in one product or another by attractive packaging which readily identifies the article with the consumer needs. Promotional packaging concentrates on creating excitement and enthusiasm in the mind of the would-be purchaser at the point of sale. This applies whether dealing with seasonal consumer goods or packaging industrial goods for promotional drives to meet marketing objectives.

Advertising

We stated earlier that mass-production has to be matched by mass-consumption; this in turn requires mass-communication. Commercial advertising is the means by which a company disseminates information to the market about its products or services. In other words, it is an exercise in mass-communication.

Of all the marketing functions, therefore, advertising is the most familiar to us but it should be realised that it is only one of the tools of marketing, just as market research and sales promotion are others. It is one more ingredient in the marketing mix, just as product features and packaging are others, which leads to the ultimate sale. The contribution of advertising is to communicate the sales message to the potential purchaser in such a way as to increase the likelihood of a sale.

In practice, therefore, advertising has two main elements: the *message* (or *copy*) and the *medium*.

Advertisements usually consist of words and pictures. The words are prepared by a copywriter and the pictures by an artist or photographer. This work is combined by a layout artist or *visualiser*. In preparing the advertisement, this creative group will be concerned with answers to the following questions:

To whom is the advertisement addressed?
What benefit does the product (or service) advertised offer the people to whom it is addressed?
What should be the basic appeal of the advertisement?

Note that the *appeal* of an advertisement is usually directed towards basic human needs (which are discussed in Chapter 5). This is why potential customers are persuaded to identify with characters portrayed in advertisements. Products are often 'sold' on the basis of fulfilling some deep psychological satisfaction which goes beyond the direct function of the product; this explains the portrayal of human (and non-human) responses in relation to such relatively humdrum products as washing-up liquid, cubes of beef extract, etc. The *message* is conveyed by the *medium*, which is the channel of communication; thus commercial radio, popular magazines, daily newspapers and television are *media* which may connect the advertiser with the consumers he is seeking.

We have seen that an important function of market research is to identify the segment of the market to which a particular manufacturer is proposing to sell his goods. But this research must be carried further to determine the environmental circumstances and behavioural characteristics of the market group. Such market information will be essential in the proper selection of appropriate media.

Some indication of the relative importance of each of the media may be gained from the advertising expenditure figures which are shown below:

ADVERTISING MEDIA AND EXPENDITURE 1957–68

	£ million			
	1957	1960	1964	1968
Press	157	218	271	320
Television	48	72	102	132
Poster & transport	49	29	18	20
Outdoor signs			15	15
Cinema	8	5	6	6
Radio	0	1	2	1
Total	262	325	414	494

ADVERTISING MEDIA AND EXPENDITURE IN 1968

	%
National newspapers	20
Regional newspapers	20
Magazines and periodicals	10
Trade journals	9
Other	6
Total press	65
Television	27
Poster and transport	4
Outdoor signs	3
Cinema	1
Radio	0
	100

Source: *The Advertising Association.*

Advertising costs will depend on the media used. For instance the cost of a square inch of space in the *Radio Times* may be £55 whereas the same amount of space in a local newspaper may be bought for a few pence. With regard to advertising expenditure by product groups, some interesting facts are revealed in a survey of 1968 expenditure by *Legion Publishing*. The three most heavily advertised groups were chocolate and confectionery, cigarettes and soaps, and detergents. Expenditure on chocolate and confectionery was in excess of £10 million. Financial advertising also reached new records with the banks spending £3·7 million and unit trusts a further £3·3 million. In the battle for supremacy in the razor-blade market, Gillette spent £791,000 to Wilkinson's £870,000.

In considering expenditure on advertising, it should be mentioned that the amount spent does not represent the true net cost of advertising. Of the £290 million spent on consumer advertising in 1962 it is estimated that there was a subsidy element of approximately £100 million contributing towards the costs of the press and other media. Somewhere between 35 per cent and 60 per cent of the revenue of newspapers and journals in this country is derived from advertising. Were it not for the expenditure on press advertising a number of well-known newspapers and periodicals would cease to exist and it is probable that the price of others would be doubled. In the past ten years spending on advertising has remained fairly constant as a proportion of the gross national product (about 1·4 per cent), and also as a proportion of total consumer spending (about 1·8 per cent).

The key to success in advertising, as in all other aspects of marketing, lies in proper planning. A prerequisite of planning is the setting of clearly defined objectives. Within the established overall company marketing objectives, advertising planning will be concerned with answering the questions: *What* has to be said, *to whom* and *how?* As an integral part of the total marketing function, advertising must be so planned as to convey the required company message as well as the sales message of the particular product.

There are 6 basic steps in advertising planning:

(a) Identify the market or market segment to be reached.
(b) Determine and create the advertising message.
(c) Select the most effective and most economical media to reach the market.
(d) Schedule the media to provide the best timing, frequency and impact of the message.
(e) Determine the advertising budget.
(f) Measure results of the advertising.

Advertising Agencies

The early advertising agencies in the mid-19th century were solely concerned with selling advertising space in newspapers and other journals. With the growth of competition and the evolution of marketing techniques, the role of the advertising agency changed and additional services were offered to their clients. From selling advertising space, it was a short step to producing the actual advertising copy. Nowadays the larger agencies can offer their clients complete marketing programmes and their functions include: market research, campaign planning, media planning, merchandising and public relations. The creative functions will involve work for copy-writers, script-writers, visualisers, pack designers and other artists.

It will be clear from what has gone before that advertising is a specialised function within the marketing organisation. So too within the advertising function itself there is a further degree of specialisation.

The growth of advertising has led to the formation of many advertising agencies; some, like S. H. Benson and J. Walter Thompson, have become public companies. Inevitably there develops a close association between an agency, whether large or small, and its client companies, since careful advertising planning will dictate that the agency must be in full possession of its client's forward plans for product introduction and an agent will not offer its services simultaneously to companies competing in the same market.

By retaining the services of the same agency over a prolonged period, a company may expect to develop a very close working relationship with its agency whereby the agency is able to assist in developing the company's basic marketing policies or anticipate changes with consequent benefit to both parties.

Advertising accounts are, however, continually changing hands and there is strong competition between agencies to secure accounts where massive advertising appropriations are involved. Similarly there is considerable movement of staff from one agency to another. This is inevitable in a field where new ideas are at a premium. If a company changes its marketing policy or enters a new product field or plans to enter a completely new market with an existing product it may decide to change its advertising agency. In such circumstances it will perhaps invite a number of agencies to submit outline plans from which it will select the one which it feels best meets its requirements.

Measuring Results of Advertising

It is frequently said that about half of all advertising is wasted; the difficulty is to find out which half. This may perhaps be an overstatement but it is not without an element of truth for, although it is important that a company can judge whether its expenditure on advertising is having the desired results, there are many difficulties yet to be overcome in the measurement of advertising effectiveness.

Basically advertising is a two-way means of communication, the sales message of the product is transmitted to the customer and the customer's response is transmitted back to the producer. To the extent that the effectiveness of these communications can be measured, it is possible to measure the results of advertising. Since advertising is but one of the components leading to a sale and is not a means of selling in itself, effectiveness cannot be measured in terms of sales.

In addition the marketing of a product does not take place in a vacuum, there are many variable factors, each of which will influence the market. Such factors include competitive activity, changes in the economic climate or in consumer tastes and attitudes.

By means of surveys, the return of coupons, acceptance of premium offers and so on, it is possible to measure the extent to which an advertisement has been seen and acted upon.

In America, research has been carried out in this field but very little is yet known about the relationship between the establishment of a favourable attitude in the mind of the customer and actual purchasing or intention to purchase.

Control of Advertising

Even the briefest survey of advertising would be incomplete without some reference to the controls to which it is subject. The controls which are self-imposed and complicated but effective, are based on the British Code of Advertising Practice. This stipulates that all advertising shall be legal, clean, honest and truthful; it also lays down a number of requirements to which advertisers and their agencies must adhere.

Failure to conform to the standards laid down by the Code may result in the alteration or the withdrawal of the offending advertisement. In extreme cases, advertisers are refused advertising space or time.

There are many associations connected with the advertising business and the Code of Practice is sponsored by eighteen of these associations. The senior supervisory body is the Advertising Association, consisting of representatives from companies in all sides of the advertising business. It operates the Advertising Investigation Department which, together with the Advertising Standards Authority and the Code of Advertising Practice Committee, is responsible for administering the Code of Practice.

In addition to the rigid self-imposed standards, British advertising is also governed by nearly sixty Acts of Parliament.

These include various requirements of the:

Food and Drug Acts
Betting and Lotteries Act
Merchandising Marks Acts
Television Act
Town and Country Planning Act
Trade Descriptions Act

2.6 PRICING

Pricing policy determines the major source of income for most companies, which is why it is so important. The major objectives of a pricing policy are two-fold; to achieve a target return on investment and to maintain or improve a company's share of the market. Pricing policy is subject to long-term and short-term considerations, so that a company's pricing strategy may well change markedly over time. For instance, prices may be set low in the short run in order to capture a new market segment, or in order to maintain production in a slack season and a company may bear a temporary loss as a result; this loss may be made up in the future if the company is able to increase its prices without losing sales.

Pricing strategy must include provision for many factors in addition to the income received from each sale; all the incentives that are offered to persuade the customer to buy the product (such as special discounts, trading stamps, gifts, competitions) must be accounted for when the price is set.

Methods of pricing are generally classified as follows:

(a) *Cost-plus pricing:* where total costs are calculated and a margin is added to provide an anticipated profit per unit. This method demands a very accurate knowledge of the structure of costs and the ability to distinguish how various categories of cost behave at different levels of output.

(b) *The Contribution Approach:* which is an attempt to balance market demand and costs of production by developing tables which reveal what level of sales is required to enable a company to 'break even'; sales above this level make a contribution to profits (see page 109).

(c) *Competitive pricing:* where prices are determined by competitors established in the market. Newcomers to a market may find that consumers have accepted a price structure which yields a very high profit to the companies concerned; to react to this by offering a new product at a substantially lower price invites disaster from two possible sources:

(i) The customers, who may not accept that a new and cheaper brand is as good as the brands they are used to;

(ii) The competitors, who may have large enough resources to start a price war in order to drive the new entrant out of business.

A major problem in pricing is to establish the relationships between the volume of sales and:

(a) Income (this relationship is called **Income Elasticity of Demand,** the relationship between demand and various levels of income).

(b) Price (this relationship is called **Price Elasticity of Demand** and is a measure of the reaction of demand to changes in price). Demand is said to be **elastic** when a small change in price produces a large change in demand; when demand is not responsive to changes in price it is said to be **inelastic.**

Many marketing managers argue that **price plateaux** exist for some products, above which demand becomes very elastic; an increase in price above the 'plateau' tending to bring forth a sharp slump in demand. These 'plateaux' are thought to exist around the following prices:

25p	£1	£5
£25	£50	£100
£5,000	£1,000	£2,000

and to apply, in particular, to such products as cigarettes, chocolates, products in the Christmas trade, furniture, radios, television sets or motor-cars.

2.7 THE SELLING FUNCTION

We have considered various aspects of the marketing function, such as market research, product planning, sales promotion and distribution, but all these activities represent a cost to the manufacturer. It is only when his goods are sold that the manufacturer is able to recover those costs and to show a profit from his efforts.

With the infinite variety in the needs of consumers in terms of goods and services it is only to be expected that there should be a wide range of sales methods and techniques.

The Nature of Salesmanship

What do we mean by salesmanship and why does a marketing-orientated company need salesmen anyway? After all, if the company has observed the basic precept of studying the market and is offering a product which satisfies the needs of consumers, it should not need salesmen: the product should sell itself. If there were no such thing as competition then such a situation might well apply. But we know that there are very few products which enjoy a 100 per cent share of the market and where such conditions do exist they are usually short-lived. The more usual situation is that there are available from different manufacturers, a number of similar products whose specification and price are so alike that it is only superiority in one of the marketing areas, such as advertising, sales promotion or salesmanship, that gives one or the other a lead over its competitors.

Let us consider a hypothetical case where a buyer is faced with making a choice between three products, each of which he has seen and which he believes will meet his requirements in terms of price, specification and delivery. The chances are that if his enquiry is followed up by a personal visit from the salesman for one of the products, then he is more likely to place his order for that product than for either of the other two.

In real life it is more likely that the prospective buyer will receive visits from salesmen for each of the three products and in this case it will probably be the salesman who can persuade him that his product has the features which most closely fulfil the customer's particular needs who receives the order.

We can now begin to see that salesmanship consists of (and is sometimes defined as) *personal, persuasive communication.* Despite wide differences in methods of operation and techniques, the successful door-to-door brush salesman and the sales manager negotiating a multi-million pound contract for machine tools have this in common, both are able to communicate persuasively their sales message to their customer.

Self-Service and Self Selection

A self-service store is one in which customers select and help themselves from the goods on display and then pay for all the goods they have collected at a check point before leaving the store. Almost all grocery supermarkets operate in this way.

A self-selection store is one in which the customer chooses the goods he requires but staff are available to wrap the goods, to deal with payment and with the customer's queries.

In both systems there are advantages to the customer and to the retailer. The customer is able to spend as much or as little time as he chooses, and can freely compare the goods on display. The retailer can operate the store with fewer sales staff since the customer does not receive the personal attention which is necessary in ordinary service stores.

In some stores both self-service and self-selection methods are used; for instance, in many supermarkets the meat, vegetables, and delicatessen sections are operated by counter staff who will cut, weigh and wrap the goods, whereas the general groceries are displayed on open shelves from which the customer will help himself.

The growth of both methods has been one of the most significant developments in retailing in the past decade. According to a report published in 1968 a survey by *Gallup Poll* showed that self-service and self-selection stores together account for over 60 per cent of grocery sales in the U.K. and by the mid-1970s the figure is expected to be about 80 per cent.

The following table shows the growth in supermarkets, defined as stores with over 2,000 square feet of selling area operating on self-service lines with check-outs:

	Approx. number	Approx. sales £ million	Approx. % of all grocery sales
1958	150		
1961		138	5·8
1962	1,000		
1963		268·1	11·4
1968	3,000	700	23·0
Forecast			
1973	5,000		50·0
1975	7,000		
1977	7,200	3,000	60·0

(Sources: J. Gulliver, Chairman of Fine Fare (Holdings) Ltd., D. W. Smallbone – The Practice of Marketing; Contimart Report–The British Market)

Some supermarkets are taking about £2 per square foot per week or the equivalent of about 40 family grocery shops; trading margins are 18 to 19 per cent, wage costs as a percentage of sales are about 6.3–6.4 per cent and average stock turn is 18·3 per annum. These figures compare with trading margins of 15 per cent, wage costs of 8 per cent and stock turn of 15·3 per cent in orthodox grocery shops, and indicate very serious competition for ordinary retailers who are handling similar merchandise. Much thought is given to the layout of supermarkets in order to permit customer flow; and goods are arranged so that customers will be directed past impulse purchase items before necessities are reached. Attractive packaging and prominent display has encouraged a very high degree of impulse buying; one estimate has put this at 70 per cent in self-service stores.

Since the criterion of success in the supermarket is the achievement of maximum profit per square foot, the amount of shelf space allotted to a given brand will depend on its market share. Of the 7,000 standard grocery items, 2,000 yield 90 per cent of the turnover and 1,000 yield 60 per cent of the turnover. High demand items are, therefore, given more shelf space than low demand items.

If you are wondering why this section is predominantly concerned with the retailing of foodstuffs, it should be borne in mind that food is by far the most important item of expenditure in the household budget and accounts for approximately 30 per cent of all consumer expenditure.

C

65

Automatic Vending

Although slot machines have been used in this country for many years for the sale of such items as stamps and chocolate, it was mainly during the 1960s that automatic vending machines became widely used for other merchandise. It has been estimated that the number of vending machines in use in the U.K. has grown from 42,000 in 1957 to over 200,000 today with a total annual turnover in excess of £20 million.

With the advance in technology and packaging, there has been an increase in the range of goods available from automatic vending machines so that is is now possible to obtain a wide selection of items including soft drinks, tea, coffee, snacks and even coal in this way.

The machines are usually situated out of doors, adjacent to retail outlets and at bus and railway stations. Most of the best outdoor sites have now been taken up and many of the recent installations are in factories and offices. It seems inevitable that the earlier reserve with which automatic vending machines were treated in this country will gradually diminish as the convenience of the method becomes more fully recognised. The trend towards a reduction in working hours and rising labour costs in the service industries are also likely to lead to more widespread automatic vending.

Mail Order

Mail-order trading needs little explanation. As its description implies, it is the ordering of goods by post direct from the manufacturer or mail-order company. The order is usually placed as a result of the customer having seen the goods advertised in the press or in a catalogue which has been circulated by the mail-order company.

The technique originated in the U.S.A., where a high proportion of the population lived in remote areas poorly served by local shopping facilities. Its growth in this country, while possibly less dramatic than in the U.S.A., has nevertheless been significant and at a rate of about 10 per cent per annum compared with 2–3 per cent in the retail trade generally.

The growth of mail-order business in the U.K.:

	Approximate sales in £ million
1947	47
1961	276
1968	450

Recent published results of one mail-order house show the following sales trend:

1964	£9,445,000
1965	£12,077,000
1966	£15,477,000
1967	£18,200,000
1968	£23,515,000

Mail-order firms and the methods by which they operate can be divided into three main groups:

1. Those who advertise their goods to the public in general usually through the medium of the press.
2. Those who contact consumers direct by mail.
3. Those who issue catalogues of their goods to group organisers, agents or consumers.

According to the 1961 Census of Distribution, 91 per cent of the U.K. mail-order business was handled by twenty-eight firms in category 3. The largest of these firms are Littlewood's and Great Universal Stores, both of whom also own retail stores. Most of the remaining business was conducted by about 4,000 firms in category 1, each of whom tended to specialise in certain types of goods such as clothing, watches and portable buildings.

A wide range of merchandise is sold through mail order, but clothing accounts for the greatest proportion by value.

The major problems associated with this method of selling are the high proportion of goods returned by the customer (many firms advertise a money-back guarantee) and the difficulty in finding new agents. Despite these drawbacks the sales figures show substantial increase in recent years and the trend is expected to continue, partly as a result of the more widespread availability of branded merchandise. The increasing congestion of high-street shopping centres may also contribute to further growth in mail-order sales.

Retail Trade Financing

In the previous sections, we have discussed a number of methods by which sales of goods and services are effected. In each method there is a straightforward transaction between buyer and seller whereby the goods or services are exchanged (or sold) for an agreed sum in a single transaction.

There is, however, a growing volume of business being conducted other than by outright cash purchase. Some of the methods used are considered below.

Hire purchase

This is a method of buying goods by instalments. The total cost is higher than if the same goods were purchased outright for cash, because of the interest charges on the money borrowed. When goods are bought on hire purchase, the purchaser pays an initial deposit and agrees to pay the balance by instalments over an agreed period. The amount of both the initial deposit and the length of the payback period are subject to regulation by the Chancellor of the Exchequer, who frequently uses his powers to vary these rates as one of his weapons to control the total level of consumer demand. In a hire purchase transaction, the goods remain the property of the seller until the last instalment is paid. This form of buying originated in the United States and initially met with severe prejudice in this country.

Credit sales

Credit sales are a halfway house to personal loans and security for the goods purchased rests, not in the goods, but in the credit standing of the borrower. The customer agrees to pay for the goods within a stipulated time and charges are related to the length of time over which credit is extended. Both H.P. agreements and credit sales are subject to a clause of the Hire Purchase Act, 1965, under which contracts are subject to a 72-hour 'cooling-off' period, in which the customer may withdraw from his contract without obligation.

In 1957 the total instalment credit debt in Britain was £448 million. This had grown to £872 million in 1963 and approximately £1,000 million in 1969, when roughly one quarter of the debt was owed to retailers and the balance to finance houses.

Deferred payments schemes like H.P. and credit sales were developed as a method of buying to suit people with low incomes. The expansion in these types of transaction is partly the result of improvements in design and reductions in cost of consumer durables, partly due to the rise in incomes and also a result of continued inflation. As incomes rise, it becomes progressively easier to maintain fixed repayments. It could be argued, however, that working class customers are forced to pay more for their consumer durables because they tend to be dependent on H.P., whereas middle-class customers may finance their purchases in other ways— from bank overdrafts, for example, a much cheaper form of borrowing. In recent years there has been a trend away from H.P. transactions (which involve dealers in a good deal of paperwork and the risk of having to bear the costs of repossession when customers do not keep up their payments), towards credit sale agreements and, more recently, towards personal loans.

Personal loans have several advantages. They are not subject to the changes which the Chancellor imposes frequently on hire purchase transactions, they eliminate the large commissions which finance houses pay to dealers who direct business to them and, until 1969, tax advantages accrued to borrowers who paid income tax at the standard rate. Two important sources of credit which have emerged in recent years are Barclaycard and the loan system operated by Mercantile Credit through the National Giro. These loans are more expensive than bank overdrafts, but bank overdrafts have been severely restricted in recent years by the Chancellor. This is another reason why consumers have been turning to new sources of personal finance.

Hiring or leasing

Under hiring or leasing schemes, goods remain the property of the firm which supplies them. The customer enters into a leasing agreement with the supplier, whereby he obtains the use but not the ownership of the goods on payment of a fee or rental on a regular basis for the duration of the agreement. This method is commonly used with such items as motor-cars, television sets and washing-machines. Usually under the terms of such agreements the user is responsible for providing service and maintenance whereas under leasing agreements, the lessor contracts to provide to the lessee service or maintain the goods in a usable condition at all times.

This method is becoming increasingly widely used in industrial goods, for example, tractors and other costly items of machinery in which the user does not wish to tie up his own or borrowed capital.

Stamp trading

This is a method by which retailers give their customer a small discount either on all or on selected purchases. The discount is in the form of stamps which, when saved, enable the consumer to obtain goods of his choice to the equivalent value of the stamps collected which are then surrendered.

The practice was introduced into this country in the 1920s and apart from a break during the second world war, has grown rapidly. There are some twenty-five trading stamp companies operating (of whom 'Green Shield' are perhaps the best known) claiming about 40,000 retail outlets mostly grocers, supermarkets, and petrol stations.

The economics of stamp trading are, that the retailer purchases stamps and this costs $2\frac{1}{2}$ per cent of turnover, the customer obtains the equivalent of $1\frac{1}{2}$ per cent discount off the purchase price of the goods he obtains in exchanging his stamps. The stamp trader obtains his profit from two sources, firstly his return on the face value of the stamps and secondly from his ability to purchase items in bulk at attractive terms from manufacturers. There is also the hidden profit which he derives from unredeemed stamps held by the consumer.

After-Sales Service

The importance of after-sales service cannot be over-emphasised because it is often the deciding factor in the mind of the prospective purchaser when he compares one product against another of similar specification and price and makes the decision to buy. Indeed, some buyers will base their choice of product entirely on the level of after-sales service. A good example of this is the plant hire company which may have a dozen excavators or crawler tractors working on a 'timed' contract in a national road-building programme. The company must be absolutely sure that, when the plant breaks down or needs replacement parts, the facilities will be available for them to make quick repairs and resume work in the minimum time.

In a free competitive society where shortage of most industrial and consumer goods no longer exists, the transitional period from shortage to abundance has brought with it a new dimension of the 'after-sales service' aspect in the affairs of many large companies. We have mentioned the motor industry, the agricultural machinery industry and the heavy construction machinery industry; it is equally applicable to the makers of, say, domestic appliances, television and radio sets and lawn-mowers.

2.8 EXPORTING

Overseas marketing produces many special problems which do not arise in companies which are solely concerned with home trade; the differences, however, are matters of *degree* rather than *kind* and in this section we consider briefly how marketing principles are applied to the special problems of exporting. Basically the marketing requirements are the same, but there is a greater need for co-ordination and specialised knowledge. For example:

(a) *Knowledge of the market* now extends to the need for information on economic, geographic, political, social and linguistic pheno-mena which may not exist in the home market.

(b) *Market Research* may have to be conducted at long range and will have to take into account the prospect of changes in the value of currencies, unexpected changes in taxes, import tariffs, and other factors. Knowledge is required of specialised sources of information, provided by newspapers and journals (try to find time to look at some reviews of overseas markets published by *The Economist*), the commercial banks, the Board of Trade and specialised agencies.

(c) *Distribution*, the task of delivering the product into the hand of the final consumer usually involves a number of intermed-iaries.

(d) *Finance*, the task of providing funds for expansion into over-seas markets and, in particular, of providing insurance against all the hazards involved in shipping over long distances in foreign currencies.

A large number of specialised marketing and financial institutions operate in this field, many of which are assisted and supplemented by the Government. There has been a rapid increase in government activity in this area since 1964 because of the critical state of the balance of payments. The following are some examples of specialised institutions which give assistance to exporters:

(a) The Board of Trade, which provides insurance for exports through the Export Credits Guarantee Department and which provides, through its Export Intelligence and Services branches a free service of guidance on individual export problems, information on overseas markets, status reports on foreign firms, help with overseas business visits and similar matters.

(b) The commercial banks, which provide specialised advice and finance for exporters, usually exempt from any credit 'squeeze' at home.

(c) Confirming houses, which guarantee to the supplier that he will be paid by the overseas buyer according to the terms of the contract between them.

(d) Shipping and forwarding agents.

(e) Export houses, which provide the services noted in (c) above plus such services as **export factoring** (a financial service which relieves the manufacturer of all the costs of exporting), shipping, packing, insurance and the preparation of export documentation.

(f) Overseas sales agents, who operate in overseas markets on behalf of companies in the home market.

71

2.9 PUBLIC RELATIONS

The objective of public relations in industry is to create favourable attitudes towards the company. As a matter of deliberate policy, most of the larger business organisations develop a 'public image' and their marketing policies and advertising are designed to project this image, or company philosophy.

The following quotation from a major industrial company's handbook on public relations will illustrate what we mean:

'We must provide information to show the extent of our contribution to the prosperity of the community and we must ensure that our acts merit public favour and achieve public understanding. In order to do this we must establish a reputation and demonstrate our leadership in such matters as our record of social services, our policy towards labour, the lasting quality of our goods and services, the experience and ability of our staff and our general sense of responsibility towards those whom we serve.'

We saw earlier that, in marketing a product, it is necessary to define the segment with which one is concerned. Similarly, in public relations it is necessary to define the section of the public to which any particular story or news item should be directed. Some companies, therefore, classify the public into sections such as:

Shareholders
Customers
Employees
Suppliers
Dealers
Finance and banking circles
Government departments and agencies
Local communities
Press and radio editorial staffs

By defining these various categories, the public relations officer is able to select and present his material in such a way as to provide the greatest possible interest for each group.

Public relations has a dual role in communications and will act as the voice and the listening post for the firm. The required public image cannot be created and sustained unless information is available about outside opinion and attitude. Among specific responsibilities which are usually assigned to the public relations department are:

(a) originating company newspapers and house journals for external and internal circulation;

(b) handling all editorial contacts with the press, radio and television on a national and regional basis, by the issuing of press releases to daily newspapers and trade journals, holding press conferences, answering press enquiries, and by offering articles and photographs to the press;

(c) receiving visitors to the company and arranging visits programmes;

(d) arranging external and internal lectures, film shows, and other functions;

(e) making films about aspects of the company's affairs or co-operating with film-making organisations for the purpose;

(f) instituting and operating schemes and programmes designed to enhance the company's standing with the public, or sections of it.

The benefits to a company of good public relations are usually long term in their effect. It may take a number of years for the required 'public image' to percolate through the various media to the extent where public opinion towards the company is generally favourable. There is a short-term role which can be played by public relations when, for instance, it is called on to assist in the promotion of a particular product or service. It can also fulfil a useful advisory role when advertising and other promotions are being planned. Of course there is bound to be some overlapping between the functions of public relations and product promotion and it is right that these two should be closely co-ordinated.

As with most marketing activities, the role of public relations becomes increasingly important when competition between companies' products or services is greatest. But whereas it is the function of sales promotion to sell the product, it is the function of public relations to 'sell' the company image or philosophy.

FURTHER READING

Davies & Coy, *Economics from Square One*, Allen & Unwin, Chapters 1 and 2.

Delens, *Principles of Market Research*, Crosby Lockwood.

Rodger, *Marketing in a Competitive Economy*, Hutchinson.

Smallbone, *The Practice of Marketing*, Staples.

Organisation for Overseas Marketing, Board of Trade Export Handbook.

QUESTIONS

1. Explain the significance of the market research function within the marketing concept and describe briefly how the Market Research Department might be organised in a firm engaged in the manufacture of domestic appliances, such as washing-machines, refrigerators and electric fires.

2. Describe the development in the role and organisation of an advertising agency.

3. A major motor-car manufacturer in France recently announced its intention of marketing its products in the U.K. direct rather than through a chain of independent distributors. Why do you think it came to this decision and what steps will be necessary to implement it?

4. Describe briefly under the headings of (a) Market Research and (b) Distribution the problems of marketing TWO of the following products: textbooks on business organisation, insurance policies, coke, washing-up liquids, wigs.

5. 'A product is a cluster of psychological satisfactions.' Discuss.

CHAPTER THREE

The Production Function

3.1 PRODUCTION

To begin with, try to think of the term *Production* in the following contexts. Without reading further, what problems would you expect in trying to 'produce' the following goods and services (and what kind of specialist help would you need to solve them)?

a First Division football match, to be watched by 60,000 people every Saturday in the season;

a new steel works for a desert site in Israel;

sufficient cans to supply a manufacturer of baked beans for five years;

a new toothpaste for the teenage market;

a camera, to be the same size as a small cigarette lighter.

The discussion which follows relates mainly to the production of *goods*.

Production may be defined as the process of transforming raw materials into finished products, or of input into output. *The Employment and Productivity Gazette* shows that in March, 1968, 11,051,700 employees, or 49 per cent of a total labour force of 22,561,000, were engaged in production as follows:

Mining and Quarries	516,800
Food, Drink and Tobacco	809,500
Chemicals and Allied Industries	511,800
Metal Manufacture	583,900
Engineering and Electrical goods	2,305,200
Shipbuilding and Marine Engineering	193,800
Vehicles	810,200
Metal Goods	559,400
Textiles	693,400
Leather, Leather Goods and Fur	55,500
Clothing and Footwear	485,100
Bricks, Pottery, Glass, Cement, etc.	345,400
Timber, Furniture, etc.	301,400
Paper, Printing and Publishing	629,000
Other Manufacturing Industries	335,300
Construction	1,495,600
Gas, Electricity and Water	420,400
	11,051,700

You should note that production in this context differs from the definition used by economists in that it excludes *service* industries such as the retail trades, the Civil Service and the professions.

Types of Production System

It is possible to distinguish four types of production system, normally dependent upon the scale of operations employed:

Job Production (such as the making of a turbine for a large ship, like the *Q.E.2*) involves the output of a single product to specific requirements. Each product is a 'one-off' job, which may not be repeated and thus the prime features of job production are normally:

(a) a relatively high-priced product;
(b) the use of highly skilled labour;
(c) low capital costs of production system;
(d) a high degree of flexibility;
(e) centralisation of management.

Batch Production (such as the making of turbines for standard aircraft) involves the output of a batch or quantity of a product without there being continuous production. It often involves the production of goods for stock, such as standard components for the machine-tool industry. Its prime features are essentially the same as job production although in each case modified by the increase in scale so that although 'batch' production operatives will normally be less skilful than 'job' production operatives, a relatively high degree of skill is still demanded.

Mass Production (such as the manufacture of soap powder) involves the output of products of a uniform and standardised nature. Production is continuous and all units of production are so highly specialised that each is employed continually upon the same operation. The range of products made is usually very restricted and consequently output is very high. It requires a highly developed marketing organisation to make continuous production possible. Since mass production is production on a large scale, its prime features are in decided contrast to job production:

(a) a relatively low-priced product;
(b) a high proportion of semi- and unskilled labour;
(c) high capital costs of production system;
(d) little flexibility (because plant and equipment often has a very specialised use);
(e) less centralisation of management and a greater emphasis upon specialist services to management.

Process Production (such as oil refining) involves the output of a product whose nature is determined by the technological process used, as in the chemical industry. Production is continuous with an even higher degree of automation than in mass production. Like mass production, process production requires an effective marketing organisation, so that its expensive machinery can be employed without interruption. In fact just as batch production may be regarded as an extension of job production, so process production may be viewed as an extension of mass production, since the process production system is even more inflexible and highly capitalised than mass production.

Within any one industry, one type of production system may be dominant as is mass production in the motor industry. But in other industries all four types of production system may be found.

Scope of the Production Function

The production function encompasses all activities concerned directly with the manufacture of goods and materials. A typical production division within a company might be sub-divided into at least four distinct activities:

1. **Production Administration,** which may be defined as the process of effectively planning and regulating the operations of that part of an enterprise which is responsible for production. It usually incorporates such activities as production engineering, production planning and production control.
2. **Production Management,** which may be defined as the organisation and supervision of the actual production processes. It is important to remember that successful production management, whether at works manager or foreman level, demands an ability to regulate and co-ordinate human effort. It is therefore concerned with such aspects of production as supervision, reward, performance and control.
3. **Production Design,** which may be defined as the designing of products that consumers need and the factory can produce. It is likely also to involve the preparation of estimates and quotations, and research and development.
4. **Production Ancillaries,** which may be defined as those departments ancillary to the main production process but nevertheless providing a specific service to production. The most important is usually *purchasing*, which is the buying of all materials and supplies required in the productive process. Other typical ancillaries are *storekeeping* and *works engineering*. It is convenient to include *inspection* as an ancillary, although it is properly part of production control. However, it often operates as an independent acti-

vity because of its specialised nature and because it is desirable to have an independent check on the performance of production departments, in order to ensure that satisfactory standards are maintained.

Such a production division could be expressed in diagrammatic form (Fig. 3.1). You should note that this diagram is a functional model.

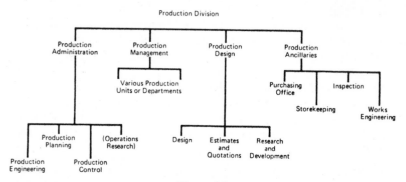

Figure 3.1

You must appreciate that this is no more than a model. There is no ideal production division and the organisation of any one will be largely a question of administrative convenience and company practice. Certainly the arrangements in any two companies are unlikely to be identical; in one company, the compilation of estimates and quotations may not be the responsibility of the production division at all; in another, works engineering may be attached to production administration; in a third research and development may be part of an entirely separate technical division. A worthwhile exercise would be to relate your own firm's production structure to this model. You may well find that the exercise is not an easy task! Remember then that this is simply a model and in practice there will be numerous variations from this model.

The question of titles is also worthy of comment. In a particular firm, any one of a number of titles may be given to the heads of the various departments. For instance, the head of production administration may be either the production **engineer** or the production **controller.** The actual title is again essentially a matter of company practice and it is much more important that you understand the nature of the functions exercised than that you memorise a string of titles.

78

Let us now examine the four areas of activity in much greater detail:

Production Administration
Production Management
Production Design
Production Ancillaries

3.2 PRODUCTION ADMINISTRATION

As we have seen, production administration is the process of effectively planning and regulating the operations of that part of an enterprise which is responsible for production. What you should grasp at the outset is that the setting up of a production administration division is a consequence of the realisation of the benefits to be derived from separating production administration from production management. Originally, production administration was indistinguishable from production management; the same person performed both functions at the same time and usually in the same place. By divorcing the two, effective planning and regulation is made more likely, production can now be planned by specialists away from the hubbub of the shop floor. At the same time, efficiency on the shop floor is likely to rise once the executive has been released from administrative responsibilities to concentrate on getting the product manufactured.

In a large firm, production administration is likely to incorporate such activities as:

(a) *Production Engineering*, which is concerned with the determination and specification of work processes. The functions of a production engineer are to investigate methods of production, prepare process specification, design tools and equipment, measure the rate of work and establish standard times.

(b) *Production Planning*, which, in addition to both short- and long-term production scheduling, usually includes the maintenance of material and stock records, progress charting and machine loading.

(c) *Production Control*, which concerns initially the recording of results and their correction for deviations from programmes.

Other activities such as *Operational Research* may fall equally within the province of either the production or administration functions. Whenever operational research is part of the production function, it will be within the production administration department (see page 210).

We shall now look at each of these in more detail:

Production Engineering

The prime aim of the production engineer is to find the best method of production. His three major functions are:

(a) *Work Study*, which entails an analysis of work performed in order to eliminate unnecessary labour.

(b) *Work Measurement*, which entails a measure of work content in order to make production planning, production control and the payment of operatives by results possible. Work study and measurement are closely allied and together involve three separate processes: observation of a particular job, analysis, and finally, the setting of work standards, based upon the concept of a 'fair day's work' so that the measurement of work in a common unit is possible.

(c) *Jig and Tool Design*, which involves the improvement of existing jigs and tools and the design of new jigs, tools and machinery. In jig and tool design the production engineer will work closely with production design and the works engineer.

Production Planning

The aim of production planning is to implement production policy as logically and effectively as possible. To be successful, production planning must be:

(a) geared to a suitable production policy. The most obvious policy would be to produce *what* is required, *when* it is required at minimum cost;

(b) realistic and based upon the facts, which is why production administration should logically include stock control in order, for example, to be able to ascertain the availability of materials;

(c) the result of a careful analysis of the facts so that production schedules, machine loading schedules, labour schedules do not conflict with sales forecasts, or involve delivery dates which are excessively optimistic;

(d) explained to the labour force through a series of targets, so that they have some conception of objectives;

(e) flexible, so that inevitable delays can be offset;

(f) not merely for the short term, but based upon long run considerations in order to obtain a balance of work between departments;

(g) subject to controls, which enable adjustments to be made when the plan 'is off target';

(h) above all, sensitive to the state of demand for the company's products as evidenced by the order book.

The order book will show the pattern of demand for the company's products in the coming months. Orders may be categorised into home and export, by product, by type of customer and if the order book shows a falling away in demand provision will have to be made for such action as:

(a) maintaining existing production schedules and letting stocks accumulate;

(b) discontinuing overtime, or going over to short-time working perhaps by bringing in the labour force only four days a week, or even less frequently;

(c) making some of the labour force redundant.

When there is a sharp increase in demand, production planners will examine the following possibilities:

(a) cutting stock levels to the barest minimum;

(b) introducing rationing (by permitting customers only a proportion of their orders);

(c) introducing overtime and week-end working;

(d) sub-contracting work to other manufacturers;

(e) the scope for long-term expansion and re-equipment.

Investment appraisal, or taking decisions on major changes in the stock of plant and equipment, is a major management function which is reserved to the highest levels in the organisation; it is the task of production planners to report the need for increased investment as soon as it becomes apparent. In doing so, account will be taken of:

(a) seasonal factors influencing demand, and

(b) the overall budget for activity in the works in the current financial year. For example, the budget may provide for a deliberate increase in stocks of certain products in order to support increases in demand anticipated in the following year.

In essence, Production Planning is the link between the marketing function and the production or works management structure. In many firms it is the rule that marketing and works personnel must not communicate directly. Works people may find it intolerable if sales personnel are constantly telephoning about the state of a particular order and sales people do not wish to be told by works personnel that they are accepting orders for the wrong products. The buffer between the two is production planning and, in practice, this means that production planners have to put up with the worst of both worlds. The marketing and production functions demand different types of skill and tend to attract different kinds of people. Sales and works personnel often find it impossible to understand each other's problems; it is the task of production planning to bridge this gap and the job requires diplomacy, the ability to compromise and the ability to explain the problems of one side to the other.

Having listed the products which are to be manufactured during the next production cycle on the *production schedule*, the next task is to convert the products listed into their component parts. The amount of work necessary at this stage depends on the complexity of the product. Lists of parts required are broken down into machine loading and manning schedules; where the components are being manufactured from a raw material, production planning will originate schedules, on which is shown the quantities of raw materials required and also the requirements necesary to replace materials used in production. These schedules are then made available to the purchasing department. The activities set out above are sometimes known as **product explosion** and they must be undertaken whenever a new manufacturing schedule is set up. You will realise the complexity of this problem if you consider 'product explosion' in relation to a cigarette lighter (ten components), and a motor-car (how many thousand components?).

Two other activities come within the ambit of production planning. Firstly, the receipt of despatch documentation from the marketing departments. Typically, this will comprise despatch notes and advice notes to enclose with the goods when they are despatched and also paperwork to be returned to the department responsible for invoicing and billing.

Secondly, production planning is usually responsible for ensuring that supplies of materials for packaging are available, with which to pack the finished product.

Production Control

Production control is an inevitable consequence of the need for production planning. Any plan must incorporate certain controls to ensure that targets are achieved. In particular, there must be provision for managers to be informed of, and to investigate, unexpected variances from the plan. In a large organisation a wide range of production controls will exist:

(a) *Progress Control*, which is the control of production programmes and schedules in order to ensure that planned output is attained.

(b) *Cost Control,* which is the control of a whole series of budgets, including such aspects as material cost control and labour cost control, in order to ensure that the original budget for costs of production is observed (see page 109).

(c) *Quality Control,* which is the control of the quality or standard of the product. This is closely allied to, and indeed will often be the responsibility of the inspection department.

(d) *Machine Utilisation Control,* which is the control of machine loading, in order to ensure that the 'load' is related to machine capacity.

(e) *Stock Control,* which is the control of stocks and stores, in order to ensure that supplies are available as required and that their availability will not, therefore, interrupt production schedules.

(f) *Computer Control,* which is the control of some operation which is entirely automatic. If differs fundamentally from the other controls in that, whereas, they involve taking corrective action in response to a detected deviation from target, usually some time after the deviation has been detected, computer control involves an immediate and automatic adjustment to maintain the required target. In other words, control is 'in-built' and there is no separate control process.

3.3 PRODUCTION MANAGEMENT

As we have seen, production management is the organisation and supervision of the actual production process. The prime aim of management is common to all areas of company activity; not merely to get the job done, but rather to get others to do the job in response to effective leadership and adequate supervision. Moreover, the management process—of establishing aims, of settling relevant performance targets, of taking corrective action when necessary in order to ensure attainment of target and therefore aim—does not differ fundamentally whether the management is in production, sales or any other area of activity. What we are concerned with here are some of the more important aspects of management in production or in the factory: supervision, reward, performance and control, aspects which are equally applicable to other departments.

Supervision and Leadership

The successful supervisor must have the following qualities:

83

(a) He must be able to plan, to organise to achieve that plan and motivate the personnel involved in that plan; in short, he must be a *leader*.

(b) He must be technically proficient—so that he can understand operational problems.

(c) He must have an appreciation of human needs and of personality differences, so that he is able to appoint the right person to the right job, whilst remaining alert to such problems as the need for adequate and fair rewards and man's traditional desire for justice.

(d) He must have the ability to communicate both with his superiors and subordinates—the major cause of friction on the shop floor, indeed at any level of production, is failure to communicate.

(e) He must have a ready acceptance of responsibility, without letting it distort his judgment, or indeed his personal life—shop floor problems should be left on the shop floor rather than be taken home in the evening.

(f) He must be a decision taker, because to manage is to take decisions based upon a careful and objective analysis of the facts and circumstances.

(g) He must have the respect of his subordinates, for respect is the essence of *any* worthwhile human relationship.

(h) Finally, he will preferably be more extrovert than introvert, a good 'mixer', who can lead without forfeiting popularity, who is not only respected, but also liked—and, in this last respect, an invaluable asset is a good sense of humour.

Clearly, the number of persons with these qualities is limited, but a recognition that these are the qualities demanded would be an important step in improving middle management on the shop floor.

Rewards

The most important incentive to work is reward. One aspect of this is monetary payment and this takes the form of:

(a) **Time Rate,** which is payment for hours worked—the oldest means of payment, time rate has the virtue of simplicity but has one supreme defect: it offers no incentive to work harder, indeed there is no relation between effort and reward since there is no distinction between more or less efficient operatives, as each receives the same pay.

(b) **Piecework,** which is payment for work completed, or for 'piece' completed, offers a solution to the problem of relating effort to reward, but there arises now the difficulty that operatives may be so eager to increase quantity that they forsake quality. In addition it is, of course, much more complicated than time rate and requires careful explanation to operatives.

(c) **Co-partnership,** which is frequently used in addition to, rather than instead of, time rate and piecework. Its aim is to give workers a stake in industry by giving them some share of profits. Two problems arise here, the amount of profit due to operatives is often small in relation to the rest of their earnings and therefore offers little inducement to work harder. In some years there may be no profit, even a loss, and the effects upon morale may then be disastrous.

Finding a fair means of payment is, however, only one aspect of the pay problem. Not only does production management wish to ensure a fair means of payment within a production unit, but also between operatives within the one production unit. This topic is discussed further on page 165.

Performance and Control

It has been continuously emphasised that good management involves achieving targets. It is obviously necessary to measure performance in order to know whether targets have been achieved. A further advantage of measuring performance is that such measures are invariably also useful means of control; and control is clearly necessary if production targets are to be attained. A number of controls (production budgets, planning schedules, production reports and machine utilisation reports) exist, all of which can be used as measures of performance. However, other measures will not become available in the normal production routine but will have to be calculated. For instance, **productivity** which may be defined as output per man hour. Clearly the higher the productivity the better is the performance, although care must be exercised in comparing productivity between different factories, even departments, as so many circumstances may be entirely different (particularly quality and quantity of the labour force, capital equipment and raw materials).

3.4 PRODUCTION DESIGN

Whatever name is given to the department concerned—production design, technical department, design department or drawing office— production design is the designing of products which consumers need and the factory can produce. Whilst in one respect it services production, nevertheless it occupies a crucial position in the chain of production, for it is production design which will translate consumers wants into the reality of what can be produced.

In some industries production design will be concerned with products which will be sold in thousands, such as television sets or packets of biscuits; the designer may never come face to face with the consumer. In other industries, the designer will work closely with the consumer in the design of a product exactly tailored to the consumer's requirements (such as a specific type of crane or diesel turbine) and in such industries as these, the design department will spend much of its time preparing estimates and quotations for customers.

One particular aspect of production design which creates a unique management problem is **Research and Development,** an activity which may vary in scale from an academic investigation into the property of matter to building a pilot plant for a new industrial process. Two specially difficult problems in the management of research and development are:

(a) The results of research are not amenable to prediction. A firm might spend huge sums on research only to find no opportunity for commercial application at the end; research work on a new product may result in loss because a rival firm is first to reach the stage of development.

(b) The costs of research effort on quite a small scale, in terms of specialised staff and equipment, are quite considerable and may often be beyond the reach of all but the largest firms. Many small firms face this problem by entering into co-operative *research associations* (such as the British Steel Castings Research Association), where research programmes are financed by levies paid by member firms.

The importance of increasing the application of science in industry has received considerable emphasis in Britain in recent years, notably by the setting up of the Ministry of Technology in 1964 and through the establishment of regional offices of the Ministry, supported by area Industrial Liaison Officers.

Factors Influencing Design

A well-designed product must satisfy at least four basic criteria:

(a) *Function:* The product must be functional in that it must serve its prime purpose effectively. You must at some time have used a tin-opener which simply did not open tins and was therefore not functional.

(b) *Appearance:* As far as is practicable, the product must be attractive to look at and this is especially important where goods are produced for mass consumption. But care should be taken not to sacrifice the consumers' convenience and comfort to appearance.

(c) *Quality:* In order to retain consumer goodwill, many products are expected to have a reasonable life expectancy and therefore must be durable. This is especially true of consumer durables such as motor-cars and lawn mowers.

(d) *Cost:* However much the preceding criteria are satisfied, no product will be a success unless the price is right. That is to say, unless the price is such that consumers will be prepared to pay for the product, while leaving a sufficient margin for a profit over and above costs.

Each of these criteria must in turn be considered from the three viewpoints:

(a) *Consumers' needs:* Normally the designer will begin with the consumer's needs, which intially his design will be aimed to satisfy. Where mass-production is involved, market research will help clarify exactly what the consumer needs and later it will pronounce his verdict upon the product. But where job production is involved, the designer will work hand in hand with the consumer and the finished design will often be the product of their joint efforts.

(b) *Production Potential:* A successful designer must possess a high degree of technical expertise. He must know exactly the potentialities of:

  (i) his labour force;
  (ii) his machinery;
  (iii) the available materials, such as plastic or metal;
  (iv) the available processes, such as press or mould.

Only then can he decide whether or not his firm can meet the consumers' requirements.

(c) *Design for Economical Production:* Production design will usually have close contacts with departments concerned with work study (or O & M) but essentially the approach will differ according to the type of production. The larger the scale of production, the greater the opportunities to gain economies through **standardisation**, which may be defined as the setting of known types, dimensions, qualities and performance, so that like components, materials, processes and tools are immediately interchangeable. Originally many components were 'hand-fitted' to a particular product and could never be used in any other product. As technical skills improved, components became interchangeable between like products. Standardisation is an extension of interchangeable components in that like components are now interchangeable between many products. An example of design standardisation is the production of an auto engine interchangeable between a wide range of vehicles, say from a 30 cwt. van to a small family saloon.

By and large, the more a designer can standardise the greater the economies of production which can be reaped. Clearly standardisation is part and parcel of mass production, but in all types of production the consumer has a limited budget and the designer will, therefore, be eager to restrict costs in order to secure his custom.

Estimates and Quotations

The distinction between an estimate and a quotation is a legal one; an estimate is not legally binding upon a supplier but a quotation is. As we have seen, a designer of mass consumption products will not usually be involved in providing estimates and quotations, but designers of firms engaged in jobbing, for example the manufacture of plant and equipment for other manufacturing companies, will often have to provide one or the other. The amount of time spent upon any one estimate or quotation will normally be governed by the ratio of estimates and quotations to sales, but the aim in each case is to estimate, as accurately as possible, the ultimate cost of producing a certain product. You will quickly appreciate the consequences of over estimating: the contract will go elsewhere to a cheaper competitor, but under estimating is equally disastrous for it is always the profit which is being eaten into and a firm which does not work for profit has no purpose.

Estimates are best handled by following a set procedure:

1. The designer must first establish exactly what the consumer wants. He will find it useful to agree a data sheet with the customer, as it is essential to avoid mistakes at this stage.
2. He then has to clear the design with other departments such as:

   Production Engineer (work processes);
   Production Planning (delivery date);
   Legal Department (copyright);
   Sales Department (future sales).

3. The next step is to prepare cost data using standard costs if available, but if not, basing the price upon past experience and previous contracts.

4. The design department will produce a figure of total works cost only, which will be handed to a senior executive, perhaps the general manager, to add a percentage to cover overheads and the profit margin. The senior executive will consider a wide range of factors, such as state of order book, current spare capacity, production capabilities, necessary capital expenditure, size of order, strength of desire to retain the customer's purchases, working capital outlay, the size of contract, the terms of payment, before arriving at a final price.

3.5 PRODUCTION ANCILLARIES

There are a number of departments or sections in any firm which service the production unit and which do not fall naturally into either of the three previous divisions. The most usual example is the purchasing department—but there are others and we shall consider storekeeping, works engineering and inspection. The exact location and influence of these departments in any firm is largely a matter of convenience; in one firm the purchasing officer may be directly responsible to the works manager and in another to the managing director, in another the purchasing officer may be part of production administration and in some cases a small service department, quite independent of the main production divisions. You should examine the role of these departments in your own firm and then compare your findings with another firm with which you may be familiar.

Purchasing Office

In many firms the purchasing office enjoys an aura of prestige denied to the other offices in the production division. Purchasing is clearly a vital function but its influence in the firm arises, neither from the sumptuous lunches which supposedly the purchasing officer enjoys daily at the expense of eager representatives, nor the bottles of whisky which submerge him at Christmas. Purchasing is placed in its proper perspective when it is realised that in some industries, such as process industries, the total value of purchases in any one year equals about two-thirds of sales. Let us consider two firms, *United Milk* and *City Dairies*, both engaged in milk distribution and having the same annual turnover and expenses:

	United Milk	City Dairies
Purchases	£60,000	£70,000
Expenses	£30,000	£30,000
Sales	£100,000	£100,000
Profits	£10,000	Nil

A simple example, but one which illustrates very clearly the truth that whilst good purchasing does not of itself make profit, bad purchasing inevitably wastes money. In other words every penny spent upon purchases decreases profit by the same amount and no expenditure can be justified which is not essential to the operation of the firm. The ideal purchasing policy is one which offers maximum value by providing, with reliability and dependability, *what* is wanted, *when* it is wanted, at a *fair* price. Like any firm, your supplier is in business for profit and it is not in your firm's interests to squeeze his profits too tightly, for if you do he will either attempt to sell to other purchasers or perhaps quit the industry.

What has emerged so far should have offered some insight into the qualities demanded by a successful purchasing officer: administrative ability, business acumen, a knowledge of economic trends, a tactical skill in bargaining, an understanding of human behaviour and above all, experience. A successful purchasing officer is invariably a career specialist, whose major asset is his experience. Besides interviewing suppliers and advising other departments, he will need to spend much of his time studying markets, of which he may well maintain his own records as the best aid to forecasting future trends and thus avoiding the ill-effects of sharp price changes. In many cases, of course, the purchasing officer will enter into a contract with his suppliers which may extend well into the future, but normally he will buy according to current market conditions, exercising his judgment in the prevailing situation. If he believes prices will rise sharply due to a shortage of the commodity, he will clearly buy, but if his experience leads him to predict a sharp fall due to a glut, he will obviously only buy for immediate requirements.

In any case, where large sums are involved, he will act with the approval of either the financial controller or the general manager, for clearly purchasing policy must be integrated with financial policy. Usually a ceiling is placed upon purchases and all over some defined value will have to be referred to a higher authority.

Most firms follow a stated purchasing procedure: the department requiring purchases sends in requisition forms to the Purchasing Officer; if necessary he secures estimates which he refers to the department concerned; once accepted, the order is placed and once received, is checked by stores against the original order form; finally the purchasing office checks the invoice against the order too, before passing on for payment. An apparently simple procedure which, however, requires a great deal of paper work. In view of the large number of parties concerned, an order form, for example, may run to a dozen copies. Purchasing therefore involves much documentation and clerical work, for the efficient purchasing officer in a large firm has at his command not only extensive records of his own transactions but information relating to dozens of different markets.

Storekeeping

Closely allied to purchasing, the keeping of stores is nevertheless most effectively executed as a separate department, directly responsible to the works manager. Further, store-keeping should be essentially a physical task with a minimum of clerical work, for the maintenance of stock records should be the responsibility of the production planner rather than the storekeeper. In fact the storekeeper has four functions:

(a) To store stocks neatly and efficiently.
(b) To receive new supplies.
(c) To issue supplies when requisitioned.
(d) To operate a periodic stocktaking—in some firms a perpetual inventory check is maintained but this is often both expensive and duplicative of work done elsewhere—in order to check stock in hand with production planning.

The ideal storekeeper is one who can produce *what* is required, *when* it is required, with a *minimum of cost*, a *minimum of space* and a *maximum of speed*. It is not a job for a low grade of employee; effective storekeeping requires that the storekeeper should be neat and tidy, accurate and consistent, trustworthy and honest, highly numerate and possessed of a good memory. The tendency in the past to place the storekeeper in the labouring category is clearly misjudged and does much to explain the high degree of pilfering which remains a major concern to industry. Products purchased usually become products stored and it is not realistic to pay a man a trifling wage to ensure the safekeeping of many thousands of pounds worth of goods, perhaps, as we have seen before, equivalent in one year to two-thirds of the total turn-over.

There are a number of ways in which storekeeping can be made more efficient:

(a) To make maximum use of height in order to minimise space.
(b) To make full use of storekeeping aids: shelves, bins, racks.
(c) To have an active and reserve store—the reserve store for goods not required in the immediate future.

(d) To divide the store according to the nature of the products to be stored, such as raw materials, general supplies, tools and finished products.

(e) To operate a series of code numbers in order to minimise paperwork.

(f) To restrict forms used to:

(i) Goods Received or Internal Delivery Notes.
(ii) Release Requisition or Issue Notes.
(iii) Stock Control Sheets.

Inspection

Inspection is in fact an aspect of production control but, since it must be independent to be effective, it usually operates as a separate section or department, directly responsible to the works manager or production administrator. Its function is to maintain standards of quality and prevent faulty workmanship. It may also initiate improvements in work technique. Obviously, in the wrong hands, inspection could prove a source of great discontent and friction amongst the operatives; inspectors must therefore be impartial and tactful as well as possessed of sound judgment and be deliberate and careful, courageous and firm in the face of unpopular but necessary decisions. Inspection can be of several different types (such as process or quality control) and can occur at different stages of the work process (maybe inspection of raw material or a running test of the finished product to see if it performs satisfactorily). The form of inspection depends upon the nature of the finished product, but 100 per cent inspection, rather than sampling, may well require an increase in the work force of the order of 25 per cent. Inspection is therefore costly and not directly productive—but it is necessary in order to combat human nature, especially where payment is by piece-work and it is in the operatives' interest to secure quantity before quality.

Works Engineering

In many firms the functions of works engineering are divided amongst a number of executives such as the production engineer and works manager; in other firms there will be a works engineer who should not be confused with the production engineer. The functions of the works engineer may include:

(a) the construction of the factory;
(b) the internal layout of the factory;
(c) the utilisation and maintenance of plant and equipment.

In factory construction, the works engineer will work closely with the architect in charge of the project but the following considerations are all pertinent to factory location:

(a) Availability of skilled labour—if a pool of skilled labour is not readily at hand, skilled labour will either have to be attracted or trained;
(b) Suitability of land for building—and subsequent expansion;
(c) Availability of power fuel supplies;
(d) Availability of raw materials;
(e) Availability of public utilities and facilities for employees;
(f) Suitability of climate;
(g) Proximity to markets;
(h) Availability of transport facilities and other external economies common to the industry;
(i) Location of other company factories;
(j) Government location of industry policy—today, a most important factor and often of overriding importance in determining location as with the motor industry in Merseyside;
(k) The advantage of the single-storey factory in relation to the multi-storey. Single-storey factories are usually more convenient but are frequently more costly.

The internal layout of the factory will be based upon one of four systems:

(a) *Group or Batch:* where operatives are grouped into sections according to their occupation. It enables centralisation of control and specialisation of skill.
(b) *Work Flow:* where the factory is organised according to the flow of operations, so that ideally the raw material enters one end of the factory, proceeds continuously through the different stages of production and emerges at the other end as the finished product.
(c) *Line Flow:* which is properly an improvement upon work flow in that it aims to erase 'down-time'—the proportion of time in which a machine or operative is idle. Let us say a factory produces 1,440 cars in a 24-hour day giving a rate of flow of 60 cars an hour and a basic time of one minute per car, if one operation takes 15 minutes then 15 machines of that type

93

must be in operation in order to ensure complete continuity and line flow. Line flow is used for example in the automobile industry and is a phrase to remember in the same breath as mass-production and standardisation.

(d) *Process:* where essentially the technological process of production determines the layout. The chemical industry, with its huge and costly plant, is an example; clearly the nature of the process will determine location.

The efficient utilisation and maintenance of plant and equipment is essential to greater productivity. The toolroom is often the key to industrial advance and the maintenance engineer is a key employee. In some firms there will be a maintenance foreman too, and together they are responsible for maintenance of plant and machinery, periodic inspection and overhaul of all plant and machinery, the repair of breakdowns and the minimising of operational costs.

FURTHER READING

Brech, E. F. L., *The Principles and Practice of Management*, Longmans, Part 2.

Massie, Joseph L., *Essentials of Management* Prentice-Hall, Inc., Chapter 12.

Vance, Stanley, *Industrial Administration*, McGraw Hill Book Co., Part 2.

Timms, Howard L., *The Production Function in Business*, Richard D. Irwin, Inc.

Batty, J., *Industrial Administration and Management*, Macdonald & Evans.

QUESTIONS

1. Distinguish *four* types of production system. Why may all four types exist within a single industry?
2. Compare and contrast the problems facing production managers in the manufacture of:

   (a) baked beans
   (b) cylinder blocks.

3. What attributes should a good supervisor have? Give reasons (U.L.C.I. 1968).

4. Consider the influences of equipment availability and consumer demand on product design (A.C.C.A. 1968).
5. Discuss the appropriate terms of reference for a Purchasing Officer in a large public company (U.L.C.I. 1968).

CHAPTER FOUR

The Financial Function

4.1 THE ACCOUNTING FUNCTION

IN Chapter One we saw that the main objective of a business enterprise is the achievement of a satisfactory profit. In barest outline, the profit earning process is as follows:

First, available cash is invested in buildings, machinery, materials and labour.

Second, the application of labour and the use of production facilities adds utility to the raw materials, creating a product with increased economic value.

Third, the product is converted into cash by means of sales and the cycle begins again.

If the utility created is positive, the resulting cash balance will be larger than it was before the investment was made. The conversion of cash into real assets is known as **expenditure**; the conversion of real assets into cash is known as **revenue** and the difference between revenue and expenditure for a given investment is its **profit or loss**.

The basic objective of the financial functions is to assist management in formulating policies so that the most effective use is made of resources, so that the company will make the best use of the funds at its disposal and will also select the most favourable sources of additional funds to finance future activities. By far the most important source of information employed in financial analysis and planning is that located in the accounting records. Accounting, by a process of measurement, analysis and communication, has developed to reflect and control economic activity. Accountants measure such things as performance, sales, expenses, profits, assets and liabilities and express their findings in numerical terms. This data is analysed and communicated to individuals, both inside and outside the enterprise, who have an interest in its affairs. The prime objective of this process is to enable rational economic decisions to be made. Accounting may, therefore, be defined as *the measurement, analysis and communication of economic data to permit informed judgments and decisions by users of the information.*

Since accounting is an instrument of economic behaviour, it is possible to distinguish an evolutionary pattern which reflects the changing requirements of economic development. Accounts have been found amongst the earliest of man's surviving records. Accounting, as we know it today, has developed through the following phases:

Stewardship Accounting, which involves the orderly recording of business transactions. Accounting concepts, systems and procedures in use today have stemmed from a development that began to take shape in the accounts of the merchants in the Italian city states during the Renaissance. The main principles were set out by Luca Pacioli, an Italian monk, in his famous treatise of 1494. Stewardship accounting developed from the need of commercial firms to keep track of their relationships with outsiders, to maintain records of how and where they had invested their money and to determine the amounts accruing to the owners of the business.

Financial Accounting came into existence in the middle of the 19th century, when the information contained in the stewardship accounts was put to a new use. The Industrial Revolution resulted in the development of large business units, most of which found it necessary to raise capital on a large scale from members of the public. The advent of limited liability, whereby an investor was liable merely up to the amount of cash he had invested in a business, vastly increased the supply of capital to business enterprises, but unscrupulous companies sometimes gave a false impression of their soundness. A parallel development was the increase in the role of the State in business affairs through company law, regulations on bankruptcy and the introduction of taxes on profits. Companies had to cope with demands from the State for periodical accounts to indicate their financial position and performance.

Accountants responded to this new challenge by developing two new accounts which give a view of the whole company: the **Balance Sheet,** which indicates the wealth of a company at a certain point in time, and the **Profit and Loss Account,** which shows what additions to wealth have been made over a period. Another financial statement which is becoming an increasingly common supplement to the published accounts of many companies, especially in the U.S.A., is that relating to funds. The **Funds Statement** gives details of company investment and the source of funds for the investment in a given period.

97

D

Management Accounting also developed as a consequence of the growth in size of business units, which creates problems not only of external finance, but also of internal control. This development has answered the demands of managers of companies for detailed information about the cost of manufacturing individual products and represents a shift of emphasis to current and future periods, in order to assist management decision making.

Today, therefore, the function of accounting is to provide information for three broad purposes:

1. External reporting to shareholders, government and other interested parties.
2. Internal routine reporting to managers to help them to plan and to control their activities.
3. Internal non-routine reporting to managers to assist them in deciding what products to make and how to sell them.

The Financial Statements

The information contained in the financial statements of a business enterprise indicates many of the problems which a firm has to resolve and is designed to answer such questions as: What financial resources are available? How much and to whom is the firm in debt? Is the business profitable? Is it possible to finance future growth without recourse to outside sources?

The answers to these questions have an important bearing on managerial decision-making. The larger and more complex the business organisation, the more dependent are the managers on financial reports. Financial statements are used by management as the basis for planning operations, of procuring finance and of exercising control over the financial position in order to make the most efficient and profitable use of assets. A firm must have cash or credit at the time of acquiring assets or entering on expansion projects; in addition, the firm's cash flow must be adequate to meet current obligations. Interest in financial statements is not, however, confined to internal analysts alone. Suppliers, financial institutions, investors, potential investors and speculators all have a vital interest in the health of a company as interpreted in its financial reports.

The Balance Sheet is a list of assets and liabilities, plus capital. All assets or repayments of debt require funds which are secured by liabilities and capital. Whenever a company makes a purchase of goods or services, either cash on hand is reduced, or accounts payable are increased, or a loan is obtained to finance the purchase. The Balance Sheet, by depicting the assets of an enterprise and the sources of capital used to finance them, provides a picture of the financial condition of a company at a particular point in time. This point is emphasised by the vertical form of the Balance Sheet, illustrated in Fig. 4.1.

Figure 4.1 THE BALANCE SHEET

ASSETS EMPLOYED

Fixed Assets	Cost	Accumulated depreciation	Net
	£	£	£
Premises	5,000	1,800	3,200
Fittings	1,000	200	800
	6,000	2,000	4,000
Current Assets			
Stock		2,000	
Debtors		1,000	
Cash		1,000	
			4,000
			8,000
FINANCED BY			
Capital		5,000	
Retained profits		1,000	
			6,000
Current Liabilities			
Creditors		1,500	
Expenses owing		500	2,000
			8,000

The Balance Sheet demonstrates the truism that, the investment in assets must be equal to the sum of the creditors' and owners' claims on those assets, in other words:

Assets = Liabilities + Owners' Equity

In the example in Fig 4.1 the owners' equity is £6,000. Note how the accountant classifies both the sources of capital and assets on a long or short term basis.

Although the Balance Sheet shows the financial position of a company very clearly, it has serious limitations as regards its usefulness for analytical purposes. It is essentially a statement of historical costs and may, consequently, be irrelevant for use as the basis for future decisions. The economist would argue that the real value of an asset is represented by the *future* profits which an asset is expected to make and not by its actual cost. Furthermore, the value of labour is not disclosed by the balance sheet despite its significance, with land, plant and machinery, as a factor of production. Goodwill is also omitted from the balance sheet, although it would appear in the valuation of a company if it were up for sale. Other resources, such as leased items of plant and machinery, are also not shown in balance sheets.

Despite these limitations, the balance sheet contains information which is essential for internal management and the external analyst, because the relationship between assets and liabilities present a vital key to the understanding of a company's financial status. Do the company's assets safely cover the claims of creditors? Is the company able to repay its creditors? Although additional funds may be secured from future profitable operations, it is unwise to rely on uncertain future events. For this reason, prime dependence is placed on the resources on hand in relation to the calls on them.

The Profit and Loss Account (or **Income Statement**) presents a moving picture of the course of profit or loss over the period of time between balance sheet dates; it explains the change in retained earnings from one balance sheet to the next.

FIGURE 4.2   PROFIT STATEMENT FOR THE YEAR ENDED......

		£
Sales		10,000
Cost of Sales		4,000
Gross Margin		6,000
Expenses	£1,000	
Dividends	2,000	3,000
Net Profit		
before tax		3,000
Corporation Tax		2,000
Total Retained Profit		1,000

The main purpose of financial accounting is the determination of profit. Accurate profit measurement is important for the following reasons:

(a) Profit is used as the basis of one of the principal forms of taxation;

(b) Profit is used in public reports as a measure of the success of a company's activities;

(c) Profit is used as a basis for establishing withdrawals by owners or dividend policies by directors;

(d) Profit is used by lenders of short-term loans and by suppliers in making decisions to grant credit;

(e) Profit is used to guide the management of an enterprise in the conduct of its affairs. It provides a basis for the development of policies on asset acquisitions, marketing and research programmes, production and manpower planning and it is also used to evaluate decisions taken in the past.

Frequently, profit and loss statements are nothing more than convenient records which form the basis for calculations of liability for tax. Since accountants use historical costs in measuring profit they fail to take into account the effect of changes in the value of money. In a period of rising prices, this may lead to an over-statement of profits, so that dividends and taxes are paid out of profits that have not been made! A further limitation arises from the fact that a sale has to be made before a profit is recognised. Consequently, the financial position which is disclosed, excludes holding gains or losses which may have accrued during the period arising from changes in the value of money. The profit and loss account may therefore be regarded essentially as a statement for persons outside the company; internal management require much more information and more frequently.

The **Funds Statement** provides an analysis of the flow of funds through an organisation. Projections of future transactions involving cash or other working capital items are essential for the preparation of comprehensive budget and other reports for senior management. Analyses of past transactions are similarly helpful in evaluating the performance of managers and explaining the results of operations.

A continuous flow of working funds is present in every firm. At the beginning of an enterprise a proportion of funds is raised from shareholders and long-term debenture holders and is spent on purchasing land, buildings, plant and machinery. This particular use of funds is termed **sunk** or **fixed capital** and the assets are classified under the heading **fixed assets**, which are kept in the business for the purpose of earning profit. Every year a charge is made for their use by including depreciation in the accounts. In addition, other

101

assets are retained in the business for a short period only; these are continually changing their form and are known as **current assets**, whilst the funds needed to purchase them are called **circulating capital**. For a manufacturing firm, a portion of funds subscribed is used to pay for raw materials and manufacturing expenses, which bring into existence a stock of finished goods. A further portion goes to meet the costs of administration and selling. Sales generate cash, which then becomes available for expenditure on raw materials and other requirements, and so the cycle is completed. This movement of circulating capital through different forms within a business is called the **Working Capital Cycle** and it is illustrated in the form of a diagram in Fig. 4.3.

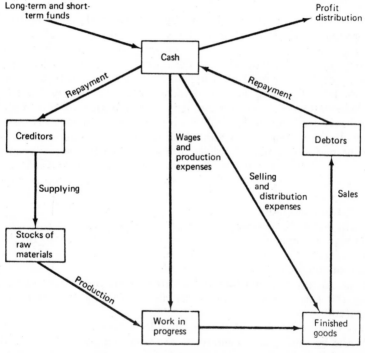

Fig. 4.3   The Working Capital Cycle

All phases of the working capital cycle take place concurrently. Cash is continually being expended on raw materials, operating, selling and administration costs and is being received continuously from debtors. In a successful business, cash always tends to increase

102

due to profit and it is either retained in the business, or distributed to shareholders.

If the flow of cash is interrupted, a firm may find that it is not able to continue to trade. This is why it is important to analyse the past behaviour of the cash account and to prepare projections of what the future cash position will be. This vital topic is discussed in detail in Section 4.2 below. Our present concern is to determine the new uses to which resources have been applied and to bring to light the sources from which the funds used were obtained. We wish to answer the questions:

What new assets have been acquired and how was their purchase financed?

Has any new debt been incurred and, if so, for what reason?

What has been done with the profit retained in the business?

The answer to the last question may be illustrated by means of the following example, which is an extension of the Balance Sheet presented in Figure 4.1 on page 99. We compare the position on 1st January with that a year later on 31st December:

	1st January	31st December	Change
	£	£	£
Assets	6,500	8,000	+1,500
Less Liabilities	1,500	2,000	+ 500
Owners' Equity	5,000	6,000	1,000

Owners' equity has increased by £1,000, which is reflected in an increase in assets of £1,500, less an increase in liabilities of £500. We may express the changes in the two Balance Sheets as follows:

Funds provided

Increase in Owners' Equity	£,1000
Increase in Liabilities	500
	£1,500

Funds applied

Increase in assets	£1,500

Details of changes in individual assets and liabilities are not given here, but it is useful to distinguish between these items in compiling a more detailed statement, which should include the following:

103

Sources of funds

1. Profits from operations before charging depreciation
2. Capital contributions by owners
3. Increases in long-term liabilities
4. Increases in short-term liabilities
5. Reductions in short-term financial assets
6. Reductions in long-term financial assets
7. Proceeds from the sale of fixed assets

Uses of funds

1. Withdrawals of profits or capital by owners
2. Reductions in long-term liabilities
3. Reductions in short-term liabilities
4. Increases in short-term financial assets
5. Increases in long-term financial assets
6. Expenditure on fixed assets

By including these items the analyst is able to use the funds statement to determine the manner in which the distribution of the firm's resources changes with the passage of time. For example, the funds statement will show if working capital is liquidated in order to procure fixed assets, the sources from which finance is derived and the influence of profits or losses upon the composition of assets and liabilities.

The Analysis of Financial Statements

People who are interested in financial statements seek answers to two questions:

Is the company earning satisfactory profits?

One of the objectives of financial analysis is to evaluate the success of a business enterprise in earning profits. The results of this analysis are of particular interest to potential creditors and owners as well as to management.

Is the firm solvent?

Solvency is the ability to meet obligations as they become due. For the firm to be solvent over the short term, it must be capable of paying its current liabilities promptly as they mature. Clearly, management must be able to evaluate this capability if the firm is to survive. It is also important for lenders to be able to identify poor credit risks if losses through bad debts are to be avoided.

Return on Investment shows how effectively the operating assets of a company are being employed in generating profits. The calculation of the return on investment involves three basic factors: capital employed, sales and profit and may be represented by formula as follows:

$$\text{Return on Investment} = \frac{\text{Profit}}{\text{Sales}} \times \frac{\text{Sales}}{\text{Capital Employed}}$$

'Profit' here refers to the total available net profit after tax which is at the disposal of the directors before dividends are declared. Capital investment, from an investor's viewpoint, consists of capital and reserves; from the point of view of management, however, capital investment consists of total assets. Using the information given in Figures 4.1 and 4.2 we may calculate:

(i) Return on investment (for investors)

$$\frac{£3,000}{£10,000} \times \frac{£10,000}{£6,000} \times 100 = 50\%$$

(ii) Return on investment (for managers)

$$\frac{£3,000}{£10,000} \times \frac{£10,000}{£8,000} \times 100 = 37 \cdot 5\%$$

In spite of the limitations which are inherent in financial statements, the return on investment is one of the most common methods used by management to measure the effectiveness of business organisations. The overall performance of a company may be evaluated by comparing current performance with predetermined standards. A special advantage of this analytical tool is that it may be used to measure not only the operational efficiency of its capital employed but also the efficiency of its production and sales departments. For example, if investment turnover (sales÷capital employed) meets the desired standards and the firm's rate of return is still below the predetermined level, management can direct its attention to the efficiency of its sales and production departments.

Return on investment is also a valuable yardstick in the measurement of performance at the divisional level in large organisations, provided that all costs and capital can be allocated correctly. Measuring the rate of return on investment at the divisional level makes it possible for the results of one division to be compared with the other divisions in the group. Return on investment may also be used to measure the profitability of individual products. Through the use of a satisfactory product cost system, capital and costs may be allocated to the various products, so that it becomes possible to calculate the profitability of each product. This allows management to allocate its capital to those products with the greatest potential for profits in the long run.

Liquidity Ratios are used to determine the degree of liquidity. The **Current Ratio** is the ratio of current assets to current liabilities and measures working capital available at a particular point in time. Using the information given in Figure 4.1, you should be able to establish that the current ratio is 2 : 1 (£4,000 to £2,000). The larger the ratio the more liquid the firm is said to be. The current ratio may also be used to measure operational efficiency. If the ratio is too high it indicates that the firm's investment in cash, stock or debtors may be too high for the present volume of sales. On the other hand, a firm may have a favourable current ratio and yet be unable to meet its current obligations because its stocks may include a large proportion of immovable products which cannot be converted into cash. In other words, the current ratio does not indicate the *quality* of current assets. A further example of this occurs when debtors include accounts which are overdue and perhaps not collectable. It is for these reasons that financial analysts tend to be suspicious of current ratios of less than 2 : 1.

The **Quick** or **Liquid Ratio** is an analytical device that provides a measure of performance which deals with the problem of stocks noted earlier (i.e. that stocks may include goods which are not readily convertible into cash). In this ratio, stocks are eliminated from the equation thus:

$$\frac{\text{Current Assets} - \text{Stocks}}{\text{Current Liabilities}}$$

which, from our previous example, yields a ratio of 1 : 1. In this case the solvency of the firm is assured because it has sufficient current assets, which can be converted into cash to liquidate all current obligations. If a financial manager should find that his current ratio is favourable, but the 'quick' ratio is less than 1 : 1, his first reaction would be to investigate the stock-holding policies.

Managing Current Assets

Fundamentally, the objective of the financial function is to see that cash is on hand to pay bills on time and to assist the firm in earning a satisfactory profit. In a sense, these two objectives are contradictory.

The more a firm protects itself against the risks associated with the inability to pay bills on time, the more it loses income that might have been gained from investing the idle cash. Similarly, a high turnover of debtors may be gained only through restrictive policies in granting credit and aggressive policies in collecting debts. Thus, the high turnover of debtors and the resulting liquidity will be gained at the expense of profitable credit sales. We shall now examine the factors which affect the size of a firm's investment in current assets.

Cash is kept in two forms, in the bank and on hand. The famous English economist, J. M. Keynes, formulated two chief motives for holding cash. The *transactions motive* is the need to hold cash for carrying out normal business functions. The size of the holding required for this purpose depends on such factors as the size of transactions that the firm is called upon to make and the frequency of cash payments and receipts. When the cash flowing in and out of a firm is steady and continuous, less cash may be held than if these flows were irregular. The *precautionary motive* is the need to provide a buffer to meet abnormal demands for cash, as, for example, when abnormal conditions interrupt sales (perhaps because of a dock strike).

Cash balances are expensive to maintain. The cost of holding them is their **opportunity cost,** i.e. the income that could be earned if they were put to some alternative use (e.g. invested outside the business). If the best use is to be made of resources, surplus cash must be suitably invested. If the cash surplus is likely to be available for a long time, it may be invested inside the business by expanding facilities, alternatively, it may be invested in shares or debentures of other companies. If cash is available for a short time only, it may be invested in bank deposits. Treasury Bills, discount houses, finance companies or with local authorities.

Debtors are created when goods sold are not paid for immediately. Their size is determined by the quantity of sales made on credit, the length of the credit period allowed and the vigour with which credit control is pursued. Some firms will supply goods to customers who failed to pay for previous supplies, in the hope of stimulating future sales and preserving a certain amount of goodwill; others may demand payment of outstanding bills before future orders are accepted. Similarly, the policies pursued by firms in accepting potential customers vary from firm to firm; some firms grant credit on application, others have rigorous procedures for classifying their customers by means of credit rating. The credit-worthiness of potential customers may be established directly or indirectly. Direct methods involve an analysis of the customer's past records, seeking the opinions of staff who have dealt with the customer in the past and utilising information volunteered by the customer. Indirect methods involve the use of bank references, trade references (where firms which have previous knowledge of the customer act as referees) and the use of protection associations and enquiry agents. Protection associations collect and disseminate information relating to the credit-worthiness of consumers at regional and national levels.

The cost of investing in debtors involves more than the loss of income which could be earned by investing elsewhere. A credit department is necessary to investigate applicants, maintain accounting records and to police the accounts. There are also additional costs of collecting overdue debts and of meeting bad debt losses when the customer is not able to pay. In theory, the credit controller attempts to relate these costs to future revenue. If a firm accepts high credit rated customers only it limits its share of the market, but the more the firm sells to customers with a low credit-rating, the higher the costs of maintaining accounts, collection and losses due to bad debts.

Another factor which affects the cost of debtors is the type of credit terms offered. This involves the size of cash discount, the length of the cash discount period and the length of time before the payment of debt becomes due. A lengthening of these periods, or an increase in the discount will, perhaps, attract more sales, but any additional revenue would have to be related to the increases incurred in costs.

Stock consists of raw materials, work in progress, finished goods and other supplies which are not themselves sold or manufactured, but are used in the process of manufacture. In addition to the opportunity cost element noted earlier, a wide range of supplementary costs are incurred in maintaining stock: costs of equipment, rent, heating, lighting, personnel, insurance and the costs of deterioration and obsolescence. Over-stocking clearly has potentially serious consequencies for the level of profits. On the other hand, under-stocking may result in loss of sales, loss of goodwill, penalty payments and may disrupt production. Stock control procedures predetermine for each item of stock the maximum and minimum levels and also stipulate re-order levels and re-order quantities. The maximum level is that which must not be exceeded and is set after taking the costs of storage into account. The minimum level is that below which stocks should not be allowed to fall and depends on the rate of production and the 'lead time' (the time taken from ordering to the receipt of fresh supplies).

4.2 COST INFORMATION FOR MANAGEMENT

You will probably find this section rather formidable at first reading and you may choose to skim through it and return to the subject later. The detail in this section is provided in order to show how the jig-saw of the budgeting process fits together; it also serves to illustrate the importance of the need for co-ordination between the main business functions.

The control of a business can only be effective where the information service is tailored to the specific needs of every key executive. The required information should be available when it is wanted and it should be adequate for its purpose, provided that the cost of supplying the information is reasonable.

Information is required at every stage of the management control process, which includes:

1. Forward planning to achieve the objectives of the business.
2. The ascertainment of what constitutes good performance for each key executive.
3. The appraisal of the performance of executives given specific responsibility for aspects of business operation.
4. The decision on corrective action to be taken where this is considered necessary for the benefit of the business.

This section is concerned with cost information provided to managers in the context of the management control process beginning with a review of cost behaviour as a basis for planning and the interpretation of cost data.

The Profit Graph

Planning concerns the future of the business and the decisive factor is usually *sales*. This activity level governs costs and profit, and if plans have been made in advance on a particular volume the manager requires an answer to the question: 'What will happen to profit if the sales level changes?' This is a significant question and a graph may be useful in giving the answer. Figure 4.4 shows a chart known as a profit graph which may be used as an aid to interpreting the cost-volume-profit relationships.

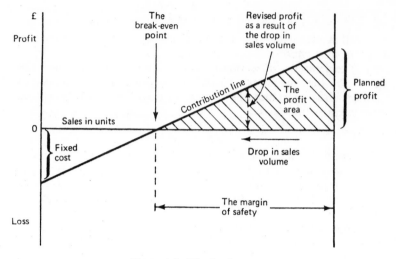

Figure 4.4   The Profit Graph

The horizontal axis of the graph gives the sales volume and the plan shows a profit at a given volume of sales. If this volume is reduced, on the basis of the planned cost structure of the business, the extent of the reduction can be measured on the horizontal axis and a revised profit calculated.

This illustration shows that a number of important assumptions have been made regarding the business.

The assumptions particular to the period covered by the chart in Figure 4.4 are:

1. That certain costs will be unaffected by a change in the level of activity—these are known as **fixed costs.**
2. That the remaining costs will vary in direct proportion to changes in the level of activity; or, in other words, they will be constant per unit of volume—these are known as **variable costs.**
3. That the sales price per unit of sale will be a constant.
4. That manufacturing efficiency will be as planned and, therefore, production costs will not vary owing to this factor.
5. That costs can be divided into strictly fixed or strictly variable elements.
6. That in the case of a multi-product business the sales mix will be constant.

The point arises as to whether these assumptions are valid. A

110

study of cost behaviour is relevant to this question and features of the problem are examined in the sections that follow.

The Behaviour of 'Fixed' Costs

The word 'fixed' is placed in inverted commas in this section because in the context of cost-volume-profit analysis, although it may be assumed that a certain cost will tend to be unaffected by a change in the level of activity, if a long enough period is taken it is known the cost will change. This fact is illustrated in Figure 4.5 in the case of rent.

A **fixed** cost which is constant for a particular range of output, as in Figure 4.5, and then increases or decreases to a new level for another range of output is sometimes known as a **stepped** cost.

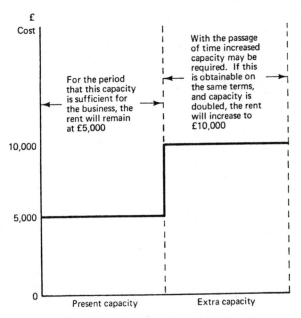

Figure 4.5   Cost Behaviour—Rent Cost

Variable Cost Behaviour

The linear relationship assumed with costs that are constant per unit is illustrated in Figure 4.6 using direct material costs as an example.

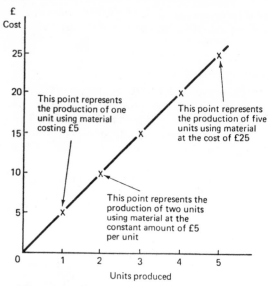

Figure 4.6   Cost Behaviour—Direct Material Cost

Power is a variable cost but showing its behaviour graphically it may appear as in Figure 4.7.

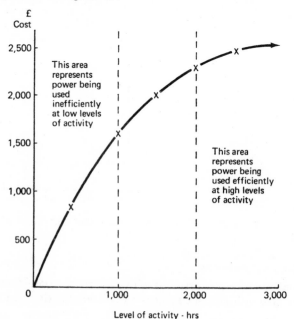

Figure 4.7   Cost Behaviour—Power Cost

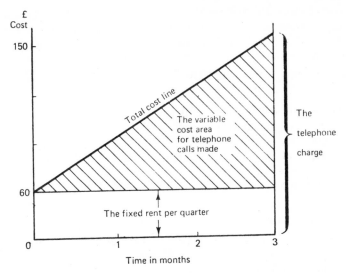

Figure 4.8   Cost Behaviour—Telephone Cost

In the above illustration it has been assumed that a minimum cost has not been incurred, whether the power supply was used or shut down for the period. Sometimes, such a charge must be incurred as, for example, in the case of a telephone charge—shown in Figure 4.8.

A **variable** cost, showing a behaviour pattern as illustrated in Figure 4.7, is known as a **semi-variable** cost. A cost showing the behaviour pattern illustrated in Figure 4.8 is known as a **mixed** cost. These costs may, therefore, be defined as follows:

A **semi-variable** cost: A cost which does not vary or tend to vary in direct proportion to a change in the level of activity, but does vary indirectly to the level of activity.

A **mixed** cost: A cost with fixed and variable elements.

The Division of Costs into their Fixed and Variable Elements

With mixed costs, the fixed cost component can be placed in the fixed cost classification and the variable cost component in the variable cost classification. The use of scattergraphs or the application of the statistical technique of least squares may assist in identifying these components. Regarding semi-variable costs, the classification may be on the basis of the predominant characteristic

113

of cost. For example, plant maintenance cost is normally predominantly variable so that it may be considered a variable cost. Stepped costs usually present no problem because the planned range of output is known and the costs are interpreted accordingly.

The purpose of the division of costs on the basis of units of activity is to provide data to:

(a) assist in the fixing of selling prices;
(b) assist in the control of costs;
(c) provide information for the value of stock;
(d) assist in the determination of the profitability of company activities; and
(e) measure the efficiency of company operations.

The Planned Range of Activity

The reference in the previous section to the 'planned range of output' is a key factor in cost-volume-profit analysis. Figure 4.9 illustrates the importance of this point.

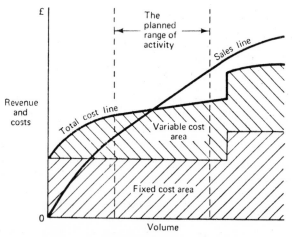

Figure 4.9   The Planned Range of Activity

The 'straight line' relationships shown within the planned range of activity change outside these limits; therefore, linear assumptions in cost-volume-profit analysis should be re-examined if data is used outside these limits. For planning purposes, the planned range of activity makes possible the use of conventional cost-volume-profit formulae as being not significantly in error within the limits given.

114

Marginal Product Cost and Contribution

Given the ability to segregate fixed and variable cost, it is possible to calculate the marginal cost and contribution per unit of product. **Marginal Cost** may be defined as the total variable cost per unit of product. **Contribution** equals the selling price, minus the marginal cost per unit, and is the amount available to contribute to fixed costs and profit.

The contribution per unit makes possible the plotting of the contribution line as illustrated in Figure 4.4 and it will be noted that up to the point where this line crosses the sales volume axis, the contribution has been used to cover the fixed costs. From this point on the chart, contribution gives profit.

The contribution per unit may be useful information to the management that plans to sell a product at the usual price in one market and to sell the same product at a reduced price in another market. The emphasis to be placed on sales of particular products, for a given volume of sales to achieve maximum overall profitability, may be calculated by the use of the contribution per unit for each type of product.

The Break-Even Point and the Margin of Safety

Where the contribution line crosses the activity line is known as the **break-even point**. The break-even point may, therefore, be defined as the level of activity where total costs equal total revenue. If the level of activity increases beyond the break-even point, a profit is obtained; if the level of activity drops below the break-even point, a loss is incurred. The profit graph, therefore, in disclosing the estimated profit or loss at different levels of activity also gives the extent to which a planned activity level can fall before a loss is experienced. This is known as the **margin of safety**, and is the difference between planned sales and the break-even point.

If reference is made to Figure 4.10, where the cost-volume-profit structures of two companies are illustrated, it will be noted that two companies with the same total costs and sales amounts may have differing break-even points and, therefore, different margins of safety.

In the case of company A once the break-even point is reached, large profits will be quickly made as volume increases. With company B, once the break-even point is reached, profits will be achieved but at a slower rate than in company A. Where trading conditions are difficult, the activity level in the case of company B can drop much further than in company A before a loss is sustained.

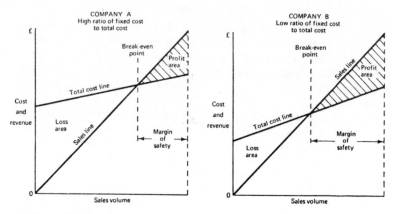

Figure 4.10 The Effect of Company Cost Structure on the Break-even Point and the Margin of Safety

In other words, the 'margin of safety' of company B is greater than in company A.

Cost-Volume-Profit Analysis Formulae

On the assumptions described for the conventional profit-planning chart it is now possible to represent the graphs given in this chapter by formulae. These are as follows:

May also be calculated by using the formulae:

Fixed cost = contribution − profit

Profit/Volume Ratio × Sales − Profit

Contribution = fixed cost + profit

Profit/Volume Ratio × Sales

Break-even point:

$$\text{in sales: £s} = \frac{\text{Fixed cost}}{\text{Contribution}} \times \text{Sales}$$

$$\frac{\text{Fixed cost}}{\text{Profit/Volume Ratio}}$$

$$\text{in sales: units} = \frac{\text{Fixed cost}}{\text{Contribution per unit of product}}$$

Margin of safety = Sales − break-even point

Profit = Contribution − Fixed cost

Profit/Volume Ratio × Margin of Safety

The term **profit/volume ratio** has been introduced into the above formulae. It is calculated as a percentage and represents the relationship of contribution to sales as follows:

$$\text{Profit/Volume Ratio (P/V Ratio)} = \frac{\text{Contribution}}{\text{Sales}} \times 100.$$

The P/V ratio determines the slope of the profit graph.

The inter-relationships of these formulae may be illustrated by the following example:

Given data for an accounting period:

	£
Sales	£8,000
Variable cost	4,000
Contribution	4,000
Fixed cost	3,000
Profit	1,000

$$\text{Profit/Volume ratio} = \frac{£4,000}{£8,000} \times 100$$
$$= 50\%$$

Inter-relationships of the data:

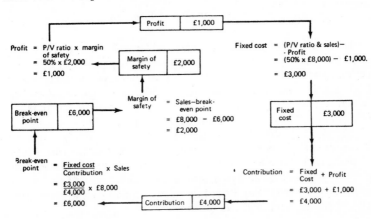

The Elements of Cost

Total cost may be analysed as required and four possible classifications are given in Figure 4.11.

117

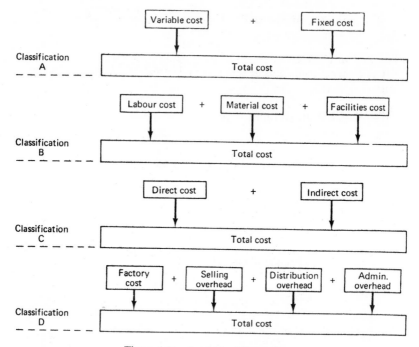

Figure 4.11   Analysis of Total Cost

Classification A has already been considered for business planning purposes; classifications B and C are used for product and departmental costs; and the functional classification D serves as a link with the conventional manufacturing, trading and profit and loss accounts. The use to be made of the cost information for management dictates the classification method adopted.

Costs directly identifiable with the manufacture of a product are known as **direct costs** or **prime costs**. Prime cost plus other manufacturing costs (also known as factory overhead) equals **factory cost**. Indirect cost may be analysed into factory, selling, distribution and administration overhead according to the organisational responsibilities of the managers of the business.

Absorption Product Cost

The elements of cost may be summarised for product costing purposes as follows:

118

	£	
Direct material cost	—	
Add: Direct labour cost	—	
Prime cost	—	
Add: Factory overhead	—	
Factory cost	—	
	£	
Add: Selling overhead	—	
Distribution overhead	—	
Administration overhead	—	—
Total product cost		—

The identification of prime cost with the unit of product presents no problem but overhead **allotment** (known as **cost absorption**) involves the use of an overhead rate compiled from the detailed application of the general formula:

$$\text{Overhead rate} = \frac{\text{Overhead}}{\substack{\text{Absorption base considered suitable to reflect} \\ \text{the incidence of the overhead to product units}}}$$

The choice of the most appropriate base depends on a knowledge of the business. For example, if the overhead is concerned with a labour intensive manufacturing process, direct labour hours may be used to give an overhead absorption rate per direct labour hour. The factory overhead absorbed to the product might then be calculated by the application of the formula:

Direct labour time involved in the manufacture of the product	×	Factory overhead rate per direct labour hour	×	Factory overhead absorbed to the product

The absorption process may be accomplished by the use of a percentage. If, for example, direct labour cost is used for the absorption base, the factory overhead percentage may be calculated as follows:

$$\text{Factory overhead percentage} = \frac{\text{Factory overhead}}{\text{Direct labour cost}} \times 100$$

The factory overhead absorbed to the product might then be calculated by the application of the formula:

119

| Direct labour cost incurred in the manufacture of the product | $\times$ | Factory overhead percentage | $=$ | Factory overhead absorbed to the product |

The rates or percentages of overhead absorption should be chosen and calculated with care, and the desire to achieve greater accuracy may dictate the analysis of the rates or percentages by departmental responsibility.

Responsibility Accounting

Management responsibility may be delegated to departmental managers and the identification of costs incurred and controllable by a manager may be an essential requirement in appraising the effectiveness of executive performance.

Certain costs appropriate to a department may not be directly controllable by the departmental manager and these are known as **uncontrollable costs.** For example, rent paid for the space occupied by an assembly shop is a departmental cost but the allocation of the space available in the factory is usually outside the control of the departmental manager.

Where total departmental costs are required, expenses not directly identifiable with the department are apportioned by the use of the formulae:

$$\text{Appropriated cost} = \text{cost} \times \frac{\text{The factor considered suitable to reflect the incidence of the cost to the department (departmental amount only)}}{\text{The factor considered suitable to reflect the incidence of the cost to the department (in total)}}$$

For example, rent may be the cost to be apportioned. If it is assumed that the area occupied is the factor considered suitable to reflect the incidence of the cost to the department, the calculation on given data may be as follows:

GIVEN DATA FOR AN ACCOUNTING PERIOD

Rent	£1,000
Total factory area	50,000 sq. ft
Departmental area	10,000 sq. ft

$$\text{Apportioned departmental cost} = £1,000 \times \frac{10,000 \text{ sq. ft}}{50,000 \text{ sq. ft}}$$

$$= £200$$

Like the choice of the absorption base, care should be exercised in identifying the most appropriate apportionment factor for a given cost.

The identification of cost and cost responsibility is an important factor in the control system but the technique known as 'budgetary control' can develop responsibility accounting to include all aspects of the management control process.

Budgetary Control

In the terminology of the *Institute of Cost and Works Accountants*, **budgetary control** may be defined as:

The establishment of budgets relating the responsibilities of executives to the requirements of a policy, and the continuous comparison of actual with budgeted results either to secure by individual action the objective of that policy or to provide a basis for its revision.

A **budget** is:

A financial and/or quantitative statement, prepared and approved prior to a defined period of time, of the policy to be pursued during that period for the purpose of attaining a given objective. It may include income, expenditure and the employment of capital.

The overall control budget, or **master budget** is the end product of detailed functional or sectional budgets and their relationship is illustrated in Figure 4.12.

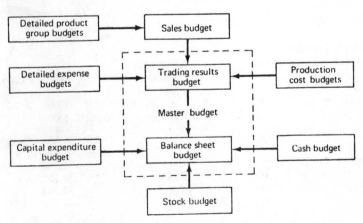

Figure 4.12   Relationship of Sectional Budgets to the Master Budget

If budgetary control is introduced into a company, the management is forced to examine the problems which the future will present. The recognition of possible difficulties before they arise is an advantage to any business, because the alternative is the constant attempt to avoid trouble at the last moment. At this stage, the problems may have developed beyond the point where effective remedial action can be taken.

Where conditions change suddenly, the availability of the relevant information, as provided by budgetary control, can indicate all the effects on the business because planned management action is co-ordinated in financial terms.

Where managers know that figures they submit for budgetary purposes will subsequently be used as a measure of their efficiency, there is built in the system an incentive to submit estimates that are not too demanding on their performance. Senior management therefore require the experience and skill to recognise this type of budgeting and order the pruning of the estimates to a more realistic level.

To show the inter-relationship of the figures in a budgetary procedure a simple illustration is given. Quantity information is not given and analysis that would be provided in practice, such as accounting period detail, has been eliminated to show the essentials of the budgetary system.

GIVEN DATA FOR THE BUDGET PERIOD

BALANCE SHEET AS AT 1ST JANUARY 19....

	£	£	Fixed Assets:	Cost £	Deprecia-tion to date £	Book Value £
Share capital		50,000				
Revenue reserves:						
General reserve	15,000		Land and buildings	20,000	—	20,000
Profit and loss balance	8,000		Plant and equipment	45,250	15,000	30,250
		23,000	Vehicles	10,000	5,000	5,000
				75,250	20,000	55,250
Current liabilities:			Current assets:			
Trade creditors	3,000		Stock		20,750	
Bank	30,000		Trade debtors		30,000	
		33,000				50,750
		106,000				106,000

	Product A	Product B	Product C
Sales in units	20,000	10,000	30,000
Selling price per unit	£4	£6	£3
Costs per unit:			
Direct material:			
X (at 1s per lb)	10 lb	20 lb	—
Y (at 6d per lb)	10 lb	—	20 lb
Direct labour:			
Department 1 (at 10s per hour)	½ hour	½ hour	1 hour
Department 2 (at 20s per hour)	½ hour	1 hour	½ hour
Variable overhead	£0.50	£0.75	£0.50

The above figures give the following information per unit:

	Product A £	£	Product B £	£	Product C £	£
Direct material:						
X	0·5		1·0		—	
Y	0·25		—		0·5	
		0·75		1·0		0·5
Direct labour:						
Department 1	0·25		0·25		0·5	
Department 2	0·5		1·0		0·5	
		0·75		1·25		1·0
Variable overhead		0·5		0·75		0·5
Marginal cost		2·0		3·0		2·0
Selling price		4·0		6·0		3·0
Contribution		2·0		3·0		1·0

The sales budget may now be given as follows:

SALES BUDGET   YEAR ENDED 31ST DECEMBER 19....

PRODUCT GROUP	SALES £	MARGINAL COST OF SALES £	CONTRIBUTION £	PROFIT VOLUME RATIO %
A	80,000	40,000	40,000	50
B	60,000	30,000	30,000	50
C	90,000	60,000	30,000	33⅓
TOTALS	230,000	130,000	100,000	

BUDGET SUBMITTED BY...   DATE.................

The column details are calculated by multiplying the unit prices and costs by the sales in units for each product

UNIT STOCK MOVEMENTS

	Product A	Product B	Product C
Work-in-progress (complete as to materials only):			
Opening stock	2,000	2,000	2,000
Materials issued	20,000	8,000	28,000
	22,000	10,000	30,000
Production	21,000	9,000	29,000
Closing stock	1,000	1,000	1,000
Finished Goods:			
Opening stock	1,000	2,000	3,000
Production	21,000	9,000	29,000
	22,000	11,000	32,000
Sales	20,000	10,000	30,000
Closing stock	2,000	1,000	2,000

The following budgets may now be given:

The Production Cost Budget
The Materials Cost Budget
The Labour Cost Budget

PRODUCTION COST BUDGET   YEAR ENDED 31ST DECEMBER 19....

	PRODUCT A £	PRODUCT B £	PRODUCT C £	TOTAL £
DIRECT MATERIAL COST	15,000	8,000	14,000	37,000
DIRECT LABOUR COST	15,750	11,250	29,000	56,000
VARIABLE OVERHEAD	10,500	6,750	14,500	31,750
MARGINAL PRODUCTION COST	41,250	26,000	57,500	124,750
ADD OPENING WORK-IN-PROGRESS	1,500	2,000	1,000	4,500
	42,750	28,000	58,500	129,250
DEDUCT CLOSING WORK-IN-PROGRESS	750	1,000	500	2,520
MARGINAL COST OF FINISHED PRODUCTION	42,000	27,000	58,000	127,000

BUDGET SUBMITTED BY ....   DATE...........................

The multiplication of the closing stock of finished goods in units by the marginal cost per unit gives the marginal cost of finished production. The use of the stock movement figures and the relevant unit costs provides the input data shown in this budget.

Reconciliation between the budgeted sales at marginal cost and the marginal cost of finished production:

	Product A	Product B	Product C	Total
	£	£	£	£
Sales at marginal cost	40,000	30,000	60,000	130,000
Add Closing stock–finished goods	4,000	3,000	4,000	11,000
	44,000	33,000	64,000	141,000
Deduct opening stock–finished goods	2,000	6,000	6,000	14,000
Marginal cost of finished production	42,000	27,000	58,000	127,000

MATERIALS COST BUDGET   YEAR ENDED 31ST DECEMBER 19....

MATERIAL TYPE	PRODUCT A	PRODUCT B	PRODUCT C	TOTAL
	£	£	£	£
X	10,000	8,000	—	18,000
Y	5,000	—	14,000	19,000
TOTALS	15,000	8,000	14,000	37,000

BUDGET SUBMITTED BY...   DATE................

LABOUR COST BUDGET   YEAR ENDED 31ST DECEMBER 19....

DEPARTMENT	PRODUCT A	PRODUCT B	PRODUCT C	TOTAL
	£	£	£	£
1	5,250	2,250	14,500	22,000
2	10,500	9,000	14,500	34,000
TOTALS	15,750	11,250	29,000	56,000

BUDGET SUBMITTED BY...   DATE................

The above budgets are subsidiary to the Production Cost Budget, explaining in greater detail the summary information for direct material and direct labour costs.

125

RAW MATERIAL STOCK MOVEMENTS

	Material X lb	Material Y lb
Opening stock	20,000	50,000
Add Purchases	370,000	770,000
	390,000	820,000
Deduct Closing stock	30,000	60,000
Raw materials issed	360,000	760,000

The following budgets may now be given:
  The Purchasing Budget
  The Stock Budget

PURCHASING BUDGET   YEAR ENDED 31ST DECEMBER 19....

	MATERIAL X £	MATERIAL Y £	TOTAL £
MATERIALS CONSUMED	18,000	19,000	37,000
ADD CLOSING STOCK	1,500	1,500	3,000
	19,500	20,500	40,000
DEDUCT OPENING STOCK	1,000	1,250	2,250
PURCHASES	18,500	19,250	37,750

BUDGET SUBMITTED BY..   DATE........................

STOCK BUDGETS   YEAR ENDED 31ST DECEMBER 19....

	MATERIAL X		MATERIAL Y		TOTAL	
	OPENING STOCK £	CLOSING STOCK £	OPENING STOCK £	CLOSING STOCK £	OPENING STOCK £	CLOSING STOCK £
RAW MATERIAL	1,000	1,500	1,250	1,500	2,250	3,000

	PRODUCT A		PRODUCT B		PRODUCT C			
	OPENING STOCK £	CLOSING STOCK £	OPENING STOCK £	CLOSING STOCK £	OPENING STOCK £	CLOSING STOCK £		
WORK-IN-PROGRESS	1,500	750	2,000	1,000	1,000	500	4,500	2,250
FINISHED GOODS	2,000	4,000	6,000	3,000	6,000	4,000	14,000	11,000

BUDGET SUBMITTED BY............................   DATE................   20,750   16,250

The unit cost information for raw materials, work-in-progress, and finished goods, enables the management to value the units of stock and a comprehensive picture of investment in this important asset is indicated.

Fixed Expenses:	£
Factory	30,000
Selling	20,000
Distribution	7,000
Administration	20,000
	77,000

The Trading Results Budget may now be given:

TRADING RESULTS BUDGET   YEAR ENDED 31ST DECEMBER 19....

		PRODUCT A	PRODUCT B	PRODUCT C	TOTAL
		£	£	£	£
SALES	(A)	80,000	60,000	90,000	230,000
DIRECT MATERIAL COST		15,000	10,000	15,000	40,000
DIRECT LABOUR COST		15,000	12,500	30,000	57,500
VARIABLE OVERHEAD		10,000	7,500	15,000	32,500
MARGINAL COST OF SALES	(B)	40,000	30,000	60,000	130,000
CONTRIBUTION	(A–B)	40,000	30,000	30,000	100,000
PROFIT/VOLUME RATIO		50%	50%	33⅓%	

	£	
DEDUCT FIXED EXPENSES		
FACTORY	30,000	
SELLING	20,000	
DISTRIBUTION	7,000	
ADMINISTRATION	20,000	
		77,000
Net Profit		23,000

BUDGET SUBMITTED BY...   DATE..................................

In this budget the fixed expenses are deducted from the contribution, as shown in the Sales Budget, to give the final net profit.

Two capital expenditure projects have been approved for the budget year as illustrated below:

127

CAPITAL EXPENDITURE BUDGET   YEAR ENDED 31ST DECEMBER 19....

PROJECT NO.	DETAILS OF PROJECT	£
1	ACCOUNTING MACHINE	2,000
2	CONVEYOR	7,000
	TOTAL	9,000

BUDGET SUBMITTED BY..   DATE........................

Customers are allowed an average of 1½ months' credit and one month's credit is normally taken from suppliers. For this illustration, it is assumed that all other outlays are for cash.

The following budgets may now be given:

The Trade Debtors' Budget
The Trade Creditors' Budget

TRADE DEBTORS BUDGET   YEAR ENDED 31ST DECEMBER 19....

	£
OPENING BALANCE OF DEBTORS	30,000
ADD SALES ON CREDIT	230,000
	260,000
DEDUCT CASH RECEIVED FROM CUSTOMERS	231,250
CLOSING BALANCE OF DEBTORS	28,750

BUDGET SUBMITTED BY..   DATE........................

The opening balance of debtors is taken from the opening balance sheet and the sales on credit from the Sales Budget. The closing balance of debtors, allowing 1½ months' credit is, therefore, one eighth of £230,000.

TRADE CREDITORS BUDGET   YEAR ENDED 31ST DECEMBER 19....

	£
OPENING BALANCE OF CREDITORS	3,000
ADD PURCHASES ON CREDIT	37,750
	40,750
DEDUCT CASH PAID TO SUPPLIERS	37,600
CLOSING BALANCE OF CREDITORS	3,150

BUDGET SUBMITTED BY..   DATE........................

The opening balance of creditors is taken from the opening balance sheet and the purchases on credit from the Purchasing Budget. The closing balance of creditors, taking one month's credit is, therefore, one twelfth of £37,750 (rounded to the nearest £10).

Included in the fixed expenses is £7,000 for depreciation. The Cash Budget is illustrated below:

CASH BUDGET   YEAR ENDED 31ST DECEMBER 19....

		£
OPENING BANK OVERDRAFT		30,000
ADD RECEIPTS FROM CUSTOMERS		231,250
BUDGETED NET RECEIPTS	(A)	201,250
DEDUCT: PAYMENTS TO SUPPLIERS		37,600
CAPITAL EXPENDITURE		9,000
WAGES AND SALARIES / OTHER PAYMENTS		157,750
BUDGETED PAYMENTS	(B)	204,350
CLOSING BANK OVERDRAFT	(A–B)	3,100

BUDGET SUBMITTED BY............................ DATE....................

The total of cash payments from the earlier budgets and the cash received from customers figure from the Trade Debtors' Budget explains the change in the bank overdraft in the Cash Budget.

The Balance Sheet Budget is illustrated below with the supporting Budgeted Fixed Assets Analysis:

BALANCE SHEET BUDGET AS AT 31ST DECEMBER 19....

		£
Fixed Assets:		
LAND AND BUILDINGS AT COST		20,000
PLANT AND MACHINERY AND OTHER EQUIPMENT AT COST LESS DEPRECIATION		33,250
VEHICLES AT COST LESS DEPRECIATION		4,000
TOTAL FIXED ASSETS	(A)	57,250
Current Assets:		
STOCK-IN-TRADE		16,250
TRADE DEBTORS		28,750
	(B)	45,000

Continued overleaf

BALANCE SHEET BUDGET AS AT 31ST DECEMBER 19.... *Continued*

		£
Current Liabilities:		
TRADE CREDITORS		3,150
BANK OVERDRAFT		3,100
	(C)	6,250
WORKING CAPITAL	(B–C–D)	38,750
NETT ASSETS		96,000
REPRESENTED BY:		
ORDINARY SHARE CAPITAL		50,000
GENERAL RESERVE		15,000
PROFIT AND LOSS ACCOUNT BALANCE		31,000
CAPITAL AND RESERVES		96,000

BUDGET SUBMITTED BY........................... DATE....................

BUDGETED FIXED ASSETS ANALYSIS   YEAR ENDED 31ST DECEMBER 19....

	COST (A) £	CAPITAL EXPENDI- TURE (B) £	TOTAL COST (A+B = C) f	DEPRE- CIATION BROUGHT FORWARD (D) £	DEPRE- CIATION BUDGET YEAR (E) £	TOTAL DEPRECIATION (D+E = F) £	BOOK VALUE (C−F) £
AND AND BUILDINGS	20,000		20,000				20,000
LANT AND MACHINERY AND OTHER EQUIPMENT	45,250	9,000	54,250	15,000	6,000	21,000	33,250
EHICLES	10,000	—	10,000	5,000	1,000	6,000	4,000
TOTALS	75,250	9,000	84,250	20,000	7,000	27,000	57,250

UDGET SUBMITTED BY...................................... DATE.................

The changes in the financial status of the business are clearly presented in the Balance Sheet Budget. The net asset figures are taken from the budgets named by each item and the Budgeted Fixed Assets Analysis above. The ordinary share capital and general reserve figures are taken from the opening Balance Sheet and the profit and loss account balance is calculated as follows:

	£
Opening balance per the opening Balance Sheet	8,000
Add Net Profit per the Trading Results Budget	23,000
	31,000

Budgetary Control and Period Reporting

After the budget is approved and becomes a commitment for the organisation in the budget period, the reporting of actual results against the budget figures and an indication of the differences (variances) becomes part of the reporting system. A typical outline report is illustrated below:

TITLE . . . .

PERIOD . . . .

	THIS PERIOD			TO DATE		
	ACTUAL	BUDGET	VARIATION	ACTUAL	BUDGET	VARIATION
	£	£	£	£	£	£
ANALYSIS						
SUB-TOTALS						
HEADINGS						
SUB-TOTALS						
TOTALS						

In these reports the word 'actual' should not be interpreted literally. Information, if it is to be of any use to management, must be produced as quickly as possible, and in some instances approximation may be desirable rather than hold up the production of information which is sufficiently accurate for management purposes. These estimates, prepared on the best information available, are shown under the heading 'actual'. There is nothing wrong in this, providing it is understood by management and the possible error in the figures is not liable to lead to erroneous conclusions.

The difference between the actual and the budget figures may be further analysed by causes to assist managers in improving their performance. This aspect of the subject is often developed in a business by the use of the standard costing technique.

131

Standard Costing

The techniques of budgetary control and standard costing are inter-related. Each technique is based on:

1. A predetermined standard of performance—in budgetary control it is called the budget; in standard costing, the *standard*.
2. A comparison of 'actual' performance with the standard of performance.
3. An analysis of variances by cause to point the way to managers where their action can improve performance.

The application of these principles to the business as a whole is the province of **budgetary control;** the application of the same principles to detailed operations, particularly on the production side of the business, is the area covered by **standard costing.**

When standard costs are calculated, a standard cost card is prepared for each product. The basis of the standard cost card detail is the technical specification for the product, which provides full information on quantities and times, qualities and grades of the elements of cost. Standard cost prices and rates developed from the budget complete the factory cost of the products to be produced. The standard product cost card is used to provide the basic information against which, actual costs are compared to calculate the variances. This detailed information linked to the technical factors associated with the control of the business provides valuable data for management, analysing the causes of unsatisfactory performance, which may be as follows:

Paying more for material or using more material than intended
Paying more for labour or using labour inefficiently compared with the standard
Spending more than intended for overhead or using facilities inefficiently
Falling short of the sales volume intended or selling products under the standard selling price

The above information may be used by managers to assist in the day-to-day decision-making process, but other data may be required. In the next section, decision-making theory is examined in sufficient detail to form the basis of a consideration of relevant cost information in the context of the management control process.

Decision Making

The essentials of the decision-making process are illustrated in Figure 4.13.

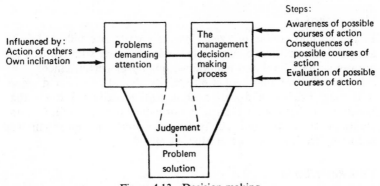

Figure 4.13   Decision-making

Of the facts required as a basis for decision-making, financial information is vital to assess the likely profit impact of a decision on the trading results of the business.

Relevant Costs

The purpose for which the cost is to be used affects relevancy and in decision-making what is relevant is the difference in the cost arising from one course of action as compared with another course of action. Since the decision is concerned with the future, all costs considered should be anticipated future costs—historical costs are not relevant except as a guide to the assessment of future costs. In choosing relevant costs for decision-making the following terms are recognised:

Avoidable costs: These are costs avoided if a particular course of action that would originate these costs is not taken.

Imputed costs: These are costs not recognised as a transaction in the accounting records of the business but a necessary factor in the decision-making process, such as interest on capital.

Opportunity costs: Revenue unobtainable as a result of not taking a particular course of action.

Available time may be limited for the collection of relevant data, but as much relevant information should be provided to reduce the probability that an incorrect decision may be made. If correct decisions are made the profitability of a business should be improved. Decision-making, with the specific intention of securing a profit improvement, is clearly part of the cost reduction activities of a business.

133

Cost Reduction

In the normal course of events business costs rise unless definite action is taken either to keep costs stable or, better still, reduced for a given activity level and maintained quality or performance.

To be effective, cost reduction activity should be directed where it is most needed, and cost analysis will identify the items that account for the highest cost. It is normally easier to obtain a substantial cost saving from such items, than obtain an equivalent cost reduction from a low cost product element.

Cost Reporting

The stage where managers obtain the information they need by direct observation alone is rapidly passed as businesses expand. In this section, the attempt has been made to show that the cost accounting system captures a volume of data, that is directly relevant to the management control process.

4.3 INVESTMENT AND GROWTH FUNCTIONS

Very often we hear of people who would be willing to start a business if they had the capital to do so; and of businesses which have collapsed due to insufficiency of capital. In both cases 'capital' means **cash,** an ample supply of which is necessary for the day-to-day running of a business and, if expansion is contemplated, additional finance must be found to make this a reality.

All business involves a waiting period. Even before production begins, a manufacturer must buy or lease plant and buildings. Other payments are made for raw materials, labour and services before production begins, during the production process and before proceeds from the sale are received. Therefore, two kinds of finance are required: **long term,** to finance fixed assets and **short term,** to finance each round of production before cash is finally received.

When additional cash becomes necessary, a business should consider several factors before deciding on the source to be used:

1. The need for cash must be defined. Is it required to finance new plant, or for additional working capital? The error of borrowing money needed for the long-term from a short-term source, or tying up long-term sources when the need is for short-term money must be avoided.
2. How much money is required? It could be disastrous if the funds required to finance a development programme were under-

estimated. Conversely, if large amounts of funds which are surplus to requirements are borrowed, the interest payments on them could make serious inroads into the profitability of the project. Cash requirements are determined by careful cash budgeting.

3. Is it possible to economise on the cash requirement by utilising more efficiently the funds already tied up in the business?

Internal Finance

Despite the existence of a highly developed capital market, industry still continues to obtain the major share of its financial requirements from its own sources. In fact, 75 per cent of the total capital raised by all industrial and commercial companies come from retentions of profit. This form of finance is as marked in private as in public companies.

Sources of External Finance

(a) *Short-term* (*up to two years*)

Bank Credit: An overdraft from a joint stock bank is the most familiar form of finance for the smaller company. In recent years English banks have lent for medium- and long-term purposes, but they still continue to regard themselves as essentially short-term lenders, engaged in financing working capital, especially that of a self-liquidating nature such as finished stocks. Therefore, bank advances are usually made for a short period, say six months, but they can be renewed again and again and run on for years. In theory they are repayable on demand; in practice, in time of 'credit squeeze' the banks may well refuse an increase, or demand a reduction, in the agreed limit. The Bank of England, on behalf of the Government, has imposed 'qualitative' lending restrictions on the activities of banks in certain areas (such as finance for imports), which have been regarded as against the interests of the economy.

Bills of Exchange and Acceptance Credits: The bill of exchange has been used for centuries to finance trade throughout the world, and it can be equally suitable for financing domestic trade. Arrangements may be made in appropriate cases for customers to accept bills of exchange at an alternative to making payment for goods received after an interval of two or three months. Such bills may be discounted with (or, sold to) a commercial bank or a discount house, thus providing funds immediately.

A refinement of the use of the bill of exchange is the **acceptance**

credit. This involves the borrowers drawing bills on a merchant bank, or acceptance house, which can then be discounted with a discount house. By this technique it is possible to raise three or six months finance at rates comparable with the cost of an overdraft. The use of such facilities have the advantage of leaving the bank overdraft free for profitable use elsewhere in the business.

Trade Credit is an important source of short-term finance. A firm receives trade credit when it pays in arrears for goods and services received from its suppliers. This source can always be used during the normal course of business, but care must be taken not to damage the reputation of the business by extending the period of credit and not sacrificing cash discounts for prompt payment.

Factoring facilities are more expensive than overdraft finance, but in circumstances where the provision of funds is a necessity, the firm will be willing to pay the price. The **factor**, a finance house, buys from his clients the invoices representing their debts, and collects the sums due from the debtors in the normal course of business. Therefore, the client has immediate access to the cash tied up in the trade debtors, less a charge for the factoring service, which can be used elsewhere in the business, perhaps to exploit favourable buying opportunities, or to take more favourable terms from suppliers.

(b) *Medium-term (two to five years)*

Hire Purchase of Plant and Machinery:

'The significance of hire purchase in the financial structure of the economy is that it is a convenient source of medium-term credit on fixed terms for the purchase of equipment, where the equipment itself can provide adequate security for the loan, and the loan can be paid off by regular instalments. The purchaser is free to employ his personal credit in other directions if he wishes, a circumstance of particular importance to business users.'

(*Radcliffe Committee Report on the Working of the Monetary System.*)

The repayment period is from three to five years and it tends to be a relatively expensive form of credit. One advantage to the hirer is that the terms fixed at the outset of the agreement cannot be varied whatever happens to Bank Rate, and the agreed credit cannot be withdrawn as long as the hirer fulfils his side of the contract.

Equipment leasing is similar to hire purchase, in that regular payments have to be made under both methods. The main difference between the two is, that with hire purchase the ownership of the asset eventually passes to the user, whereas with leasing, it does not. The advantages which are claimed for hire purchase also apply to equipment leasing:

1. It helps to preserve other sources of credit.
2. It enables the use of equipment and buildings, and it is this aspect which is vital to profitability, not ownership.
3. The equipment and buildings can be used immediately after the first payment.
4. Since the amounts to be paid are known in advance it helps the budgetary process.
5. It minimises the risks of large capital losses arising from obsolescence.
6. It prevents the broadening of the ownership of the company which equity (ordinary share) financing involves.

Equipment leasing and hire purchase cost about the same, and the advantages of one rather than the other will be determined by the tax position of the business.

(c) Long-term (over five years)

Long-term borrowing may be undertaken by both private and public companies. Land and buildings may be purchased by means of a mortgage, or loan, from an insurance company, or pension fund, which is usually payable over a specified period by direct payment, or by life insurance. A typical loan from an insurance company would amount to two-thirds of the cost of an asset and would be repayable over 20 to 25 years. Building societies are usually reluctant to lend on the security of business premises.

Sale and lease back transactions occur when a firm, which requires additional finance, sells the property which it already owns to an insurance company, or pension fund, and at the same time takes back a long-term lease. The former owner now becomes the lessee of the property at a stated rental. It gives the company instant finance, but it loses any appreciation on the value of the asset. This method is especially useful where the firm occupies premises which represent a large proportion of the total assets and where such tied up capital can be better employed in the business as working capital.

The Issue of Shares and Debentures

The sources of long-term finance are divided into two distinct areas:

137

those which are available to all concerns, which have been discussed above, and those available only to the public company. The development of a business could involve the following four stages: one-man business, partnership, private company and public company. Many big companies, whose names are now household words, started as one-man businesses in small premises. For the **one-man business and partnership** finance will be obtained from similar sources. Both will be based on the savings of the owner or owners; this may be increased by borrowing from friends, from the bank and by utilising trade credit. Fixed assets may be acquired by hire purchase, or in the case of premises by a lease. In both cases constraints will be imposed on the growth of the business by shortage of finance. Furthermore, in both cases the owners are liable for all the debts incurred.

Consequently, as the concern begins to grow in size, serious thought must be given to the formation of a **private company,** which may consist of from two to fifty persons, exclusive of employees. As each shareholder has limited liability (that is to say that, if the company fails they are only responsible for the debts of the firm up to the amount of the capital subscribed) the private company has a great advantage over the partnership. In a private company, shares are not transferable without the consent of the other shareholders and it is not allowed to offer its shares for sale to the public. The disadvantage of not being able to raise capital from the general public has been partly offset by the fact that Issuing Houses today cater for private companies by 'placing' their unquoted shares with investment trusts and insurance companies. But the cost to the private company can be high because it has to compensate the investor for the limited marketability of the shares sold in this way.

If the private company is expanding rapidly and is making good profits and huge sums of permanent capital are required, these can be obtained only by converting to a **public company.** By taking this step, a business can make use of the capital market, that section of the London Money Market which is concerned with the issue of shares and debentures to the public. A company's capital may consist of one or more classes of shares. **Preference Share** holders as the name implies, have the first claim to the profits available for distribution. If the company goes into liquidation they will receive payment before other shareholders. Most preference issues are what are called *cumulative*, which means that if there are not enough profits in any year to pay the dividend, the arrears must be paid the following year, or at the first opportunity. With the rare exception of some which 'participate' in surplus profits, preference share-holders, never get more than a fixed dividend.

Ordinary Shares are referred to as the **equity** of the company. They are the risk capital and are last in line for dividends and any return if the company goes into liquidation. Hence whether or not they get a dividend and how big a dividend will depend entirely on the fortunes of the company and on the financial policy pursued by the directors. Since ordinary shares carry the risks, they also usually carry with them a right to vote at company meetings. **Debenture** capital is loan capital. Rather like a mortgage, they are usually secured on all, or some of, the assets of the company, receive a fixed rate of interest, and are usually repayable at fixed dates. Interest is paid whether profits are made or not, and is, therefore, unlike dividends, a *charge* against profits rather than an *appropriation*. If the company gets into difficulties, and fails to pay this interest, the debenture holders can sell it or take over the management.

Under the Finance Act 1965, corporation tax replaced income tax and profit tax on the profits of a company, and this became a distinct advantage taxwise in having loan capital rather than share capital. There was consequently a tendency for companies to issue debentures rather than share capital to obtain this advantage.

The Capital Market includes the following institutions:

1. The **Issuing Houses,** who act as an intermediary between those who need capital and those who are willing to provide it by investing. They are commercial concerns including the merchant banks, approximately fifty in number, who organise a public issue on behalf of a company, or who purchase a block of shares and then make an 'Offer for Sale' to the public. Issuing Houses advise on the terms and timing of the issue, attend to the legal and Stock Exchange formalities, arrange for printing and circulating the prospectus and arrange underwriting if necessary. They generally see the chosen plan through to a successful conclusion and the very fact that a new issue is launched by an Issuing House of repute is itself an important factor in ensuring the success of the operation.

2. **Underwriters** are financial institutions, e.g. merchant banks and insurance companies, who guarantee, for a commission, to subscribe for any shares not taken up by the public. A common practice is for the issuing house to underwrite the complete issue itself and then to pass on part, or all, of this responsibility to a number of sub-underwriters.

3. The **Stock Exchange** provides a free market for securities and is the only regular market for stocks and shares. By providing a ready

market for invested capital, whereby investors can turn their holdings into cash, it plays an important role in stimulating the issue of new capital. Secondly, individual members of the Stock Exchange may 'introduce' a company's shares to the market, thereby providing finance especially in the case of the smaller companies. Finally, it provides a service by protecting the investing public against fraud.

4. The term **Merchant Banks** is normally used to describe a number of banking institutions, whose main business differs from that of the clearing banks. They provide long- and medium-term finance to companies normally by means of shares or loans.

5. **The Insurance Companies** invest 40 per cent of their funds in industry on a medium- and long-term basis, usually by advance on a mortgage. There is no doubt that, but for the support of the insurance companies, the raising of capital in post-war years would have been more difficult.

6. **Investment Trusts** raise their capital by floating securities on the Stock Exchange and use that capital to invest in other securities in their turn. In effect, they say to the personal investor

'Left on your own you are very likely to pick all the wrong industries at all the wrong times for investment of your money. Entrust your money to us and your investment will be undertaken by a body of experts, and you can share the fruits of our wise decisions.'

As in the case of Insurance Companies, they are an important outlet for 'placings', often taking unquoted securities, and are active as underwriters.

7. **The Finance Corporations** (discussed in detail below).

The methods by which shares and debentures are issued are classified below:

(1) **Placings** are the most popular method of issuing shares and occur when shares are sold at a fixed price through the company's broker to investors in the private or public sector. Before the shares concerned can be dealt with on the Stock Exchange, details of the company's history and prospects have to be advertised in the press. Some stocks which are not quoted on the Stock Exchange may be placed privately with financial institutions; in this case advertisement is unnecessary and the costs of issue are very small. If the amount of the issue is not large enough to justify a public issue, considerable expense may be saved by adopting this method.

(2) **Rights issues** are issued to shareholders by circular. New issues are offered to shareholders in proportion to their existing holdings and on advantageous terms. The shareholder may accept the offer

himself or renounce all or part of his rights in favour of someone else. The great advantage of such issues is that costs are kept to a minimum.

(3) **Public issues by prospectus** are direct issues to the public by public companies. Established companies usually make an offer to existing shareholders, while a company which is coming to the Stock Exchange for the first time is much more likely to float away its existing shares on to the market first, by way of an offer for sale, a placing, or an introduction. A company which is floating a size-able public issue would have to face costs of 5 or 6 per cent of the money raised to meet the cost of the issue; for a newcomer it would be much heavier than this.

(4) **Offer for Sale** occurs when an Issuing House buys the shares and puts them up for sale. The system can be a sensible substitute for a direct issue for any company which finds it difficult, or inconvenient, to get a direct issue underwritten in the normal way in which a newcomer can float his shares on the Stock Exchange for the first time.

(5) **Issues by tender** have been revived recently. Subscriptions by tender are invited and the investors making the highest bids are issued with the shares. The object of these issues is to obtain capital as economically as possible by equating demand and supply, thereby removing the profit which often occurs to 'stags', people who buy shares with the object of making a profit when the share price is set too low.

The Finance Corporations

A number of specialised institutions have been established to provide medium- and long-term capital in cases where it cannot be easily provided from traditional sources.

The Charterhouse Development Company was set up in 1934 through the co-operation of the Prudential Insurance Company, Lloyds Bank and the Midland Bank in response to the findings in the Macmillan Report on Finance and Industry, which in 1931 recommended that such a company should be established with the object of providing finance for small businesses and to act as intermediary between small companies and the capital market by issuing its own shares.

The Industrial and Commerical Finance Corporation was established in 1945 by the Bank of England and the clearing banks to provide long-term debenture or share capital to the smaller company. The amounts involved range from £5,000 to £200,000.

It was thought that amounts less than these could be provided by the banks, and amounts larger by the new issue market.

The Finance Corporation for Industry was established in 1945 by the larger insurance companies, the Bank of England and investment trusts, and was designed to make loans to large basic industries for re-equipment and modernisation. The object was to supplement, and not to replace, the activities of other lenders. Therefore, the Corporation does not provide finance unless, first, the funds required exceed £200,000 and cannot be obtained on reasonable terms from any other source, and, secondly, the project appears to be important for the national interest. A subsidiary, **Technical Developments Ltd.,** was formed in 1962 to finance innovations and improvements and draws its funds from various insurance companies throughout the Commonwealth.

Seven major insurance companies co-operated to finance the **Estate Duties Investment Trust,** which was established in 1953 in order to provide funds to private companies, or small public companies, to meet current, or future, death duties, which might otherwise lead to financial embarrassment.

Investment Appraisal

Economic growth, which is the rate by which a country increases output per head, is held by many economists to be the prime economic objective. With a fast rate of growth most economic problems can be solved more quickly, and generally the people of a country can enjoy higher living standards and better social services. Of the factors affecting economic growth, investment is considered to be the most important. **Investment** means an increase in the stock of capital goods—raw materials, plant and machinery, factory buildings and transport facilities. Capital goods enable other goods (consumer goods) to be produced. For example, the quickest way of increasing output of motor-cars is to increase the amount of machinery which produces cars.

The economic growth of the U.K. since the second World War has been widely regarded as unsatisfactory. The growth rates of our European competitors have been double that of the U.K., while Japan, with average increases of 10 per cent per annum, has made even our European competitors seem sluggish! Comparison of investment as a percentage of national income with national income trends reveals a strong correlation between growth and investment, and leads to the conclusion that the prime reason why other countries have grown faster than the U.K. is that they have diverted a greater proportion of their resources into investment.

Another important correlation is that between growth and profits. The long-term objective of a firm in a competitive industry is to maximise its profit; and its ability to do this is the chief criterion by which the performance of a firm is judged. In fact, it is difficult for a firm to achieve a high rate of growth unless it achieves a high rate of return on capital employed. Without a high rate of return a firm can neither finance expansion internally, nor obtain capital through the market on satisfactory terms. Therefore, it is of crucial importance, both for economic growth and for an individual firm's profits, that the best methods of evaluating the return on investment—**investment appraisal**—are used. Otherwise, a firm may invest in projects which give inadequate rates of return and may miss opportunities for more profitable investments. The conventional method of investment appraisal, the pay back and rate of return on investment methods, both have serious limitations and may lead to bad decisions being made. The most superior methods by far are those involving *discounted cash flow techniques*.

The **pay back** method attempts to forecast how long it will take for a project to 'pay for itself'. If, for example, it is estimated that a firm will receive £5,000 profit over five years from an investment of £5,000, then the pay back period is five years. The main weaknesses of this method is that it ignores both the timing of the returns from the investment and the returns after the payment period.

The **rate of return** method is also unsatisfactory. It is the average annual profit expressed as a percentage of the original capital outlay. If, for example, an investment of £200,000 will result in cash inflows of £40,000 per annum over the next ten years, the rate of return is 10 per cent calculated as follows:

$$
\begin{aligned}
\text{Profit} &= \text{cash inflows less cash outflows} \\
&= £400,000 \text{ less } £200,000 \\
&= £200,000 \\
\text{Average annual profit} &= £200,000 \div 10 \\
&= £20,000 \\
&= 10\% \text{ of original capital outlay}
\end{aligned}
$$

This method ignores the earning life of the investment and the *timing* of cash inflows. A sum of £1 received now, assuming no change in the value of money, is worth more than £1 to be received in 10 years. A more realistic approach is to discount future cash flows to *present value*.

Discounted cash flow (D.C.F.) techniques overcome the disadvantages inherent in conventional methods of investment appraisal of comparing a present expenditure (the cost of the project) with future income. Consequently, they ignore the obvious fact that money available immediately is of greater value than an equivalent amount to be received at some future date. The missing factor is the compound rate of interest the money might be expected to earn between the present time and the date of receipt of income. Consider the effect of investing £1 per annum for five years at 10 per cent. The value at the end of 1 year is £1·100; after 2 years $(£1·1)^2$ = £1·210; 3 years $(£1·1)^3$ = £1·331; 4 years $(£1·1)^4$ = £1·464; and after 5 years $(£1·1)^5$ = £1·611.

Conversely, we can express the *present values* of £1 which is received at a future date (assuming an interest rate of 10 per cent) as follows:

$$\text{In one year} \quad \frac{£1}{1·100} = £0·9091$$

$$\text{In two years} \quad \frac{£1}{1·210} = £0·8264$$

$$\text{In three years} \quad \frac{£1}{1·331} = £0·7153$$

$$\text{In four years} \quad \frac{£1}{1·464} = £0·6831$$

$$\text{In five years} \quad \frac{£1}{1·611} = £0·6208$$

This means that £1 received in 5 years' time is worth a mere £0·6208 compared with £1 received today, because the £1 received today can be earning interest at the rate of 10 per cent over the next 5 years.

Although there are many variations of D.C.F. techniques the two most popular are the net present value and yield methods.

The **net present value** method utilises the rate at which capital is borrowed, which we assume is 10 per cent. The present value of the cash proceeds are then determined using this rate, the original cost of the investment is subtracted therefrom and the resulting surplus, or deficit, which shows the net present value, represents the net worth to the business of the investment.

Assume the cost of two schemes are £3,000 each, and the net cash proceeds expected from the projects are as follows:

144

End of year	Project A	Project B
	£	£
1	500	2,000
2	1,000	1,500
3	1,500	1,500
4	2,000	1,000
5	2,000	500
	£7,000	£6,500

By applying the present value factors for 10 per cent we may determine the present value of these proceeds:

End of year	Multiplying factor per £1 at 10%	Project A	Present value A	Project B	Present value B
		£	£	£	£
1	0·9091	500	454·6	2,000	1,818·2
2	0·8264	1,000	826·4	1,500	1,239·6
3	0·7153	1,500	1,073,0	1,500	1,073·0
4	0·6831	2,000	1,366·2	1,000	683·1
5	0·6208	2,000	1,241·6	500	310·4

Present value of cash inflows	4,961·8	5,124·3
Less original cost of investment	3,000·0	3,000·0
Net present value	1,961·8	2,124·3

Since the net present value of Project B is higher than that of Project A, Project B iş the most profitable investment and should, therefore, be the one chosen by management. It may be noted that the total cash inflows is greater for Project A and that the rate of return method would incorrectly show this to be the more profitable investmetn. The fact that a greater inflow occurs in early years for Project B is ignored by this method, but this is remedied by using D.C.F. techniques.

The **yield** is the rate of interest which if used to discount the cash flow would make the net present value zero. This rate is obtained by trial and error from interest tables. A return of between 28 and 29 per cent will accrue from Project A:

Project A Cash inflows	Multiplying factor per £1 at 29%	Present value	Multiplying factor per £1 at 28%	Present value
£		£		£
500	0·7752	387·6	0·7813	390·7
1,000	0·6009	600·9	0·6104	610·4
1,500	0·4658	698·7	0·4768	715·2
2,000	0·3611	722·2	0·3725	745·0
2,000	0·2799	559·8	0·2910	582·0
		2,969·2		3,043·3
Less original cost		3,000·0		3,000·0
		−31·2		43·3

Using the same method it can be deduced that the yield for Project B is 39 per cent, which again demonstrates that this project is the more profitable.

FURTHER READING

Davies, Alan, and Coy, John, *Economics from Square One*, Allen & Unwin, Chapter 5.

Wood, Frank, *Business Accounting 2*, Longmans, Chapters 41, 42 and 47.

Friedland, Seymour, *The Economics of Corporate Finance*, Prentice Hall, Chapters 1–5.

Anthony, Robert N., *Management Accounting: Texts and Cases*, Irwin, Chapters 13, 15, 16 and 17.

N.E.D.C., *Investment Appraisal*, H.M.S.O.

QUESTIONS

1. Define the terms:

   (a) Fixed cost
   (b) Variable cost
   (c) Semi-variable cost

   Why is the distinction important?

2. Two competing businesses sell the same type of product in the same type of market. For the year ending 30th June 19 . . . their budgeted profit and loss accounts are as follows:

146

	Red Ltd.		Green Ltd.	
	£	£	£	£
Sales		300,000		300,000
Less: Variable costs	240,000		200,000	
Fixed overhead	30,000	270,000	70,000	270,000
Budgeted net profit		30,000		30,000

You are required to:

(a) calculate the break-even points of each business;
(b) state which business is likely to earn greater profits in conditions of:

   (i) low demand for the product;
   (ii) heavy demand for the product.

Give your reasons (I.C.W.A.).

3. What costs are involved in maintaining debtors?

4. Why are short-term funds referred to as 'circulating capital'?

5. In what ways are the D.C.F. techniques superior to older methods of investment appraisal?

CHAPTER FIVE

The Human Element

5.1 WHY WORK?

WORK is done by individuals and the differences between individuals are significant factors in organising the working environment. An attempt is made in this chapter to provide an understanding of human aspects of work by studying the relations between the individual and his working environment.

In Chapter One the point was made that a primary objective of any business is to operate at a profit. To do this, management has to organise its resources to achieve maximum performance. One of its major resources is, of course, human beings. Whilst the output of some factors may be predetermined (such as the output from a machine in a workshop, or a budget in the accounting system), activities which involve people are not so easily calculated. Even if they are calculated, then the results may very well vary owing to what is described as the 'human element'. People are social beings subject to many pressures and influences. How a man does a job is a complex of many variables—for example his attitude at the time, his physical condition, how well he has been trained, or how much 'work' he thinks at that point in time he should do in return for his *rewards*. The term *rewards* in itself has a complex meaning, for as a result of research into human behaviour in work situations, we now know that wage or salary is only one of several important needs of the worker. Persons at work in the present technological and advanced industrial society require that the firm treats them as human beings and not as a commodity. The late Hilaire Belloc once wrote:

'Workers have certain inalienable rights as important as those of the persons who employ them, and it is the duty of industry to recognise these rights.'

How well the employees work is important in terms of the results of the firm. *How well* requires the manager to understand *why* the employee works. The diagram (Figure 5.1) illustrates the point that a worker has *needs* which the work situation may satisfy or may frustrate. The degree to which satisfaction of needs, or frustration of need satisfaction, takes place will be reflected not only in measured work but in the morale and environment of the firm. To maximise the personal contributions of all the human constituents in an organisation is a major objective of the organisation and is implemented, not solely through the Personnel Function (policy procedures and plans as implemented by a personnel department), but through the whole management process itself; managers get work done through people. How these individual persons are organised directly influences their own need satisfaction.

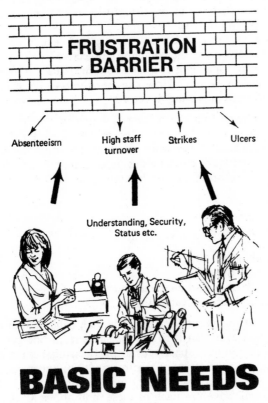

Figure 5.1

Work Satisfaction

In the past, many a manager could be heard to remark, 'Give them another penny an hour and it will keep them happy'. To improve work performance studies were made, for example by work study engineers to minimise waste or scrap. Working conditions may well have improved this way, but many payment schemes as a result still limited the reward to a narrow range of human activity. If we accept that satisfaction of non-material needs is as important to workers as satisfaction of financial needs, the questions then must be asked:

(a) If only some needs are being satisfied, what happens to those which are not in any way fulfilled—are they being in part satisfied by unofficial outlets, or by negative attitudes and behaviour towards management and the firm?

(b) What is the cost of low morale and lack of workers' co-operation in achieving the company's objective?

(c) How can something be done about the situation? What should be done and by whom? How can *co-operation* be achieved from junior worker to managing director?

A real awareness that the worker is bounded by the mechanisms of society at large and by the social processes within the firm, will help the organiser of the work situation to assess the human element. A knowledge of the individual is, therefore vital to the manager to achieve the co-ordination of the abilities and efforts of people.

Individual Differences

Characteristics of the individual are:

Mental abilities
Emotional demands
Personality traits and characteristics
Physical and sensory capacities

The most obvious general feature of human behaviour in any of the above categories is that it is not the same from one person to the next. We differ in our capacity for seeing, hearing, tasting and touching. We differ in the extent of our imagination, our memory, our intelligence, our powers of thought, our attitudes, our sentiments and our emotional make-up. Each of these, and above all the universal drives which make people 'tick', are found in varying degrees in each individual in differing circumstances.

What is the significance of this for human relations at work? Not only may these differences be seen to exist, but, they will be seen in different ways by different people. What we perceive of our environment is very much the product of the world we wish to see and we all construct different interpretations of the world. The past experience of an hourly paid worker in a strike-ridden factory may influence the worker's attitude towards wage negotiations. Equally, the past experience of a salaried professional monthly paid manager will influence his acceptance of long-term salary negotiations.

Fortunately the differences are of degree and not of fundamental distinction. The human element then follows the same principles of behaviour, the actual behaviour being of difference in degree. In the work sense then, the highly intelligent person requires from his work intellectual stimulation and satisfaction, while the person of low intelligence demands a more habit-formed routine, and different rewards or satisfaction of needs. Thus, behaviour is not totally unaccountable, and we can say behaviour is *caused*. Men and women have innate tendencies to certain forms of behaviour which form the basis of the way they do things. These are the needs or wants, or drives, which we all have within us, which we call *motivation*.

Motivation

When we study motivation, we are studying what goes on inside a human being to bring about his behaviour. For example, when we ask someone to perform a certain task which we know to be within his capability and experience and it is not done satisfactorily, this failure may well be the result of weak motivation rather than lack of ability. Some motivating factors, which are easy to identify for they are basically biological or physiological, may be looked upon as 'natural' or unlearned. They are necessities which include air, water, food, sleep, the sex impulse, clothing and housing. For their satisfaction, money and security are usually required. An old-established firm paying its shop-floor workers by piece rates (work output) and time rates (hourly paid) has recently introduced weekly staff rates throughout the firm in an attempt to reduce **labour turnover** (the rate at which workers leave the firm) and to provide the workers with a reasonable guarantee of security, both at work and *in the home*. The worker may now enter into contracts for hire purchase of a television set, a car and so on, without 'losing face' before his family if they are repossessed due to the effect of 'short time' working on his earnings. The managing director reported that after twelve months labour turnover had dropped and that productivity had increased.

Other motivating factors are learned. Motivation depends on the existence of a desire, arising from an awareness of a need, which comes, in its turn, from an instinctive drive or pressure creating a need. If such a need is not satisfied at once, a desire forms and with it a will to satisfy that desire. If an activity occurs in which the pressure is not removed, the restraints imposed on the will create for the individual a feeling of frustration. It is here that the individual's *egoistic* needs operate. **Egoistic needs** are those that an individual has for a high evaluation of himself, and include such needs as self-respect, achievement, status, recognition, knowledge and a sense of being wanted and appreciated. To maintain a high estimate of ourselves, most of us never stop needing reassurance that we are held in esteem by others. Thus, if we satisfy our egoistic needs today, we continue to seek such satisfaction today and tomorrow, and the days following. Physiological and social needs may be satisfied and cease therefore to motivate. The continuing satisfaction of egoistic needs, then, would seem to offer the way to motivate employees to better job performance and thus utilise the human element in seeking to achieve the objectives of the firm. This is becoming of increasing importance when we recognise that the educational level of all employees is rising due to later school leaving, society's recognition of formal qualifications, 'worker participation' and the new emphasis on industrial training.

However, the satisfaction of egoistical needs in itself is not enough, for the individual has the needs in relation to his social needs and to the way he sees the world he has constructed. This will be influenced by both the formal and informal organisation of the work situation. Many studies have examined the effects of these, the most famous being the Hawthorne Investigations of Elton Mayo. Other studies by Professor Tom Lupton (*On the Shop Floor*) show the effects of informal groups on workers' attitudes and motivation in two British factories, ranging from heavy electrical engineering to rubber garment clothing factories. From these studies, it may be seen that the size, cohesiveness and motives or 'goals' of the group act as controls on the members' own motives, or goals, and that its organisation should create a situation in which group and individual goals coincide to as great a degree as possible.

It is, therefore, important to recognise the wide diversity of factors which can influence the needs of a single individual at work, and it is with these in mind that a company must attempt to harness the human element to achieve the company's objectives through its organisation.

Understanding the Employee

One of the major factors which can influence worker output is the way in which the employee thinks that the firm thinks of him. In other words, how the employee sees his role as a member of the firm.

You will find below a list of opinions frequently expressed about workers. Tick the appropriate column to indicate your own opinions as follows:

YES = emphatically yes
NO = emphatically no
yes = on the whole yes
no = on the whole no

Are your answers consistent? Was it difficult to answer? Now you should ask yourself what the completed list *really* signifies. You have been asked in a simple way to conceptualise your attitudes towards why people work and how people work. Further, depending on your answers, would be indicated how something gets done, and in what way it gets done.

Behind every managerial decision or action are assumptions about human nature and human behaviour. Professor Douglas Mac-Gregor in his book, *The Human Side of Enterprise*, identifies two opposing attitudes towards the organisation of people at work: Theory X and Theory Y.

CHECK YOUR ATTITUDE	Your opinion is			
	YES	NO	yes	no
1. Good social relationships are very important work factors for employees				
2. No one really enjoys working: we work because we have to				
3. Most people like to be told what to do				
4. Most people like to be given responsibility for the job				
5. Most people can learn to accept responsibility if the boss has the right attitude towards them.				
6. Most people can be imaginative and creative in the work they do				

	Your opinion is			
	YES	NO	yes	no
7. Wage earners are not paid to show initiative or think constructively about the job				
8. It is only human nature that people will do as little work as they possibly can				
9. Most people really want to work, and like to do a good job				
10. There is usually a valid reason for the way people behave at work				
11. The more 'rope' you give workers the more they want				
12. Most people who work in industry, commerce are not called upon to use their intellectual capacity to the full				
13. People will work better when they can see and feel that what they do makes a direct contribution to company objectives.				
14. The strongest motivator is 'What is in it for me?'				
15. Only if management make it possible can workers give optimum work and not feel dissatisfied				

MacGregor suggests that in:

Figure 5.2

Theory X

(1) The average human being has an inherent dislike of work and will avoid it if he can.

(2) Because of this human characteristic of dislike of work, most people must be coerced, controlled, directed, threatened with punishment to get them to put forth adequate effort toward the achievement of organisational objectives.

(3) The average human being prefers to be directed, wishes to avoid responsibility, has relatively little ambition, wants security above all.

Theory Y

(1) The expenditure of physical and mental effort in work is as natural as play or rest. The average human being does not inherently dislike work. Depending upon controllable conditions work may be a source of satisfaction (and will be voluntarily performed) or a source of punishment (and will be avoided if possible).

(2) External control and the threat of punishment are not the only means for bringing about effort towards organisational objectives. Man will exercise self-direction and self-control in the service of objectives to which he is committed.

(3) Commitment to objectives is a function of the rewards associated with their achievement. The most significant of such rewards, e.g. the satisfaction of ego and self-actualisation needs, can be direct products of effort directed towards organisational objectives.

(4) The average human being learns, under proper conditions, not only to accept, but to seek, responsibility. Avoidance of responsibility, lack of ambition, and emphasis on security are generally consequences of experience, not inherent human characteristics.

(5) The capacity to exercise a relatively high degree of imagination, ingenuity and creativity in the solution of organisational problems is widely, not narrowly, distributed in the population.

(6) Under the conditions of modern industrial life, the intellectual potentialities of the average human being are only partially utilised.

In assessing briefly what MacGregor suggests, we find that Theory X offers management a form of control most suitable to an authoritarian or traditional-type company organisation in which the **scalar model** is used (see page 24).

The assumptions of Theory Y illustrate the fact that the limits on human collaboration and co-operation in the organisation or firm are not limited by the individual, but are limited only by management's ability or inability to harness the potential within each employee.

The potential itself is rapidly developing with the extensive development of education and higher education, as children stay at school longer and are part of an educational system which itself is changing towards liberalising the individual. The last thirty years has seen the emancipation of the woman and the wife. A similar revolution is taking place in the adolescent group, as consultation

155

involvement and participation become a feature of university, college and school environments.

Management today and in the immediate future has a responsibility to use its human assets in the best way possible. This indicates the desperate need for management to be aware of all the means possible of identifying individual differences and selecting with care for different job training, for the right job, and above all, achieving an environment of work.

Fitting the man to the job and fitting the job to the man is of increasing significance to the organisation as society's expectations change. The employer must analyse his own attitude towards workkers, and realise that the attitude of his employees is a key factor in gaining increased productivity. In the following sections we briefly examine methods of selecting, training and rewarding the employee. We then return to the key question of organising the worker, both in the formal and informal institutions and mechanisms.

5.2 RECRUITMENT, SELECTION AND TRAINING

Job Description and Job Analysis

Only in very recent times has industry started to place real value on its most valuable and, in many cases, its most costly resource—*the human element*—and to draw up a human element budget. Current forces such as the Industrial Training Boards and Selective Employment Tax returns, are pushing firms into drawing up Manpower Plans, or Manpower Budgets.

To do this, the individual personnel manager or director for labour relations must analyse the present situation in terms of the structure of the organisation and the competence of the people working for it. An organisation chart should indicate the jobs being undertaken. For any further use such as recruitment and selection or manpower planning, detailed job descriptions will be necessary.

Job description: As a term, it includes job analysis or job specification—a process of establishing the elements of a job and the nature of the human qualities required to perform it. A job description provides a title to the job, e.g. *capstan lathe turner*, or *general office filing clerk*, a summary of the job, the equipment used in the job, job factors in relation to other job factors in terms of evaluation of skills or characteristics and usually merit rating.

Job analysis or **job study** is the process of examining a job in order to identify its component parts and the circumstances under which it is performed. There are different approaches to the methods of job analysis, depending on the purposes for which the resulting information is to be used. Some of these are:

1. Gives specific evaluated information for a job specification.
2. Assists an individual to make a job choice.
3. Assists in selection during a recruitment selection process.
4. Provides a basis for the design of a training programme (of increasing importance since the setting up of the Industrial Training Boards; see pp. 175).
5. Aids evaluation of the worth of the job and remuneration paid, on a scientific basis.

Thus, job evaluation presents additional benefits, in that it is applied to the appraisal of each job performed in an organisation as a comparative yardstick or measure. Its common application is to the fixing of basic rates of pay for jobs, and in allowing the establishment of an equitable wage structure and the elimination of anomalies in the payments for jobs of approximately the same value. It is of vital importance in union collective bargaining talks and in the writing of a productivity agreement—discussed on page 168.

Detailed job descriptions indicate the physical, mental and psychological qualities demanded of the person who is to perform it. Thus the kind of information in general is:

(a) A statement of duties showing what is done, how it is done, and the limits of the job.
(b) The standards of performance expected—quantity, quality, time, and tolerances allowable.
(c) Specific job information.
(d) Responsibility: to whom, and for what, in relation to the company organisation chart.
(e) Any special working conditions.
(f) Any specialised training required over and above those shown by (a).
(g) Negotiated earnings/actual earnings.
(h) Any established reason for high labour turnover, if it exists.

Each organisation or personnel manager may well have his own design for the job specification card.

The above features are fairly common and, although generalised, can usually be found in varying forms. What is important is that the information given is utilised.

Whilst most people are familiar with the terms 'job description', 'job analysis,' 'job evaluation', 'job rating', and so on, distinction between the terms and their exact meaning is often blurred. The

Department of Employment and Productivity and the Industrial Training Boards have drawn up agreed definitions. General use of agreed definitions would greatly assist communication in the factory, as well as in the classroom. It is suggested that for a full list of definitions, you should consult the *Glossary of Training Terms*, Ministry of Labour, Published by H.M.S.O., 1967.

Recruitment

Recruitment is knowing what staff are required and where to get them. This procedure itself involves the existence of a manpower plan, and the availability of a detailed job description based on job analysis, as discussed above.

It is not possible, within the limitations of the size of this book, to discuss recruitment factors in detail, but they may be taken as implicit in the operation of a selection process as seen below. It is worth noting, however, one distinction between recruitment in the public service and that in industry and commerce. In the former, references are taken up prior to interview, whereas in the latter, references are usually taken up following provisional offer and acceptance of the appointment. It is the author's experience that practices in the two sectors are quite distinct and different in content of references and the importance attached to references. Some large firms, as policy, decline to give references. Other firms prefer to dodge any likely responsibility and give superficial generalised comments which are virtually useless, or even worse, dangerous in that what they fail to say may be construed adversely.

Recruitment itself is a costly process, both in time spent and time wasted, if the job description and the subsequent advertisement produce applications which prove to be totally unsuitable. Thus the next stage, selection, is of major importance.

Selection

The term **selection** relates to the individual differences referred to in the preceding sections. For revision purposes these are listed again under broad heads of: Physical, Mental, Emotional. These give us specific factors to examine when we try to fit a man to a job: intelligence, personality, sociability, educational background, and so on. It is necessary to analyse on some standardised basis which of the many individual factors one can measure and evaluate. Careful job analysis is the only sound criterion on which to build reliable selection and training procedures, for it results in an itemised job specification and personnel specification. It follows that it is advisable to use a single analytical system to get valid correlation.

The Seven-Point Plan designed by Professor Alec Rodger and now used extensively is such an attempt. It is given below:

1. *Physique:* Some jobs call for specific physical capabilities or for people able to withstand certain strains—e.g. blast furnace stoker, long-distance articulated-lorry driver. General items are, health, hearing, eyesight, voice, appearance.

2. *Attainment:* Level of general education and specialised training and experience.

3. *Intelligence:* Intelligence quotient tests to associate with initiative or adaptability.

4. *Special Aptitudes:* for example, verbal or figure fluency, manual dexterity, mechanical aptitude, spatial concepts.

5. *Interests:* An attempt to assess the individual from his activities, for example, social, physically active, practically orientated, cultural activities. (From such activities, which may or may not be related to the job, one may deduce useful information on which to allow for the strain/stress of the interview.)

6. *Disposition:* Qualities of temperament, general character traits —steadiness, reliability, acceptability. It is important to restrict oneself here to a few distinct qualities, and not to allow many features to distort the image being formed during the assessment.

7. *Circumstances:* Physical environment, for instance does the job involve isolation (as with the paint sprayer), or absence from home? Is applicant seeking permanence in this job, or is he ambitious in terms of promotion? In selection procedures there must be standards. Tests must have been validated and correlation evaluated. In other words, tests should have a high correlation coefficient between test results and performance at work.

There are, broadly, four types of test which may be used in personnel selection:

Intelligence tests which are useful for a wide range of occupations, particularly in the selection of people for training programmes.

Special Aptitude Tests of the nature of the job itself, which may be numerical, clerical or spatial.

Manual Dexterity Tests are apparatus tests for mechanical skills, in addition to paper and pencil tests which are particularly important in post-school apprenticeship interviewing.

Temperament and Personality Tests exist in a very large variety, but the useful ones for personnel selection are limited to a fairly narrow range. In real terms, there are basically only two personality traits which can at present be measured by simple tests with sufficient accuracy and limited time. These are the broad temperamental ranges of *introversion* and *extraversion,* and the range from *stable* to *neurotic.* The two personality dimensions are largely independent of each other: they indicate a range only. A person will show tendencies to the left or right of the average in certain situations, such as a tendency towards extraversion in a certain situation. It is however, an indicator only of likely behaviour. For example, the introverted type tends to be self-sufficient, solitary, shy, imaginative, careful, sensitive and persistent. The extraverted type tends to be impulsive, talkative, dependent on close interaction with other people. The neurotic introverted type tends to become anxious and obsessional, the neurotic extrovert tends to become liable to excesses of enthusiasm, hysterical, aggressive and unstable when in an extreme situation. It must be stressed that these are traits or tendencies only, and the term should not be lightly applied and judgements made without validation.

Again, it must be stressed that tests are of value only in the hands of people who have been trained to administer and interpret them. Training in the use of tests is essential. The two main suppliers of tests in this country are the National Institute of Industrial Psychology (N.I.I.P.), 14 Wellbeck Street, London W.1, and the National Foundation for Educational Research (N.F.E.R.), The Mere, Upton Park, Slough, Bucks. Though tests are as objective as possible, results are still to be interpreted in probability terms, and thus tests are of value only as the final refinement of a selection system. The full weight of final selection in this country still falls on the interview. It is with the interview procedure that the greatest room for improved personnel practice lies.

The Interview

The *interview* is extensively used. It is used for (a) selecting employees; (b) transfer and promotion procedures; (c) termination meetings; (d) management development schemes; (e) personnel problems; (f) discipline; (g) fact-finding, as in market research; (h) selling/marketing; (i) dissemination of information.

Interviewing is a difficult process. It has been described as partly a science, partly an art. It is the medium for combining the subjective, or the impact of the individual personality at the interview, with the objective facts obtained from testing.

The interview, therefore, demands a systematic approach for it costs money, and research has shown that an unplanned interview

160

can have poor results and cause frustration to the applicant, thus injuring his ambition or desire to take the job, or work for the company. The interview requires therefore a system which enables the purpose to be achieved in an effective and efficient way.

Planned interviewing can give no guarantee of infallibility; it reduces the chance element in the selection process and the application of techniques can be improved with training or experience. There are two main approaches to the interview: the open or unstructured conversational type and the standardised interview with predetermined procedures and objectives.

The unstructured type does enable both interviewer and interviewee to relax, and sometimes there is value in this. However, for systematic selection, the use of a job description with recognised plan, such as the Seven Point plan, is of prime importance. It is suggested that the student undertake further reading on this subject and this is given at the end of the chapter.

Engagement

Once the selection process has been completed, the formal offer of appointment and the formal acceptance have to be documented. These stages require a letter from the employer setting out the conditions of the engagement—starting date, salary, rate of remuneration, hours, holidays, sick pay, notice of termination required on either side. A signature of the new employee is required and a contract of employment document is exchanged.

The fact that a person has been engaged is only the beginning of the employment function. It is essential to ensure that proper induction and suitable training takes place when the employee joins the firm.

Industrial Training

Once the new employee has been selected and recruited to fit the job description, one is faced with the question as to the degree of efficiency with which the job will be performed. When standards are set, it must be an objective to meet these standards as efficiently as possible. This can best be done in training the individual by means of a systematic training programme, based on the job requirement and skills analysis. A **skills analysis** is the identification of 'the psychophysiological characteristics' of a skilled performance; in simpler terms, the knowledge and movements necessary to perform a task to give (a) economy of effort, (b) rhythm, (c) speed and (d) automacity (flow).

161

F

Traditional training methods are heavily dependent on the trainee learning from sitting beside an experienced person ('sitting next to Nellie'), and by luck or by chance picking up the necessary techniques of performance. The onus falls largely on the trainee to equip himself to become as efficient as the person he/she learned from. The system is clearly suspect, for who and how was the trainer in this case trained? Further, it is now recognised that a skill is an educative process; that knowledge about the process, tools, and job, aids increased expertise. Until this decade, the background knowledge could be gained in many instances only by attending night school classes to get qualifications.

Under systematic training, as opposed to traditional training, the job is studied, analysed, and a correct training programme produced, to ensure the four basic requirements of skilled performance. The onus to train efficiently is now on the lap of the firm, and the whole philosophy of training has been revolutionised. Training is no longer considered an unprofitable cost, but an investment in human capital and in capital intensive industries particularly, one of the major ways in reducing primary cost. The manager must, therefore, be as responsible for training as he is for improvement in methods, materials, equipment, organisation and communications.

Induction

The training programme should start on the first day that the new employee reports to the organisation. The quality of reception a newcomer receives at the personnel office may influence his job attitudes for many years. A beginner should not be left to pick up distorted versions of practice from old hands, but given a well organised induction to the organisation. This is considered so important that the Training Boards (see page 175) now give grants for induction programmes for all classes of employee.

A typical induction programme should include the following features:

(a) The company, group, or other organisation—its structure of organisation, products or services, the type of industry to which it belongs.

(b) Personnel policies—location of personnel, welfare, medical services.

(c) Terms of employment, general safety rules, specific safety rules (in a chemical works this might be helmet points, for instance).

(d) Departmental organisation—promotion systems.

(e) Trade union(s) procedure and practices. Meeting shop steward if a 'closed shop' situation exists.

(f) Explanation of training programme to follow.

Before proceeding to look at the basis of a training programme, a note is appropriate at this point about the learning process itself, for this is the basis of all teaching and training. **Learning** may be defined as the process by which an activity originates, or is changed, through reacting to an encountered situation. Thus the type and quality of the experience is important in structuring a learning situation. The first requirement is to obtain interest and attention; trainees must be convinced of the need to learn the skill and progress of the trainee will depend on:

(a) An appreciation of the nature of the activity involved.
(b) The complexity of the skill.
(c) The quality of the performance the trainee has as a model.
(d) The trainee's natural endowment (aptitude).

The acquisition of a skill is characterised by a progressive change in performance; the final proficiency is not merely the performance at the beginning carried out more rapidly: it is a different performance. In addition to the time decrease, there should be also:

(a) A reduction in muscular effort.
(b) An elimination of surplus movements.
(c) An awareness of progress.
(d) Greater self-confidence.
(e) Greater precision.

The trainee should develop, as a result of this process, the ability to anticipate and plan ahead—performance becomes smoother and speed increases without any appearance of hurry. Learning a skill is not a mechanical repetition of actions, it is an educative process involving understanding. As a result the trainee is psychologically adjusted to the job, as well as functionally proficient.

If training is accepted as one of the objectives of the organisation then a *training-needs analysis* must be drawn up by the training specialist, line manager and supervisor. The analysis must be founded on sound principles.

The analysis of training needs demands the application of the following principles:

(a) Training is the responsibility of the line manager.
(b) The aim of training is to improve job performance by extending knowledge, developing skills, modifying attitudes and increas-

163

ing self-confidence so that the employee may work as close as possible to the optimum, in terms of efficiency and satisfaction.

(c) To achieve the above, a sound learning situation must be constructed.

Training needs should be identified at all levels within the organisation, through management development, supervisory training, training to acquire clerical skills, manual skills, etc. The methods used for training might include lectures, tutorial instruction, demonstrations, discussion groups, role playing, the use of case studies, etc., and should incorporate, where appropriate, the use of audio-visual aids.

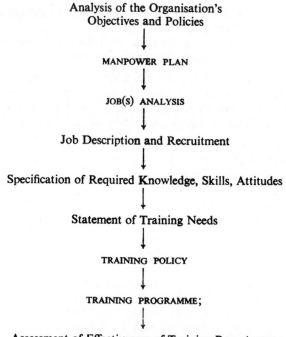

Analysis of the Organisation's
Objectives and Policies

↓

MANPOWER PLAN

↓

JOB(S) ANALYSIS

↓

Job Description and Recruitment

↓

Specification of Required Knowledge, Skills, Attitudes

↓

Statement of Training Needs

↓

TRAINING POLICY

↓

TRAINING PROGRAMME;

↓

Assessment of Effectiveness of Training Programmes

Figure 5.3

The chart, Figure 5.3, illustrates the inter-relationships which exist within the training function. Remember that these factors also operate against a background of complicated social factors, such as the economic climate, the policy of Industrial Training Boards,

164

facilities available within the educational system (at technical colleges and colleges of further education), employee morale within the organisation, and other influences.

5.3 REMUNERATION

An **incentive** is a strengthening or reinforcement of a drive which motivates the individual to both remove a need which is pressing, and to achieve his goal or objective. An awareness of incentives is both conscious and subconscious, i.e. one works for money to meet living costs and also because it is the recognised social pattern. A person in paid employment normally has some motivation to spend his day at work, and it is the offer of additional remuneration, or gaining promotion or specific needs, which adds value to his basic need for remuneration and security. A person may very well both like the type of work he is performing and be attracted by the remuneration to be earned by doing it. The elements vary in degree from one person to another, and vary also relative to any point in time and circumstance.

Wages in the form of money seems acceptable to most people in an advanced industrial society for its universal value. It can buy basic needs, it can buy power and social status. It is an incentive.

Elements in total wages

1. Basic Time Wages, according to skill
2. Additions for supervisory responsibilities and qualifications
3. Merit allowances; perhaps for timekeeping, long service
4. Special factor additions, as for danger, dirt, height, discomfort
5. Overtime and shift allowances
6. Cost of living additions
7. Incentive schemes

Wage Payment Systems

(1) *Piece rates:*

Workers are paid directly in proportion to output.

Bonus payments incentive schemes: the standard output for a day's work is determined. This and any excess above the standard is paid for at a higher rate than the ouput of the person who did not reach the standard. For example, Standard = 24 units, and the two rates are 12½p and 10p per unit. If 24 completed, then pay is $24 \times 12\frac{1}{2}p = £3$. If 20 completed then pay is $20 \times 10p = £2$ (less than the standard of 24). The real purpose of such a scheme is:

165

(a) to reward exceptional effort, (b) to persuade inefficient workers to transfer to other jobs. This basic system has undergone much modification and sophistication. Schemes known as the *Ganit Task Bonus Plan, Emerson Efficiency Method, Rowan System* have all developed from the 'scientific management' theories of F. W. Taylor.

Piece-work rates became very common in the 1940s and 1950s. Recently, the pendulum has swung back in favour of time rates. Security and stability of earnings, rather than fluctuations beyond their control, makes most workers prefer basic time rates, plus a small piece-work rate.

(2) *Time rates*

By **time rates** is meant, *flat rates*; *merit rating*; *measured day work*. Under time rates, the employer has the advantage of ease of calculation and administration of wages, but has increased responsibility for supervision. For the employee, there is greater security and ease of calculation of his earnings.

Rates per hour and hours per week are specified. Overtime is paid for at progressively higher rates. Various types of 'bonuses' (which are unrelated to output) and 'fringe' benefit may increase earnings.

Typical basic scheme:

	£
Time rate (40 hours at £0·25 per hour)	10·000
2 hours at time-and-a-quarter, 2 × £0·3125	0·625
2 hours at time-and-a-half, 2 × £0·375	0·750
4 hours at double time, 4 × £0·50	2·000
	13·375

Merit rating attempts to recognise and reward the personal abilities that an individual brings to his job, measured by the extent to which his output or the quality of his work exceeds the minimum that can reasonably be expected for his basic rate of pay.

(3) *Measured day rates*

Among the recent applications of incentives to time rates has been an extension of measured day-work rates, a system of payment which combines elements of job evaluation and merit rating. Under such a system, production standards for a job are fixed, based on: skill; working conditions; mental/intellectual demands. Each employee is paid on an hourly rate, based on his measured performance in a previous period (e.g. four weeks). Standard hours and actual hours for the period are compared, and standard and actual performance is expressed as a percentage, based on a formula. For example, a standard performance expectation of 140 standard hours, and an actual performance of 160 standard hours. The employees' efficiency is then calculated as

$$\frac{160}{140} \times \frac{100}{1} = 114\%.$$

The employee's hourly rate is then calculated on the 114 per cent efficiency he has achieved.

Systems based on these principles have found favour in the larger mass-production companies and with consultants. However, such a scheme necessitates accurate time standards, confidence of the workers and trade union co-operation.

Collective Bargaining

Collective bargaining is the method of determining wages and conditions of employment of over seventeen million work-people in Great Britain. It supplants the concept of individual wage bargaining between an individual employer and each individual worker in his employment. It is conducted by employers' organisations on the one side, and trade unions on the other.

The principles of collective bargaining are:

1. The principle of voluntary association.
2. The principle of mutual consent.

Advantages:

1. All workers of the classes or grades covered by agreements are secured basic wages and conditions of employment.
2. Employers are protected against competition by firms paying low wages.
3. Individual disputes are settled on the basis of the common agreement.

Consequences:

1. Agreements are not legally enforceable.
2. Employers and trade unions both want the system to work.
3. Some aspects of agreements become indirectly enforceable through individual contracts of employment which incorporate, expressly or by implication, the terms of collective bargains.

167

4. Under section 8 of the *Terms and Conditions of Employment Act, 1959,* a non-participating employer may be compelled to apply the terms of a collective agreement to his workers.
5. Public contracts generally require the contractor to apply established terms and conditions to his employees.

The Voluntary Principle is, or has been, affected by:

1. *The Wages Councils Act, 1959.*
2. *The Agricultural Wages Act, 1948.*
3. *The Terms and Conditions of Employment Act, 1959.*
4. *The Conditions of Employment and National Arbitration Order, 1940,* and its successor, the *Industrial Disputes Order, 1951* (both revoked, they imposed compulsory arbitration).
5. *The Prices and Incomes Act, 1965,* (which made collective agreements temporarily subject to 'national interest').

Modern Collective Agreements

The main sections of a modern collective wages and conditions of employment agreement are:

1. Wages (minimum hourly rates).
2. Hours of work.
3. Overtime payments.
4. Piecework percentages and procedure for the fixing of piecework prices.
5. Annual holidays.
6. Statutory holidays.
7. Shift allowances.
8. Guaranteed week.
9. Termination of employment.
10. Amendment or termination of agreements.

Productivity Agreements

In Great Britain, systems of wage payment have been characterised very broadly by three periods of development:

1. *Payment for time at work:* Piece and time rates are older than the Industrial Revolution in Britain.

2. *Payment for measured work:* As stated earlier, this was first achieved by F. W. Taylor and was developed alongside Time and Motion Study. In Britain, I.C.I. Limited became the model as it went over from day rates to incentive system. Both earnings and productivity increased over 2 years.

3. *Payments for Changes in Work Practice:* The third major phase in wage payments was exemplified by the introduction of the 'Blue Books' at the Esso Oil Company's Fawley refinery in 1960. This was an attempt to exchange wage increases for changes in working practices, which would have the effect of increasing productivity and reducing overmanning due to restrictive practices. This sort of agreement became popularly known as a *Productivity Agreement.*

Productivity Bargaining is not an alternative to incentive systems of payment. It is possible to have a productivity agreement, which includes an individual incentive scheme; however, most agreements are based on ordinary time rates. I.C.I. Limited for example, under M.U.P.S. (Manpower Utilisation and Productivity Scheme) are changing from individual incentive schemes as above, which involve complex variables, to a system of time rates.

Productivity bargaining and productivity agreements have, since the mid-1960s, achieved national significance as increased Government influence on wage negotiation has developed. On 16 December 1964 representatives of the T.U.C. (Trade Union Congress), C.B.I. (Confederation of British Industry) and the Government, signed the **Declaration of Intent,** the main features of which are:

1. To ensure that British industry is dynamic and that the prices are competitive.
2. To raise productivity and efficiency, so that real national output can increase, and to keep increases in wages, salaries and other forms of incomes in line with this increase.
3. To keep the general level of prices stable.
4. To keep under review the general movement of prices and money incomes of all kinds.
5. To examine particular cases in order to advise whether or not the behaviour of prices and wages, salaries, or other money incomes, is in the national interest, as defined by the Government after consultation with management and unions.

As a consequence of the agreement, the Government set up the National Board for Prices and Incomes. The Government quickly recognised the economic benefit which could be gained from productivity agreements, and productivity agreements have been explicitly accepted as legitimate forms of wage increases after review by the P.I.B.

The Prices and Incomes Board defines a **Productivity Agreement** as, 'one in which workers agree to make a change or a number of changes in working practices that will lead in itself—leaving out any

169

compensating pay increase—to more economical working; and in return the employer agrees to a higher level of pay or other benefits'.

The productivity criterion first laid down in the 1965 White Paper on Prices and Incomes, and repeated in the later White Paper of June 1967, and the one published in 1968, *Productivity, Prices and Incomes Policy in 1968 and 1969* allows pay increases above the norm:

'. . . where the employees concerned, for example by accepting more exacting work or a major change in working practices, make a direct contribution towards increasing productivity in the particular firm or industry.' Thus, a productivity agreement:

1. Excludes a mere *promise* of greater effort or efficiency in return for higher pay—the contribution must be 'direct'.
2. Excludes payment based on greater efficiency where this is caused by technological advance alone.

The essential feature, therefore, is that wage increases must be *simultaneously* paid for by increased efficiency of labour, which results in a reduction of unit labour costs. Only in this way, it is argued, can inflationary price increases arising out of wage rises be eliminated.

Fundamentals of a Productivity Bargain

Productivity agreements can be partial or comprehensive, depending on whether they relate to a limited field of work, or to a wide range of activity throughout the plant or industry.

Partial, for example, the introduction of payment by results scheme to a group of workers, involving changes in working practices.

Comprehensive, when a whole range of aspects of labour utilisation are revalued, as, for example, craftsmen's mates were to be eliminated, tea breaks to be cut down, overtime removed, and so on.

Partial productivity agreements have for several years been a feature of industrial relations, before the term productivity agreement was defined. Any agreement which led to the introduction of work study and, as a result changed the system of working and the method of wage payment, could legitimately be claimed to be a partial productivity agreement.

It is clear that, whilst the Government feels a need to exert direct influence over wages by requiring wage award vetting by the P.I.B., collective bargaining must take heed of the 'gateway' to increases offered by productivity agreements. New parameters have been set on the activities of employer and employee representatives.

WORK CHANGE;	REWARD CHANGE;
1. In working hours: the introduction of shift working; elimination of routine overtime	Increased rates Ex gratia payments
2. In quantity of work, e.g. elimination of tea breaks; elimination of group restrictive practices	Increased rates of pay with improved conditions
3. In methods of working, as a result of work study, job evaluation	Fringe benefits
4. In new manning agreements, redeployment of mates	Extra redundancy payments
5. In the technology of work; management of craft divisions—avoidance of demarcation disputes by using new techniques—increased training, greater flexibility	Improving work as such—increased variety; equipping the person to do a job in a satisfying way; increased leisure
6. In the actual organisation—movement towards technic/organismic control (less authoritarianism; more a partnership)	Closer consultation as a result of reduction in levels of command
7. In responsibility and objective setting—the man actually on the job to be responsible for advising management of what and how much his plant and equipment can do	Work becomes personal and interest-centered

5.4 INDUSTRIAL RELATIONS

Industrial relations may generally be said to be the ways in which working groups, both formal and informal, behave and interact. In real terms, it is the manner of securing co-operation between management and trade unions at the work place. This is often seen as a conflict between 'authority' and worker groups.

In any discussion about collective bargaining or wage negotiation, reference to 'the unions' is bound to occur. The behaviour of unions is more easily understood if one examines their historical development, and, as a consequence, their current problems.

The definition of a trade union in the *Trade Union Amendment Act, 1867*, is still accepted today.

'The term Trade Union means any such combination, whether temporary or permanent, for regulating the relations between workmen and master, or between workmen and workmen, or between masters and masters, or for imposing restrictive conditions on the conduct of any trade or business, as would, if this Act had not been passed, have been deemed to have been an unlawful combination

171

merely by reason of some one or more of its purposes being in restraint of trade.'

Thus, a trade union by law covers both employers and work-people's associations. A collective wages agreement cannot be argued in a court of law for purposes of direct enforcement, or for the recovery of damages for a breach of such an agreement.

The main objective of a trade union is to bring together workers' aspirations into an effective force, and any interpretation of trade union attitudes should recognise that these aspirations are different from the employers', whose aim is to buy labour as a necessary cost of production.

Unions, therefore, have the following prime objectives:

(a) To minimise threats to security of employment.

(b) To improve working conditions.

(c) To develop their negotiating strength, by increasing the number of members, providing leadership for the unorganised groups and achieving strong bargaining positions.

(d) To develop the belief in collectivism, that is to encourage workers to regard themselves collectively, rather than as individuals, and thus to accept rules of conduct and conditions agreed by the union.

(e) To exert an influence over social and economic factors which may, in turn, have effects on their members' working and private lives.

Type and Organisation of Trade Unions

British trade unions are a product of historial development and tradition. There is no real uniformity in their structure and they have just 'grown'. This lack of unification is thought by many to be one of the great weaknesses of the trade union movement in Great Britain. Four main types are identifiable:

1. **Craft-type Union:** Craftsmen of a skilled trade or trades belong to a union representing their skill, irrespective of industry or location. Good examples are: Electrical Trades Union, Amalgamated Society of Wood Workers. In addition to their concern with wages, they are very conscious of the status of their craft.

2. **The Industrial Union:** The concept here is that all workers in an industry, irrespective of their occupation, belong to a union representative. Two good examples are: National Union of Mineworkers, National Union of Railwaymen. (It must be noted that

even here, there are in existence some specialised unions—so the industrial union concept is not really true.)

3. **General Unions:** Here, the pattern is that all workers below the level of skilled workers, and classified as general workers, belong to a general labour union. This is best seen by two examples: General and Municipal Workers' Union, Transport and General Workers' Union.

4. **Non-manual Workers' Union:** Within this grouping fall all workers holding a clerical administrative, or executive job, the 'staff paid', and who would belong to their appropriate professional group. Examples are: Civil Service Clerical Association, Draughtsmen's and Technicians' Association; Association of Scientific, Technical and Managerial Staffs.

The common aspect of all the above types is the Branch. Every member is attached to a branch. The branches vary in structure. They may be based on: (a) a particular factory, (b) a particular trade; (c) a particular industry, (d) on a particular administrative or geographic region.

Trade Union Membership

The Employment and Productivity Gazette, November 1968, indicates that the total number of unions in Great Britain is 555. Total membership of unions in 1967 was 9,967,730. It should be noted that 233 unions had less than 500 members each, and that only nineteen unions had more than 100,000 members.

Many of the weaknesses of the trade union movement may be seen in the above figures; for example, management problems in dealing with a multiplicity of union groups, among whom there is often unhealthy competition.

The Royal Commission on Trades Union and Employers' Associations, 1968 (the Donovan Report) provides a very detailed analysis of the functions, strengths and weaknesses of the institutional factors affecting employment.

These are, however, institutional factors concerned with the formal influences on 'the man at work'. Much stronger influences on 'the man at work' have been recognised only in the last thirty years, and then hesitantly, because they are the product of social science research. These influences are summarised by Stuart S. Chase in his book *Men at Work,* when he states, 'A factory performs two major functions; the economic one of producing goods, and the social one of creating and distributing human satisfactions among the people under its roof. . . .' 'Some day,' writes Chase, 'factory managers are

173

going to realise that workers are not governed primarily by economic motives. . . . ' The informal group in the work place has a far-reaching influence on the worker and his output.

5.5 THE PERSONNEL DEPARTMENT

In general terms. personnel management is concerned with human relations at all levels within an organisation. A personnel department will not only see that the company's policy on personnel practices is implemented, it will ensure that the policy itself is founded on sound basic principles. Examples are:

1. **Needs:** that the needs of employees are recognised.
2. **Justice:** that the environment within which the company operates is one in which fairness and justice may be seen and be felt to exist.
3. That co-operation, rather than coercion be the keynote of employment policy. This to be translated into job enlargement policy as an attempt to assist employees to utilise their potentialities.

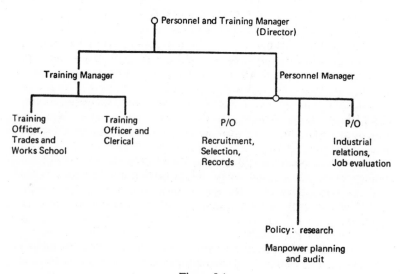

Figure 5.4

174

Personnel policies should cover the following:

1. Recruitment, selection and placement of manpower.
2. Wages and salaries.
3. Industrial relations, Joint Consultation, and Labour Policy.
4. Training, Education and Development.
5. Safety, Health and Welfare.
6. Personnel records and statistics.
7. Government legislation concerning personnel, e.g. *Contracts of Employment Act, Industrial Training Act, Factories Acts.*

The structure of personnel departments varies from industry to industry and from firm to firm. In large organisations it will serve a staff function, but will itself be organised on a line basis (see Fig. 5.4).

The development of 'job enlargement' as normal human relations practice and productivity research is likely to demand new skill, knowledge and understanding of the human element in all people in a leadership or management position at centres of work activity.

It is hoped that the student of today—the manager of the next decade—realises his own needs and satisfactions, and those of the people he will lead. Then, it is to be hoped, work will become a participative and co-operative process giving the individual satisfaction.

5.6 INDUSTRIAL TRAINING BOARDS

It is now acknowledged that, for the past twenty-five years or so, one of the main obstacles to faster economic growth has been a shortage of skilled manpower. In 1958 a report, *Training for Skill*, commonly known as the *Carr Report* was published. It urged industry to examine its apprenticeship requirements in terms of increased number of school leavers and asked employers to look again at training methods and facilities and to seek closer co-operation with those responsible for Further Education. This was stating again what had been urged in the Government White Paper of 1956 repeated again in a White Paper in 1961, as a result of which provision of Further Education facilities and courses developed rapidly. Industry failed to follow the lead, for yet another report (from the National Joint Advisory Council) in 1962 stated the solution to the shortage of skilled labour:

'. . . must remain, primarily, a matter of improving both the quality of apprentice training, in particular the greater use of systematic methods of instruction.'

175

A White Paper was published in 1962 setting out the Government proposals to remedy weaknesses in the manpower position.

In 1964 the *Industrial Training Act* was passed. It had three main aims:

1. To make sure that there is an adequate supply of skilled labour in every industry, and at every level of industry.

2. To improve the quality and efficiency of training being carried out.

3. To share the cost of training more equally between firms. Under the Industrial Training Act, the Minister of Labour (now Secretary of State for Employment and Productivity) is empowered to set up within each industry an Industrial Training Board. The members of each Industrial Training Board are appointed by the Minister on the basis of their experience within the particular industry.

Under the Act, a general advisory body called the *Central Training Council* was also set up to consider and advise on problems and occupations common to many or all Industrial Training Boards, in order to achieve some standardisation of approach. The Central Training Council publishes memoranda which deal with matters of interest to all training boards. There are also specialist committees on which independent members sit to consider more detailed aspects of training, as found in every industry.

Once it has been established, a training board has two main jobs: first to see that sufficient skilled labour is available in its industry, and secondly to publish recommendations on improving training. The main weapon of the boards in their attempt to persuade firms to undertake more and higher quality training, is the levy. A board collects from every company it covers, a levy which is expressed as a percentage of the total wage bill of the company. The levies charged by the boards vary from 2·5 per cent (Engineering Industry Training Board), to 0·025 per cent (Man-made Fibres Training Board). The levy is initially both 'carrot and stick' to encourage training. Since the establishment of the boards, companies paying levy have certainly become training conscious; whether the quality is as good as the quantity is still open to question.

The Industrial Training Act has, without doubt, meant much more importance is given to training, including induction, day release for associated further education, supervisory training courses and so on. Manpower returns to the boards from companies has also helped to make the human element in a company a valued resource in social terms.

FURTHER READING

Deverell, C. S., *Personnel Management*, Gee.
Brown, *The Social Psychology of Industry*, Pelican.
McGregor, *The Human Side of Enterprise*, McGraw Hill.
Fraser, J. Munro, *Industrial Psychology*, Pergamon.

QUESTIONS

1. Why is an analysis of individual differences important to managers in industry and commerce?
2. What is meant by the term **Productivity Bargain?** Suggest guidelines for making such an agreement and describe some work and reward changes that are likely to be negotiated in such an agreement.
3. 'The factory has two functions; one of producing goods and one of distributing human satisfactions.' Discuss.
4. How do Industrial Training Boards contribute to the efficiency of business enterprises in Britain?
5. Define the terms **Piece Rate** and **Time Rate**. Give three advantages of either and explain why the question of monetary rewards is so complex.

CHAPTER SIX

The Administrative Functions

6.1 THE OFFICE

The Nature of Office Work

In all offices, whether they are large or small, or whether they are in government, business or commerce, there is discernible a common pattern or cycle of activity. Information, usually in the form of writing or printing, is received. The piece of paper or form may have come through the post, from another office in the same organisation, or it may have originated in the office itself as the result of a telephone call. This information or 'data' is now invariably the subject of clerical activity. Broadly, this work consists of examining documents and deciding what to do with them, checking the data on the documents for completeness or credibility, sorting the documents, copying the data from one document to another, doing arithmetic on the data, summarising and analysing the data, and checking the results for accuracy. This 'paperwork', which may be performed with or without the assistance of machines, constitutes the processing of data.

Of course, office work is carried out with some end in view, data is processed to some purpose. A time sheet, listing the hours worked by men in a factory, having been received by a clerk in a wages office, is processed to produce a pay slip. An order for goods from a customer is processed with the objective, amongst others, of producing a form to send to the warehouse instructing the warehouse to deliver the goods required to the customer. A further result of the processing might be to produce statistics, about the amount of wages paid and the number of customers' orders received, for the information of management. Thus after the receipt and processing of data, results, usually in the form of words and numbers on paper, are produced. You are invited to analyse the work of an office into:

1. what is received by the office
2. what happens to it
3. what results are produced

This *data processing* activity has two further predominant characteristics. Firstly, the processing is usually centred around a record kept permanently by the office. In the above examples the wages office would keep records of every man who was being paid wages, on which would be shown, *inter alia*, his name, works number, his hourly rate, income tax code, and the amount of pay and tax to the year to date. The sales office would keep a record of the customer and his account, which would show cash charged for goods supplied, cash received and a debit or credit balance. Secondly, the processing is repetitive; wages are paid weekly and the same cycle of work is repeated, in the same fine detail each week. A customer's account is posted whenever he is debited with the value of goods sent to him, or credited with cash received from him, and each month a statement of account will be produced and posted to him. Similarly, the manager will expect his statistics in the right form on the right day. Because the processing is repetitive, it is possible to formulate a set of rules, in accordance with which the clerical work must be carried out. These rules are usually kept in people's heads and passed on by word of mouth, but sometimes they are embodied in an Office or Job Manual.

To summarise, the important points to remember about office work are:

1. The existence of a definite cycle of receiving, processing and producing results.
2. The existence of records which are the object of the processing activity.
3. The repetitive nature of the work in accordance with the rules or instructions.

If the above points have been seemingly over-emphasised it is with some purpose. So many descriptions of the office are mere agglomerations of all the different activities which can take place in it, supplemented with long catalogues of the various types of equipment and machines which are to be found in the office. A knowledge of these matters is not unimportant. But what is more important is to appreciate that activities take place and equipment and machines are used within a common or basic framework, the real nature of which is described above.

Office work embraces all the various means of communication, oral and written, by which business enterprise is carried on. The office offers its services to the business whenever and wherever they are required and in this sense an office may be said to exist wherever the activities of office work are performed.

The Growth of Office Work

A very important point to be made about office work is that more
people are engaged in it than ever before. This growth in the
number of clerical and clerical-type workers is one of the features
of any advanced economy and in this country clerical work has been
progressively absorbing more and more of the working population.
In 1921 clerks, typists and office machine operators represented
7·2 per cent of all workers; in 1961 the figure was 13·1 per cent.
Again between 1953 and 1963, though the total working population
of Britain increased by less than 1 per cent per annum, the office
labour force rose by approximately 3 per cent per annum. Some of
the reasons for this growth are:

1. The growth of government. Central government now operates
a whole range of security, pension and benefit schemes which
together constitute what is called the Welfare State. The clerical
labour force behind the administration of these services, and indeed
behind the whole apparatus of government, is enormous and still
growing.

2. Central government also uses industry and commerce to collect
certain of its taxes and social security payments. Furthermore,
government also expects industry and commerce to provide it with
data, from which a wide range of statistics can be produced for the
benefit of the nation as a whole. These activities presuppose clerical
effort in both government and business.

3. Within business itself, certain very significant developments
have taken place in the past few decades. Management is no longer
synonymous with ownership. Managements have to report on the
running of the business to the directors, who have legal obligations to
shareholders. Further, as business has, through merger and amalga-
mation, grown in size and complexity, management requires the
provision of information to enable it to control company operations
both at home and overseas. Both this external reporting and the
supply of information for the internal use of management need
strong clerically operated systems. At the same time, management
is increasingly using newer techniques, such as budgetary control
and standard costing, and more scientific methods of production and
stock control, which are often heavily dependent on clerks.

4. The growth of service industries such as banking, insurance
and building societies. Some appreciation of the scale of this problem
may be gained from the insurance industry, which had to process
9 million more insurance policies for motorists in 1970, than it did
in 1950.

5. Lastly, until recently, not nearly the same attention has been given to the effective use of resources of men, material and machines in the office, as has been the case on the factory floor. The next section is an account of one of the ways in which this deficiency is being put right.

The advent of the computer and its increasing application to a wide range of office tasks will undoubtedly have an impact on office work. But in this connection, two points should be noted. Firstly, the computer itself has created a new array of 'white collar' or office jobs. Secondly, a recent survey by the Department of Employment and Productivity estimates that despite the computer, the demand for clerical labour will continue to increase, though at a slower rate, until at least the mid-1970s.

6.2 ORGANISATION AND METHODS

Organisation and Methods, or O & M, is a term usually employed to describe the activities of groups of people in a private firm (or indeed in government or public bodies), who are asked to advise management on questions of office organisation and methods, so as to increase efficiency by providing a better service, or a cheaper one, or both. Another definition of O & M is, that it is a service giving advice on the structure of an organisation, its management and control, and its systems and methods.

It has always been part of the duty of a manager to concern himself with the organisation of his department and the methods employed in it. The justification for a specialist service concerned with these matters can be made under three heads:

(a) O & M people can take a wider view of a problem than can a line manager. They can look beyond departmental boundaries. They can build up a body of experience of office problems and possible solutions.

(b) O & M people are independent and with no prejudices in favour of existing arrangements, and are able to devote their full-time attention to the problems of organisation and procedures in a business. They have much more time than the ordinary manager for reflection and thought on the problems, not only of the day, but of the future.

(c) O & M people can be trained in, and employ, specialist techniques of, investigation. Also they may, as individuals, become experts in such matters as the design of forms or office machinery, where a line manager may be, understandably, without expertise.

181

Normally an O & M department or unit systematically considers every component part of the area of work under review, examining in detail its purpose and the way in which it operates, in order to discover how it can be made to function in the most efficient and most economical way (or to confirm in fact that it is already doing so). Design of new systems and routines, the re-layout of an office, or the purchase of new equipment may then result. Where organisation is reviewed such matters as the division of work the delegation of authority, the span of control and such issues as centralisation versus decentralisation may be examined.

There has been a significant growth in O & M activity in business and commerce in the past twenty years. Two of the more important reasons for this are:

(a) The growth of office work.

(b) The mechanisation of office work. Increasingly managements have sought to offset the steady increase in clerical labour costs by installing a wide variety of equipment and machinery (of which the electronic computer is the latest example) in their offices. The range of equipment offered by the manufacturers of business machinery is as enormous as their salesmanship is intense, and much skill and care is needed in selection and purchase.

The work of an O & M department is not easy. Among the difficulties to be faced are:

(a) Resistance to change. Most people are conservative by nature and there is no reason to expect them to change. It is often taken as an article of faith that the old way of doing things, which has stood the test of time, is the best. The known is preferred, naturally, to the unknown. O & M is often regarded as an unwarranted interference into the cosy familiar routine of the office. The natural extension of this attitude is to treat any new proposal by O & M as adverse criticism of the old method. It is in overcoming this resistance and in ensuring against introducing innovation for innovation's sake, that much of the work of the O & M department lies.

(b) Restricted terms of reference. Many companies set up O & M merely to follow the modern fashion. The department exists but its services are seldom called upon and its advice ignored. Unless O & M reports to a senior manager of the company, who is himself convinced of the useful role which O & M can play in modern business, the O & M unit cannot fulfil its function successfully. Ideally, a unit should report directly to the managing director, or chief executive. The drawback of making O & M responsible to the accountant or finance manager, which is frequently the arrangement made, is that it then becomes identified with the finance function and may thereby have to suffer the same condescending attitude which is often reserved for that function by other departments of a company.

(c) Shortage of high calibre staff. Good men are always in short supply and O & M is no exception. Turnover of staff in this field is well above average. Many people are moving over to systems work with computers. Continuity of work in the department suffers because of this and the fund of experience, which is vital to successful O & M, is not able to build up.

The O & M Function and Executive Power

O & M is an advisory function. It has no executive power, this lies with the line manager, whose responsibility it is either to accept or reject O & M proposals made for his department. It is often difficult to persuade a line manager, who has accepted revised systems, designed by O & M, that the ultimate responsibility for the successful working of those systems lies with him and not with O & M. O & M does not usurp managerial authority, rather it provides a service for that authority. Further, the fact that an O & M department exists within a company should not provide a manager in that company with an excuse for ceasing to think about problems of procedure and organisation within his department.

The Methodology of O & M

Typically, an O & M investigation, or *assignment* as it is usually called, falls into six broad stages:

* Select
* Record
* Examine
* Develop
* Install
* Maintain

* Select

The work of an O & M unit may conform to a programme previously agreed between the manager of the unit and the line managers of the company, or the O & M unit may be called in as a matter of urgency to deal with an unforeseen problem. An assignment may arise for one, or a combination of, the following reasons:

183

(a) To meet the new requirements of an expanding department.
(b) To simplify a procedure, so as to reduce costs and give greater efficiency in operation.
(c) To prevent errors or to reduce their incidence to a tolerable level.
(d) To provide a better system for safeguarding assets and information.
(e) To solve problems arising out of the timing of work and the meeting of deadlines.
(f) To investigate excessive overtime, high labour turnover, high absenteeism.
(g) To consider the introduction of new office equipment.
(h) To attend to a breakdown, for whatever reason, in the existing system.
(i) To design, from scratch, a completely new system.

Unless overruled by line management, the O & M manager should select for study an area of activity where the potential for improvement seems greatest. The O & M manager must then agree on terms of reference with the line manager. The terms of reference will be in writing and they will state:

(a) The reasons for the assignment. Why it is taking place? What benefits are sought?
(b) The scope of the assignment. What are the limitations in cost and time?

The terms of reference may need to be amended as the investigation proceeds and as new light is thrown upon the situation.

Throughout this initial period, when the first contacts are made between line management and O & M, great tact is needed by O & M personnel. A wrong word by the O & M manager or by those members of his staff whom he selects for the assignment and whom he now introduces to the line manager, can throw the whole project off course. O & M should discourage any tendency on the part of the manager to make a secret of the investigation. The staff of the line department should be told by their manager or heads of sections, what is to take place and why it is taking place.

* Record

There are two sides to this activity. The O & M man's task is to

(a) obtain all the relevant information about the existing system
(b) record, or document, this information.

There is no short cut, as all O & M men have to learn, to 'getting the facts'. It is seldom, if ever, possible to make proposals for a new or revised system unless it is known thoroughly how the existing system functions. In finding out about the existing operation the O & M man will normally examine:

(a) The forms used by an office, the papers, the documents received, the files kept, the paperwork produced.

(b) The organisation chart and job description schedule, if these documents exist.

(c) The Office Manual, again if it exists. The O & M man of course does not assume that his manual is correct.

(d) Any informal records or instructions which exist in the office.

Particularly when there is an absence of information concerning volumes, frequencies and timings, questionnaires may be devised by O & M for completion by the appropriate staff in the department.

The O & M man will obtain the bulk, and often the most important part, of his information by interviewing the staff of the department. Interviewing is an art that is difficult to teach. Every successful O & M man develops his own technique. A few of the more important points to be remembered are:

(a) Prepare well by finding out in advance as much as possible about the department, its procedures and people; be ready to answer awkward questions about redundancy and the purpose of O & M.

(b) During the interview be firm, patient, courteous; distinguish fact from opinion; do not outstay your welcome, especially if the office is busy.

(c) Take notes.

(d) Avoid being provoked by rudeness, sarcasm and the like; do not become involved in office gossip and politics.

Information obtained by the O & M man is of little use if kept in the brain or on odd pieces of paper; information so kept is lost irrevocably if the O & M man decides to join another company, or is inconveniently knocked down by a bus. So facts obtained should be recorded. Four methods of fact recording are:

(a) Procedure Narrative: This consists of a written account of the office activity. It is usually laid out as in Fig. 6.1. This method is useful for recording simple routines.

(b) Flow Chart: A flow chart is a systematic graphic representation of a procedure listing, in sequence, the operations carried out in that procedure. It is made up of symbols, lines and sometimes arrows

185

PROCEDURE NARRATIVE

DEPARTMENT: Purchase   PROCEDURE: Preparation of Goods Receiv-
                                        ed Note

PREPARED BY: John Jackson. DATE: 6 Oct. 1969. SHEET No. 1 of 3

Clerk (1)	picks up	folder containing delivery vouchers from in-tray
	sorts	vouchers into order number sequence
	stamps	vouchers with date received
	retains	vouchers until 11.15 a.m. (approx.)
	delivers	folder containing vouchers to typist's desk
Typist	types	details from vouchers on Goods Rec'd Note (G.R.N.) 1+3 copies. 12 vouchers to each G.R.N
	checks	typing
	clips	appropriate vouchers to each G.R.N
	inserts	vouchers into folder
	delivers	folder to clerk (1)'s in-tray
Clerk (1)	picks up	folder from in-tray
	checks	typing
	returns	typing for correction to typist's desk
	removes	carbon paper from G.R.N's
	delivers	copy 1 of G.R.N. to Stock Record Clerk's desk for posting
	delivers	copies 2 and 3 to office out-tray (for Accounts)
	files	copy 4 in 'Record of Goods Received' file

Figure 6.1   Procedure Narrative

which together show the relationships between activities. Its impact is visual rather than verbal and this is perhaps its chief advantage over the written account. A typical chart is shown in Fig. 6.2.

Note the use and meaning of the symbols. Other sets of symbols are in use. The ones in the flow chart opposite are known as the ASME symbols (American Society of Mechanical Engineers). This type of chart and developments of it, often extending into several columns—are known as 'multi-column' flow charts and are invari-ably used when a procedure of any complexity is being recorded.

(c) Specimens Chart: This consists of sample forms with 'live' information from the procedure under review, pasted to a backing sheet. The flow of information between the forms is shown and an explanatory narrative might be given.

(d) Flow Diagram: Neither (a), (b), or (c), above show what is the actual physical movement through space of a clerk or document. The Flow or Movement Diagram is a scale drawing of the office, and its furniture, on which such movement is plotted.

The examples shown above are sometimes known under different names and do not constitute by any means an exhaustive account of methods of fact recording.

186

FLOW PROCESS CHART

DEPARTMENT: Purchase	PREPARED BY: John Jackson
SUBJECT CHARTED: Preparation of Goods Received note	DATE: 7 Oct. 1969. SHEET 1 of 3

DETAILS OF PRESENT METHOD	Operation	Transfer	Inspection	Delay	Storage	NOTES
1. Vouchers taken from in-tray by Clerk 1	○	⇨	□	D	▽	
2. Sorted to order number	○	⇨	□	D	▽	
3. Date stamped	○	⇨	□	D	▽	
4. Held till 11.15 a.m.	○	⇨	□	D	▽	
5. To typist	○	⇨	□	D	▽	
6. Goods received note originated (G.R.N.)	○	⇨	□	D	▽	1 + 3 copies 12 lines
7. Checked by typist	○	⇨	□	D	▽	
8. Vouchers clipped to G.R.N.	○	⇨	□	D	▽	
9. Placed in folder	○	⇨	□	D	▽	
10. Returned to Clerk 1	○	⇨	□	D	▽	
11. G.R.N. typing checked by Clerk	○	⇨	□	D	▽	
12. Returns typing for correction to typist	○	⇨	□	D	▽	
13. Removes carbon paper from G.R.N.s	○	⇨	□	D	▽	
14. Top copy of G.R.N. to Stock Record Clerk	○	⇨	□	D	▽	
15. Copies 2 and 3 to out-tray (for Accounts)	○	⇨	□	D	▽	
16. Copy 4 filed	○	⇨	□	D	▽	
17.	○	⇨	□	D	▽	
18.	○	⇨	□	D	▽	
19.	○	⇨	□	D	▽	
20.	○	⇨	□	D	▽	
TOTAL						

Figure 6.2 Flow Process Chart

In preparing charts and diagrams, remember that they are a means to an end and not an end in themselves. They must be accurate and comprehensible but they need not be works of art. It should be noted that the very process of chart and diagram compilation often reveals gaps in the logic of procedures. They are a tool of analysis as well as a means of recording information.

* *Examine*

With fact finding completed, it is now possible to examine critically the existing procedures. Any inclination to jump to quick conclusions or solutions should be resisted. Analysis must be rigorous and methodical and the investigator should try to rid himself of any

Preparation of Works Production Programmes—Chart 1

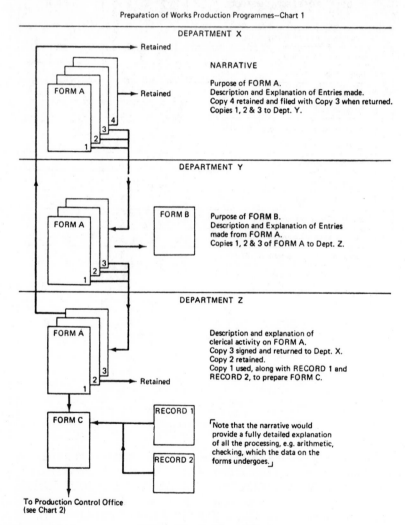

DEPARTMENT X

Retained

NARRATIVE

Purpose of FORM A.
Description and Explanation of Entries made.
Copy 4 retained and filed with Copy 3 when returned.
Copies 1, 2 & 3 to Dept. Y.

FORM A — Retained

DEPARTMENT Y

FORM B

Purpose of FORM B.
Description and Explanation of Entries made from FORM A.
Copies 1, 2 & 3 of FORM A to Dept. Z.

DEPARTMENT Z

Description and explanation of clerical activity on FORM A.
Copy 3 signed and returned to Dept. X.
Copy 2 retained.
Copy 1 used, along with RECORD 1 and RECORD 2, to prepare FORM C.

Retained

FORM C   RECORD 1

⌐Note that the narrative would provide a fully detailed explanation of all the processing, e.g. arithmetic, checking, which the data on the forms undergoes.⌐

RECORD 2

To Production Control Office
(see Chart 2)

Figure 6.3   Specimens Chart

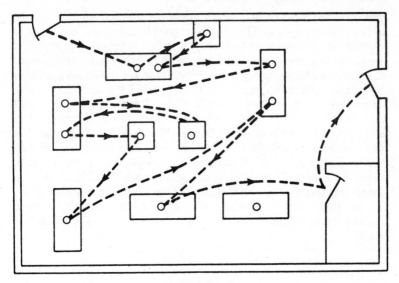

Before Study

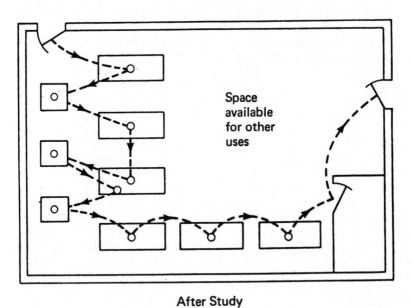

After Study

Figure 6.4   Flow Diagram

preconceived ideas or bias which might predispose him in favour of a particular proposal. The charts prepared may reveal instances of duplicated operations and checks, superfluous movements of either people or documents, unnecessary copies of documents, unnecessary filing of documents, unnecessary delays. The key questions are *Why:* Why is this operation or activity taking place? *What:* What is being done, What purpose does it serve? *When:* When does it take place? Are there bottlenecks in timing? Could operations be carried out in a more productive sequence? *Where:* Where is it taking place? Is this the best place? *How:* How are the tasks being performed? What equipment and machinery is employed? Is there a better method? Lastly, *Who:* Who is doing the work? Would it be done more effectively at another desk? In another department? *Why,* *What, When, Where, How* and *Who* are the investigator's six basic questions and he has to ask them continually and persistently at this stage.

* Develop

As a fourth step and as the result of his analysis, the O & M officer designs a new and improved method of work. The proposed new system may not be ideal or perfect, but it will be the best possible he can devise for the particular circumstances and environment of that office. He will have sought above all to *simplify* work, to produce a quicker and cleaner throughput of work. Whenever possible he will seek to *reduce* the number of operations. He will *eliminate* all superfluous activity. He may *rearrange* the steps in a procedure as a means of improving it. He will *combine* activities where it is appropriate to do so.

There is an element of creativity in this work and successful O & M men develop a flair or an instinct for sound design.

The new method will be shown in flow chart form and discussed with those whose task it will be to operate it. Useful suggestions from the department under investigation may often be made at this stage. They should be fully acknowledged. The proposed new system will invariably be embodied in a formal fully documented report. This report is for the acceptance or rejection of management (though the experienced O & M man should know in advance that his proposals will be accepted). The report will be careful to point out potential snags in the new system. Nothing should be concealed and reasons should be given why alternative methods (which the report should describe) have been rejected. Overall, the proposed new system should be self-justifying. It should be noted that this report may also provide a basis for instruction in the operation of the new system and may become part of the Office (or Job) Manual.

* Install

After acceptance, installation. Here careful planning is essential. A check list for changeover from old to new method should cover at least the following points:

(a) Timing. When to change over (better in a slack period or at the beginning of a new financial period).

(b) Equipment. Disposal of old, purchase of new. Delivery dates.

(c) Stationery: Disposal of old stocks, acquisition of new, stock levels.

(d) Personnel: Careful explanation of new system and specialist training if required.

(e) Method of change-over. Pilot running (trying the new system on old information), or parallel running (operating the old and new systems together for a period of time) are often desirable, but are expensive.

(f) Communications: Inform, at appropriate level, other offices and departments who will be affected, however indirectly, by the changed method. Inform customers and suppliers affected.

Gantt charts and Critical Path Analysis are two useful aids in helping control the change-over operation.

In the first few days of operation, there will be teething troubles and the O & M man will need to be fully available to help and advise. Some slight modifications in the system may be necessary. When the supervision of the department operating the system is satisfied that all is going well, the O & M man is, theoretically at least, free to undertake a new assignment.

* Maintain

A formal visit will be paid to the department within three months to review the new system in operation. If an O & M man constantly has to return to 'rescue' the department there is a danger that he will become a part-time member of its staff. In particular, he should be alert for slight deviations, without justification, from the agreed method. Flexibility is needed here. A drift back to the old method of work should be firmly resisted, but change and adaptation within the framework and in the spirit of the new system is acceptable. The happiest situation here, is when the O & M investigator has so

191

impressed the department with his experience and the quality of his work that the department will want to ask for his advice when it is thought that change in any procedure is required. When this happens, there has been another convert to the discipline of Organisation and Methods.

Note

The methodology of O & M, as described above, has its origin in Work Study, the argument being that 'work' in an office is as much 'work' as that carried out on the shop floor. Another approach to the technique of O & M is that suggested by the *Institute of Office Management*. Here an assignment has nine stages:

1. Ascertain the scope of the investigation — Select
2. Ascertain the purpose of the procedure ⎫
3. Study the existing procedure ⎬ Record
4. Review the situation ⎭
5. Examine the sources of information — Examine
6. Design the new procedure ⎫
7. Obtain agreement with management ⎬ Develop
8. Prepare a procedure statement ⎭
9. Arrange the installation — Install, maintain

You will note that the ground covered is pretty much the same in both the six-step and the nine-step methods.

Forms Design

Much of the work of O & M is concerned with the examination of the forms used in an existing system and the design of new forms, or the adaptation of existing forms for a revised system. The purpose of a form is to record information, so that it can be used with the maximum accuracy and economy. The design of a form, therefore, is important. Poorly designed forms, redundant forms, incorrectly entered forms cause unnecessary work and become a hindrance to the smooth operation of a system.

In O & M work the design of a new form comes after the design of a new system. Only when the new procedure is agreed upon, can one go on to design the forms to be used in that procedure. The intention in design of course will be wherever possible:

(i) To eliminate a form altogether.
(ii) To combine for entry on to one form, information which had previously been entered on two.

(iii) To reduce to a minimum the amount of information which needs to be entered.

(iv) To reduce the number of copies of a form.

(v) To rearrange the sequence in which information is entered in order to make entry easier and thereby reduce inaccuracies.

The following are among the main points to be remembered when designing forms:

1. *Layout:* Make the spacing suit the mode of entry, e.g. manuscript or typewriter; arrange the layout to facilitate speed and accuracy of entry, usually from left to right and from top to bottom; group like items together; avoid underlinings and wasted space; make the captions and instructions (which should be kept to a minimum) clear and concise; encourage brief answers or entries, making use of ticked alternatives where possible; if the form is ultimately to be filed in a binder it will need a left-hand margin of at least an inch; do not arrange for key information on the form to be entered near the margin.

2. *Paper:* Choose paper which matches use and handling of the form and which is suited to the method of entry; choose size of paper which conforms to the company's standards or, if the change-over has not been made already, consider whether the new International Standards Organisation paper sizes ought to be introduced. Is it convenient to make the forms up into pads for more economical use? Would the use of different coloured copies of a form be of use in the new procedure?

3. *Printing:* By what method of printing is the new form to be produced? Whatever method is used, avoid the use on the form of different type faces and different colours of printing ink. Prepare a good proof, whether the form is to be printed by an outside printer, or the company's own printing department. In what quantities will the form be ordered? In what quantities will it be stocked?

6.3 ELECTRONIC DATA PROCESSING

The Computer Explained by Analogy with a Clerk

The broad receiving–processing–results cycle which, as we have seen in section 6.1, characterises office work can be observed in miniature taking place at a clerk's desk. We will suppose that a clerk is responsible for keeping up to date the records of goods stored in a warehouse. For the purposes of the analogy we will suppose further, that the clerk has no memory of his own and has constantly to read a book of rules kept on his desk which tell him in complete detail what he has to do. Also on the desk is an in-tray, where forms containing information about deliveries to, and despatches from, the warehouse are placed; an out-tray where the clerk will place certain of the results of his work (such as a note for the purchasing department indicating that the stock of a certain product has reached the re-order level), a desk calculator to help him with his arithmetic and a scrap pad where any 'workings' can be carried out. Finally, next to the desk is a filing cabinet, in which there is kept a record for each of the products stored in the warehouse.

The clerk will carry out in sequence each of the instructions in the book of rules, picking up one form at a time from the in-tray, finding the record in the filing cabinet to which it relates and posting the record accordingly. Where appropriate a note for the re-order of certain goods will be written out and put in the out-tray. He will continue this activity until there are no forms left in the in-tray. Those records which have had entries made on them can be described as having been 'up-dated'. A diagram of the arrangements and activity on the desk is shown in Figure 6.5. The continuous lines show the flow of data during the up-dating activity, the broken lines indicate the control which the clerk exercises over the whole

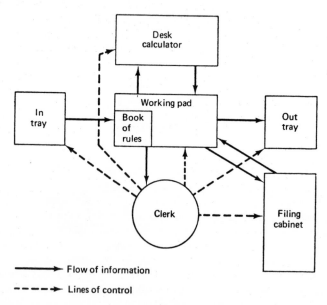

Figure 6.5

operation as he reads the rules. The passage of the rules or instructions to the clerk's brain is shown by a continuous line.

If it is to do similar work to that of a clerk, that is, to act as a data processor, a machine must have similar facilities and we can identify in the machine known as an **electric computer** the counterparts to the in-tray, the out-tray, the filing cabinet, the working pad (where both the book of rules and space to do the workings are kept), the desk calculator and the clerk himself. In Figure 6.6 are shown the computer equivalents to the clerk at his desk, the six main logical elements of an electronic computer. The lines of data flow and

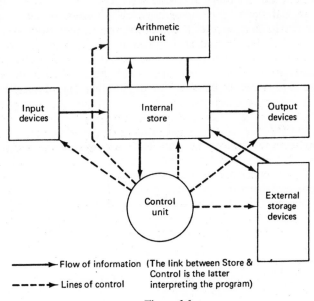

Figure 6.6

control are the same in both diagrams. The input and output devices and the external storage devices are called **peripheral equipment.** The arithmetic unit, the control unit and the internal store are collectively known as the **central processing unit** or **central processor.** The set of instructions which are placed in the store of the central processing unit (C.P.U.), whenever it is required to do a specific task on the computer are called the **program.** (This spelling of the word is now formally approved by the British Standards Institute.)

The processing of data, as has been stated more than once in this chapter, is not dependent upon the use of machines, it is at least as

195

old as business itself. What the computer does is to process data using electronic and electro-mechanical means and this activity is correctly known as **Electronic Data Processing** or **E.D.P.** By popular usage, however, the 'electronic' is dropped and the term 'data processing' is now widely understood to mean processing data by computer.

The Hardware

Hardware is the name given to the mechanical, magnetic, electrical and electronic devices from which a computer is made. The six main logical units of equipment which we have identified above constitute the hardware of a computer, or of a **computer system,** a term which indicates that a computer is not a single device but a collection of devices which work together. A detailed description of the hardware is outside the scope of this book; the outline which follows is of necessity brief, explanatory rather than descriptive.

Input Devices

The main input devices are punched card readers and paper-tape readers. A point which you will never see mentioned in an advertisement for a computer is that, generally speaking, the principal methods of getting data into a computer are tedious in the extreme. What happens is that data (words in English and numbers in decimals) are written on to forms or *source documents* as part of typical office activity (maybe, numbers of hours worked, details of customers orders received, or of purchase orders placed). These forms are now sent to the computer department where girls, sitting at key punch machines, convert the English and decimal data into holes in punched cards or paper tape. Typically another girl now performs the operation a second time to **verify** that the first girl punched the data correctly. Errors detected are put right. The tapes or cards (a computer installation may use either or both and each has advantages over the other) are then read by the appropriate device which translates the data into the computer's code and sends it in the form of pulses of electrical current to the C.P.U. The main bulk of data entering computer systems is at present prepared in this fashion. No one, however, pretends that is it a satisfactory method and other ways of picking up or 'capturing' data, which obviate the need for human punching and verification, are in use or under development. Just one of them, *viz.* **document reading,** will be mentioned. Here the characters or, in some applications, the marks

196

made on the original document, can themselves be machine read magnetically (as in the case of Magnetic Ink Character Recognition) or optically (as in Optical Character Recognition). The data is converted by these machines into punched cards or paper tape for subsequent input to the C.P.U., or sent directly to the C.P.U., cutting out punched card or paper tape media altogether.

Output Devices

Output from a computer can be in the form of holes punched in cards by a card punch, or holes punched in paper tape by a paper tape punch. But the overwhelming volume of output from computers takes the form of printing characters in English, or decimal, on paper. This should not be surprising. The whole purpose of a computer is to produce results which can be of use to human beings and we should expect it to produce these results in a form and a language with which the human being is familiar. The output device which produces results in this form is known simply as a **printer** and typically it can print at speeds of between 600 and 1,200 lines per minute, with up to 160 characters on each line. Printing is on continuous stationery, which has to be 'burst' or cut up into its separate forms and have any carbon paper removed after printing. The stationery can be blank or pre-printed (with boxes and headings already set out on the stationery), as would be the case with an invoice or a pay slip. The appearance of the stationery and the format the output takes, is of great importance as a vital factor in convincing people that the computer can do its work effectively and all the principles of good forms design apply. Many managers are understandably only interested in what the computer prints out. They want accurate output but they also want it in a form which is easy to handle and use.

Under the headings of input and output, the **console typewriter** should be mentioned. This permits two-way communication between the human operator and the C.P.U. The main form of output on the typewriter is a printed record or log of what jobs the computer is currently engaged on.

External Storage Devices

These are devices which can write data on to, or read data from, magnetic tapes, magnetic discs (both exchangeable and fixed), magnetic drums and magnetic cards, though it should be noted that only a few installations actually use this last media. Two points of clarification need to be made at the outset:

197

1. Tapes and discs are sometimes classified as input and output media under the same headings as paper, tape punched cards and the printer, and this is a valid classification insofar as tapes and discs receive data from and send data to the C.P.U. But note the distinction between these magnetic media and paper tape and punched cards. Practically all the data on the magnetic tapes and discs were put there initially from paper tape and cards which are the prime means of input, just as printing on paper (not a reel of magnetic tape, which is useless on a manager's desk) is the prime form of output. It is thought, therefore, that for the purpose of understanding how a computer operates, magnetic tapes and discs are best considered as being methods of storing data within a computer system, external to the store in the C.P.U.

2. These devices are sometimes lumped with the internal store and called **memory.** This is a confusing use of this word. The student is advised to avoid it altogether and to refer to the store in the C.P.U. as the **internal** or **fast access store** and these other magnetic media as 'backing', 'bulk', or 'external' store. All these terms are in use. It is one of the disadvantages of a new technology such as computers, that it is some time before the new words or jargon employed in it become standardised.

Magnetic tapes are typically 2,400 feet long and not more than an inch in width. One half inch of the tape can hold upwards of 500 characters, coded in the form of magnetised spots across the width of the tape. On the tapes are held records or files of information and programs. For reading data from and writing data to magnetic tape it is fitted into a device known as a tape deck or tape unit. Records held on tape are usually held in a serial fashion (one after another) and processing is sequential (the records are processed or updated in the order in which they are held on the tape). In the ordinary office, records are usually organised and posted in this way.

Magnetic discs are of two kinds. First, the *exchangeable* disc pack or store consists of six gramophone-record type devices connected by a central axle. Data can be recorded on the ten inner surfaces of the pack, being written or read by five moving arms, each with an upper and lower read/write head which contacts the recording tracks of the discs as they revolve around the axle. The storage capacity of the disc is about one-third that of a magnetic tape. Data on the disc can be held serially and processed sequentially in exactly the same way as on magnetic tape. But it is also possible to hold the data randomly (in a non-serial fashion). This facility is a very important one and makes it possible to do certain jobs on a computer which cannot be done with magnetic tape. Tape and discs are not mutually exclusive and are frequently used together in the same computer system. Exchangeable discs hold records and programs and like magnetic tapes are put on and taken off the appropriate device, as and when required.

Fixed discs operate in the same manner as exchangeable discs, but they have a much greater storage capacity and more important, they are, as their name implies, permanently attached to the C.P.U. Whenever peripheral devices are connected to the C.P.U. they are said to be **on-line,** conversely, devices not so attached are called **off-line.** Fixed discs are permanently on-line.

The magnetic drum is a metal cylinder around which data can be held magnetically in circular bands. They have a small storage capacity when compared with tapes and discs but data can be read from, and written on to, a drum at faster speeds than is the case with these devices. They are seldom used for holding programs and records; they are invariably on-line as an extension to the internal store in the C.P.U.

The Central Processing Unit

The C.P.U. is the heart of the computer system. It consists of three principal parts:

1. *The internal store:* This can best be visualised as consisting of a large number of pigeon holes or cells, each of which is identifiable by its own unique number or address. The capacity of each address is limited to a given number of digits. Into these addresses or locations, data from peripheral equipment are entered for processing, and they also hold the program, which again will have been read into the store from one of the peripheral devices. Both data and program will be in the basic machine code of the computer, the code which the computer is built to understand. This code is based on the **binary notation,** which is a system of numbering which employs two digits, 0 (zero) and 1 (one). The decimal system uses ten digits, zero to 9. The binary notation has been developed to permit, as well as numbers, all the alphabetic characters and a variety of signs such as $+$, $/$, £, $=$, and so on to be coded. And this notation is especially suited to the computer in which, for example, on magnetic tape and discs, '1' can be represented by a magnetised spot and '0' by an absence of magnetism; and in the store itself where the ferrite cores, of which most stores consist, can be magnetised with one polarity to represent '1' and with the opposite polarity to represent '0'.

2. *The arithmetic unit:* This part of the machine is where arithmetical calculations are carried out and where logical decisions, based on the units ability to distinguish between positive and negative numbers, can be made. This attribute, which enables the computer to 'know' when, for example, it has finished processing a series of records is a most important one. (See the next section.)

3. *The control unit:* The control unit interprets each instruction in the program in sequence and, acting on the instruction, causes the rest of the computer to operate accordingly.

The Advantages of the Computer

The computer may be said to possess the following advantages over previous forms of mechanised equipment for processing data:

(a) *Speed*   The speed of operating is several orders of magnitude greater than that of previous equipment. Many thousands of calculations can be performed in a second. In the most recently manufactured computers, speeds of operating are measured in **nanoseconds** – a nanosecond being one one-thousandth part of one millionth of a second. (There are more nanoseconds in two and a half seconds than there are seconds in the lifetime of the average man.)

(b) *Accuracy and reliability*   Month in, month out, the computer maintains standards of accuracy and reliability which, again, cannot be matched by previous equipment. A computer usually undergoes one or two hours' preventative maintenance daily and there are no moving parts in the C.P.U. If wrong results are produced it will be because:

(i) The wrong input has been given to the computer. Despite the double punching verification check and many other methods of screening input data, this does happen. If we put rubbish in, however perfect the actual processing, we must expect rubbish out.

(ii) The program is incorrect. If the instructions are erroneous the computer will either be unable to complete its work or will produce inaccurate results. Both the programs and the data given to a computer have been prepared by human beings, a point you should remember next time you read a newspaper report about a computer produced bill for £0.00.

(iii) There is a machine failure of some kind which corrupts either data or program and results in inaccurate output.

(c) *Versatility*   We can do any job on a computer for which it is possible to write a program. It is a multi-purpose machine which can be processing payroll one minute, and sales invoicing, literally, in the next minute. The computer can be applied to the whole range of a company's data processing tasks. It is another matter of course as to whether it is worth while to do so.

(d) *Automatic control* A computer can operate for long periods without human intervention. A computer operates under the control of a program and it is possible to write into the program instructions which permit the computer to discriminate between alternative courses of action. Thus a file of many thousands of records, requiring a wide variety of different kinds of processing can be dealt with within the one program without any need to make reference to the human operators of the computer.

(e) *Capacity* It is possible to carry within the external store of the computer large volumes of information in a relatively small amount of space, which can be made available for processing very quickly. Again, once a piece of data has been recorded accurately into the external store of a computer, it can be copied and recopied many thousands of times with little fear of corruption or errors of transcription. Only in highly exceptional circumstances do computer records get lost or out of sequence.

The Disadvantages

(a) *Equipment and staffing costs* Although more processing power per £ spent on hardware is available today than was the case in the 1950s, the cost of equipment is still relatively high and the investment still a large one. At least as big an expenditure will need to be made on the staff required to get the computer into productive use and to keep it there. An integrated system of data processing, even if the brain power is available to conceive and plan it, may take hundreds of man-years to get into operation.

(b) *The centralisation of work* In normal office activity the load of mechanisation is spread over a variety of machines and machine breakdown is a comparatively easy matter to deal with. With a computer, on which may be centred all the data processing activity of the company, a major breakdown can sometimes border on catastrophe. Few firms can afford a second machine and standby arrangements are invariably made with a neighbouring company who have a similar type of computer. Again the fact that a wide range of work may be being carried out on the computer, often to tight time-tables, means that careful job scheduling has to be undertaken and job priorities established in case breakdown should occur. The disadvantage here is the classic one of putting all one's eggs in one basket.

201

(c) *Installation and changeover* Firstly, there are the tasks concerned with preparing a site for the computer, power supply, air conditioning and the physical installation of the equipment itself. Heavy costs can be incurred here, quite separately from the cost of the hardware proper. Secondly, there is the actual process of changeover from the old system to the new computer-based ones. Staff training will need to be undertaken. And there is the frequently forgotten but very real and burdensome problem of assembling the data on existing records into a form which permits it to be punched into paper tape or punched cards, thence to be read into the computer for the build-up of the master files. This activity is known as file conversion and often proves to be both expensive and time-consuming particularly when, as is frequently the case, so many mistakes are found to exist in the company's existing records. Over and above this, there are the very real problems of human relations which come with the installation of a computer. Many companies, particularly those with ageing and conservative managements, are simply incapable of accommodating themselves to the changes which come with the computer. If they do not understand the computer, management are unable to give the leadership and create the right atmosphere which company staff at all levels need when a computer is introduced.

The Feasibility Survey

The broad preliminary examination of a company's activities to see whether the purchase of a computer can be justified is known as a **feasibility survey or study.** In authorising the carrying out of such a survey, management may have some of the following objectives in view:

1. Quicker processing of data
2. A saving in the costs of processing data
3. A better service to management in the form of a more accurate and timely supply of information; or the provision of information which was not possible previously
4. The replacement of worn out machinery and equipment
5. Savings in clerical labour
6. A better service to customers
7. The construction of a completely new computer based management information system

It should be noticed that not all of these objectives are compatible; for example 1 or 3 or 6 or 7 above may conflict with 1.

To carry out the survey a small team of three or four will be established reporting to a director, if not the managing director. A skilled and experienced team leader will be required, who may be found from amongst the existing management; the rest of the feasibility team should preferably be drawn from within the company. Alternatively, a firm may decide against forming a small team within the company and commission reputable outside consultants to make the survey. If, as a result of the consultants' work, a decision to buy a computer is made, the consultants may well assist in the recruitment of staff for the new computer department. The last thing a firm should do in these early stages is to approach a computer manufacturer for advice. A firm which calls in a computer manufacturer at the beginning is highly likely to finish up, willy nilly, with that manufacturer's computer.

The survey will cover all those areas of company activity where there are potential computer applications. The whole range of management and financial accounting and payroll, production and stock control, purchasing, order processing, invoicing and billing are the obvious areas of investigation. More general considerations should be:

1. What new management techniques (such as operational research) could the company make use of with a computer?

2. What will be the data processing needs, the management information needs, not only next year but in five or ten years' time?

3. Where are the heavy costs (such as stock holding in the company)? Where are the system bottlenecks? How could a computer reduce the one and eliminate the other?

4. What would be the effect of a computer on the relationships between existing departments? A computer can make nonsense of traditional departmental boundaries. What would be the effect of a computer on company organisation as a whole?

At the end of the survey, which typically might take six months, a report listing the jobs which are both feasible and justifiable will be produced with a recommendation as to whether or not to proceed. If the board of directors accept the recommendations and decide to buy a computer, the computer manufacturers (there are perhaps six principal ones and only one of these is wholly British owned) are now invited to submit quotations or proposals for a computer system to perform the tasks specified in the feasibility report.

After the receipt of the quotations and discussions with the manufacturers, a choice of machine will then be made. Whichever com-

203

puter is chosen, the basic reliability of the hardware can nowadays be pretty well taken for granted. More important, however, will be the software support which a particular computer firm can supply along with the hardware.

Software is defined strictly as the specialised computer programs, usually supplied by the manufacturer, which carry out a number of standard functions, which are basic to the effective use of the computer. A looser use of the term includes, not only those programs supplied along with the computer, but also those programs actually written by the purchaser or user of the computer. In the limited definition of the term software takes five different forms:

(a) *Assembly and compiler programs:* A program exists in the internal store of the computer in a coded form which the computer itself can understand. This code is known as **machine code** or **machine language.** In the early days of computers, programmers wrote their instructions in binary notation, or in decimal notation which the computer itself converted to the binary equivalent. Programming in machine code has several drawbacks, to overcome which, **assembly languages** and **compiler languages,** also known as **high level languages** have been developed. Instructions can be written in the form of simple sentences in English such as MULTIPLY RATE BY HOURS WORKED GIVING GROSS PAY. A compiler program then generates a machine language program from these instructions. The most widely used compiler language is **COBOL** (Common Business Oriented Language).

(b) *Generators:* The sorting of data within a computer and the printing out of results are basic to most computer jobs. Generator programs enable the programmer to prepare sort and print programs quickly and efficiently. The principle is similar to that employed in assembly and compiler programs.

(c) *Utilities:* These are programs for carrying out certain housekeeping tasks of computer operation such as printing out the contents of the store for examination by the programmer and writing data from punched cards or paper tape to a magnetic media and vice versa.

(d) *Packages:* These are of two kinds. Applications packages are standard programs for carrying out certain jobs which many of the purchasers of computers may wish to undertake. A standard program for doing payroll is perhaps the most widely used example. Applications packages are not tailored to any particular customer's requirements but are capable of being used, perhaps after some modification, by many of the companies interested in this application.

Secondly there are sub-routines, which are standardised parts of programs, which the user can fit into his own larger program. A set of instructions for calculating PAYE is a good example of this.

(e) *Operating systems:* These are programs often given such names as *Supervisor*, or *Executive*, or *Master*, which reside permanently in the store when the computer is operating and control the greater part of that operation. Their main function is to give the computer charge of its own activities, cutting down to a minimum the need for intervention by the human operator.

It will be seen from the above that the quality of the software which the computer manufacturer offers along with the hardware, is of great importance when the choice has finally to be made between the computer systems of the different manufacturers.

Staffing the Computer Installation

With the computer selected, the next main task is to build up a complete computer team from the nucleus formed for the Feasibility Survey. Four main types of staff are required:

(a) *Systems analysts:* The systems analyst:

1. Studies and analyses an organisation's systems and procedures, examines the purpose of these systems and how they work.

2. Designs a new computer-based system and specifies this system in detail.

3. Implements the new system, which includes planning the changeover and seeing the newly-operating system through the inevitable early snags or troubles.

The basic qualities of the analyst should be similar to those required in an O & M man. He will need to be skilled in human relations; able to 'get on with' or communicate with people at all levels in the organisation. He should have an enquiring mind, energy to overcome resistance, and a persevering enthusiasm. He should know how a business works and be familiar with such basic procedures as purchasing, stock control, sales invoicing and so on. To these attributes he will need to add skill in the methodology of his work and it can be argued strongly that a training in the methodology of O & M is the best that can be given to the potential analyst. Though his knowledge need not be of a technical nature, he should have a full appreciation of the hardware of a computer and the constraints this will exercise on the design of new systems. Lastly, though he may not have written programs himself, he should understand what programming is about and have a wide knowledge of the techniques of processing by computer.

(b) *Programmers:* The programmer's tasks are:

1. To receive and read the systems specification from the systems analyst and consult with him on points which require amplification or are not understood.

2. To draw flowcharts of the program(s) required and to check that the completed flowcharts are logically correct.

3. To code (i.e. write program instructions) in the appropriate programming language.

4. To arrange for the program to be assembled or compiled into the machine language program and then to test the completed program, first with trial data and then with 'live' data.

5. To amend the program as indicated by the results of the program trials.

6. To hand the completed program to the systems analyst for operational running in the new computer system.

7. To ensure that the program is correctly documented. This means arranging all the paperwork which goes into program writing in such a manner that a programming colleague in the same computer installation may, by a reading of the documentation, quickly understand what the program is about.

8. To maintain the program in working order. The elimination of program faults in the early days of operation is known as 'debugging'.

(c) *Operators:* Operators are of two kinds. First, there are those who carry out the routine work of loading and unloading the peripheral equipment. They are in charge of the normal operation of the computer as a machine. Second, there are those sometimes called *control clerks*, who receive forms containing input for the computer from the user departments, arrange the forms into batches and see them through the data preparation section; and then assemble the jobs in the right order of priority before handing them over to their colleagues—the first kind of operator—for computer processing. They then receive back the printed results from the computer and despatch them to the appropriate user departments, dealing with any routine enquiries made by these departments.

(d) *Data preparation staff:* The work of these people, invariably females, is to punch the data from the input forms into paper tape or punched cards.

The Organisation of the Computer Department

A typical organisation chart for a computer installation is shown in Figure 6.7. The type of staffing arrangement in which analysts and programmers are grouped together into project teams, under a leader who may have a systems or programming background, is now perhaps more widespread than the arrangement whereby analysts and programmers are kept separate, reporting to a chief systems analyst and a chief programmer respectively. The actual numbers of staff within the department will need to match the size of the computer, the volume of work it is possible, ultimately, to give the computer and the speed at which it is desired to transfer work to the computer.

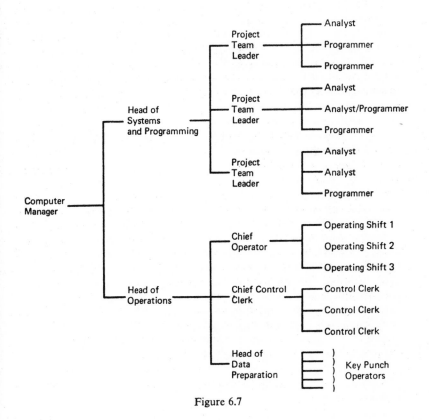

Figure 6.7

207

The Design of Systems for Computer Operation

The systems analyst will go about his work at first in very much the same manner as an O & M man would. He will often make use of the same kind of charting techniques as the O & M man. He has to understand fully the objectives of the existing systems of the organisation and the methods used within those systems. It is when he comes to design his new system, however, that the analyst calls upon his specialist expertise and parts company with the orthodox O & M man. We shall consider what is required in the design of a computer system by considering in outline what are the contents of a typical systems specification, the document in which the analyst describes in detail his proposed new system.

A systems specification may be written in a variety of different formats. The ground covered, however, irrespective of format, is the same and can be considered under seven main headings:

1. *Aims of the system:* Here the analyst, against suitable background material, summarises the main objectives he is trying to achieve in his proposed computer system. An attempt is made to justify the system to point out advantages, cost and otherwise and to mention any disadvantages.

2. *The system proposal:* Under this heading the system is described in broad outline. The main programs are listed. A diagram of the system in operation is shown.

3. *Output definitions:* All the various forms of output, printed or otherwise, from the computer are listed in careful detail. Sample forms with sample figures are given.

4. *Input definitions:* All the various forms of input to the computer are described. Sample forms with sample contents are shown.

5. *File definitions:* Here the contents and arrangement of the records required in the new systems are listed, together with the medium (such as magnetic tape or disc) on which they are to be held.

6. *Program description:* This lists in some detail the tasks to be performed by the programs, the processing of the various files which is required to produce the different outputs.

7. *Supporting material:* this consists of:

(a) Volumes (of input and output), frequencies, timings; deadlines to be met.

(b) Any new numbering schemes or reference numbers that will be required. Often an entirely new numbering system for people (customers, staff), products, etc., may need to be designed.

(c) Any changes in departmental arrangements or organisation that may be necessary.

(d) A plan of action, which will show the target date on which it is proposed to bring the new system into operation.

The above is the barest summary only of the contents of a systems specification. In practice, its chief characteristic is its comprehensiveness. No detail, if it is relevant, is too small to mention. All exceptions to the main system and the treatment of those exceptions are provided for. Nothing must be left to chance.

Implementing the New System

The problems here are a similar to those met by the O & M man at the INSTALL stage in O & M methodology. The biggest single task is file conversion, the job of transferring non-computer records to the computer and ensuring that once transferred they can be kept up to date. Even the most brilliantly organised file conversion is of no use if the analyst has failed in the task of communicating his new system to all concerned, particularly those members of staff whose job it will be to provide the computer with its input and use the results it produces. Getting people to understand, accept and use the new system is easily the most difficult of all the problems that a systems analyst has to face.

It should be noted that from feasibility survey, through computer installation, to the effective running of the first job on the computer can take from between two to five years.

Integrated Data Processing

Most of the early jobs on computers were straight one-for-one transfers of jobs previously done either manually or by office machines of one kind or another. Companies now, however, are trying to abandon this piecemeal approach. The current thinking is to consider the whole company as a network of inter-related administrative activities and to plan a 'total' computer system within the framework of which, these various activities will take place. Work, obviously, will still have to be transferred to the computer step by step, but all in accordance with a plan which will ensure that the completed and fully operational 'total' system is a rational and logical whole, not an agglomeration of several unrelated and unco-ordinated systems or activities. This finished whole would be an example of **integrated data processing.**

209

6.4 OPERATIONAL RESEARCH

Operational Research, usually abbreviated to **OR** may be defined as the application of scientific techniques to the problems of business operation, with the objective of increasing the amount of factual or quantitative data available to management when making decisions. The official definition, prepared by the Operational Research Society, is a follows:

'Operational research is the attack of modern science on complex problems arising in the direction and management of large systems of men, machines, material and money in industry, business, government and defence. The distinctive approach is to develop a scientific model of the system incorporating measurements of factors, such as chance and risk, with which to predict and compare the outcomes of alternative decisions, strategies or controls. The purpose is to help management determine its policies and actions scientifically.'

Implicit in these definitions is the idea that, with the use of OR techniques in business, the 'hunch' or intuitive element in the decisions taken by management will be reduced.

OR has its origins in the Second World War when scientists, using the techniques in which they were specialists, researched into existing and projected operations of war in order to provide their leaders with data on which to base decisions. The use of OR in wartime was generally considered to be successful and after the war it came to be recognised that there were areas of business operation which were amenable to the same kind of scientific investigation, so in the early post-war years OR teams were formed in some of the larger industrial concerns (notably, the National Coal Board, British Railways, British Petroleum). The growth of OR since has been slow and unspectacular, but probably most of the very large scale undertakings in the country and many medium-sized businesses now employ OR personnel.

Notwithstanding the above, a wider view of OR might regard it quite legitimately as a continuation, admittedly accelerated by the Second World War, of the work of F. W. Taylor in the field of *scientific management.*

OR and Electronic Data Processing

It will be obvious from the above that it is possible to undertake OR without using a computer. In other words OR could exist if the computer had never been invented. But there is a strong inter-relationship between them for two main reasons. Firstly, OR makes use of the computer as an extremely fast calculating machine able to handle large numbers of highly complex mathematical problems. Before the rapid development of the computer, certain OR techniques were not used to their full extent because of the considerable amount of time and human skill needed to apply them. Secondly, OR increasingly makes use of the large volumes of data concerning company operations which may be present in the computer as a function of its use as a commercial data processing machine.

The OR Approach to Problems

The work of OR is characterised firstly, by identifying all the significant factors in a problem. There is no attempt to limit the area to be studied. On the contrary, the intention is quite deliberately to broaden the problem to cover all those aspects of it, however remote, which are none the less considered to be significant and can be quantified, i.e. expressed in numerical terms. Next, the OR methodology is fundamentally mathemetical. It is not possible for the OR scientist to bring the production control system of his company into the laboratory for study, but he can construct a **mathematical model,** a representation in mathematical terms, of this system. By supplying the model with different data such as a higher production programme and by holding other variables in the model constant (e.g., number of operators or machine capacity), it is possible for him to experiment with or manipulate the model in which will be represented symbolically all the significant elements in the system. These manipulations will be concerned with evaluating different possible courses of action in order to determine which alternative would best accomplish a particular objective, such as minimising costs or maximising profits. Finally, much emphasis is placed in OR on the multi-disciplinary approach to problems. Because OR examines operations both extensively and in depth and from as many viewpoints as possible, there are often found in OR teams men from such different disciplines as mathematics, statistics, engineering, physics, economics and even accountancy. It is a matter of fact that the first OR workers were biologists.

The Problems Studied by OR

Descriptions of OR work are usually either *technique orientated* (a list of the various mathematical techniques which can be used, with an account of the problems on which they can be brought to bear) or *problem orientated*, in which is given a list of the types of problems

211

with some mention of the techniques usually employed in tackling them. In this section the latter method is adopted. In reading about the problems three points should be kept in mind. Firstly, by no means all the problems currently being studied by OR men are listed. Secondly, it should not be assumed that there is always a one-for-one matching between problem and technique. Some problems in OR can be examined using more than one of the typical OR techniques. Thirdly, OR is after all *research*. As industry grows in the size and complexity of its operations and as OR activity expands correspondingly, entirely new problems, as yet unidentified, will arise and come under OR scrutiny.

Broadly speaking there are two main types of problem. Firstly there are those problems of company operation or activity which have as their principal characteristic variability or unpredictability in behaviour or performance, viz.

(a) *Stock or inventory problems*

If finished stocks of a certain low level are held, what will be the cost of lost sales, given increasing levels of customer demand in the future? Or, at what stage in the production cycle should work-in-progress stocks be carried? It is cheaper to hold work-in-progress stocks early in the manufacturing process but the customer may suffer; the customer will receive better service if stocks are held at a later stage, but the costs incurred in doing this are heavier. Again, if work-in-progress stocks are kept generally too low, production breakdowns may result if, for example, scrap is heavy at one stage in the cycle and, as a consequence, machines at a later stage are idle. A high inventory means capital tied up which might be employed more profitably elsewhere in the company. The cost of inventory is thus balanced against potential losses arising from lost orders or machine down time. The OR man's approach to this problem is to build a mathematical model of the whole stock holding operation of the company and manipulate it until the overall cost to the company of carrying stock is at a minimum. (This is the more obvious form which a solution to this type of problem might take. It should be appreciated that a proposal to increase stock levels could result from this kind of exercise.) In constructing the model, the OR man may well make use of Probability Theory and Statistical Sampling.

(b) *Queueing problems*

This problem has three distinguishing features:

1. Customers (the term is used to describe products, vehicles, ships and so on, as well as people) arrive for a service.

2. There is a waiting period.
3. There is a service period during which the service is provided.

Any customer arriving whilst an earlier customer is being attended to, has to wait his turn in the queue. You will know from your own experience of waiting in a doctor's surgery, or at a shop counter, what the queueing problem is about. In industry, queueing problems are found in production control (the waiting time of parts or components at a machine), in stock control (where stock can be regarded as an idle facility awaiting customers), in deciding the level of manning of a wide variety of jobs, in deciding the amount of investment in machinery in the service area. Virtually all problems of capacity are queueing problems. Using the mathematics of Queueing Theory and Probability Theory the OR man, if he knows the average intervals between arrivals and how variable this interval is, can draw up equations indicating the average and extreme customer waiting times. In more complex problems where there might be a number of queues, a computer can simulate in minutes the formation and behaviour of queues which in practice in the real world might take weeks, months, or even years to form. By this kind of experimenting it is possible to obtain optimum solutions to what is the fundamental question in queueing problems—how costs of investment of man and machine in the service area may be minimised, how the maximum use of labour and plant may be obtained, whilst at the same time providing an adequate and timely service.

The second main kind of OR problem is identified by its preoccupation with the number and complexity of the factors which need to be considered in reaching a decision. For example, there are many thousands of ways in which a fleet of vans can supply goods from, say, five factories to fifty warehouses. Problems of this type are known as:

(c) *Allocation problems*

The allocation problem is that of assigning resources to a number of activities in the best or optimum or most effective manner. The problem has the following characteristics:

1. There are a number of jobs to be done.
2. There are resources available to do the job but sometimes the resources are limited.
3. Some jobs can be done in different ways by using differing combinations of resources and some of these ways are less costly or more profitable than other ways.

213

The task is to employ or allocate resources in the optimum way. In its simplest form the problem is known as the **Assignment Problem**. There is one job and one resource and the problem is to assign resource to job so that total costs are minimised or profits maximised; men are assigned to machines, drivers to vehicles and so on. A more complicated assignment problem is known as the **Transportation Problem**, where these are given a number of destinations (as in retail shops) and a different number of supply points (for instance, warehouses), the problem to be considered is which warehouses should deliver to which shops. A fuller treatment of this problem might take into account the optimum number of vehicles required, given certain criteria about vehicle capacity, frequency of delivery and so on, and the routes to be followed (**the Routing Problem**). Many problems of distribution in the field of marketing are of this nature.

Another variant of the problem is where resources are strictly limited and a choice has to be made as to which jobs to do. This is a problem familiar in process industries such as paint, chemicals and petroleum, where capacity is limited and the task is to decide what mix of products (it is called the **Product-Mix Problem**) best reduces costs or maximises profit. The reverse of this situation is of course that in which resources are unlimited and the decision needs to be made as to which of them can with least effect on profit be curtailed, e.g. closing down a factory, or a set of machines within a factory, or reducing the number of sales representatives.

Most allocation problems are solved by techniques called mathematical programming of which the most widely used is **linear programming**. This is basically a technique of iteration in which a succession of solutions are produced, each an improvement on (or at least equal to the previous), until the 'best' solution (that is, the one that most satisfies some originally agreed criteria) is arrived at.

6.5 MANAGEMENT SERVICES

A small but not insignificant insight into developments in business and commerce can often be obtained by a frequent reading of the appointments vacant columns of the better quality newspapers. Over the past few years, but probably not before 1960, there have appeared increasingly, advertisements in which a wide variety of companies, institutions and public authorities announce that they have 'consolidated their individual E.D.P., O & M, and OR services into a Management Services Department in order to co-ordinate the activities of the various specialists in these fields'. The advertisements then proceed to invite applications from, amongst others, 'systems analysts, programmers, O & M assistants, OR scientists and statisticians to join the newly-formed management services team'. There is little doubt that this grouping together under one manager of specialist personnel, who were previously in separate departments (sometimes, in competition with each other), is one of the most interesting developments on the adminstrative side of business during the 1960s.

Management Services may be defined then, as the name given to the management function concerned with improving the broad operation of a business and increasing its productivity by better organisation, administration and control. It involves the critical examination of the organisation, the management techniques and the systems and procedures of a business with the objective of recommending and implementing improvements. As well as E.D.P., O & M and OR men, a management services team might include work study engineers and management accountants.

The arguments for the establishment of a management services department are similar to those which can always be adduced in favour of centralisation. The activities of the different specialist groups can be co-ordinated and rationalised where previously they may have overlapped and come into conflict. Training is facilitated and within the unified department the different specialists can come to understand further each others techniques and problems. There is formed an environment which encourages the interchange of ideas between the separate disciplines.

A management services team should pay its way. Over a period of years it should be able to demonstrate that it is saving the company more money than it is costing. Those divisions or departments of the company which call upon the management services department should expect to be charged for the services they receive. But, contrariwise, they need not use those services if they are convinced that it will not be financially rewarding for them to do so. Where the benefits of improved organisation, systems and procedures and so on are not easily measured in cash, again the receiving or user department should satisfy itself that it is getting value for its money from the company's 'internal consultants', just as it would make fully sure that any outside consultants would need to justify fully the fees they charge. The details of the systems for charging for services supplied are not important. But it should be simple, and one which will not generate too much paper, too many records, so that it becomes an example of the type of business disease which it is one of the jobs of

215

management services personnel to cure. Unless over a period of time a management services department shows that it is not a drain on company resources, it will deservedly fall into disrepute. In all of this the role played by the senior managers is critical; they must actively support and encourage the management services team. Only they can create the sort of atmosphere in the company in which change will be welcomed. If they are lukewarm, or indifferent, or even worse hostile, the chances of a management services team operating successfully in a company are very much reduced. Indeed, wherever E.D.P., O & M and OR, either separately or as a group endeavour, are failing in their work, a big share of the responsibility must invariably be borne by higher management. As was suggested in section 6.2 for the individual O & M unit, the management services function should be located in the company organisation structure outside the traditional line management.

A Classification of Management Services

Brech, in his *The Principles and Practice of Management* suggests a four-fold classification of management services as follows:

(a) Diagnostic

These are activities concerned with examining and investigating the current situation within a company, finding out the facts of the existing arrangements with the intention of designing and implementing new and improved methods and formulating standards. The techniques of systems analysis, work study, O & M, and OR can all be applied in this area.

(b) Control

Following on the investigatory activities and complementary to them is the establishment of systems which give management greater control over the operations of the company. Management are given the means both to formulate valid plans or targets and to measure performance against these plans. In the light of the measurements made, decisions can be taken either to continue or amend company operations. Budgetary control and standard costing and other techniques of management accounting, increasingly associated with computer based schemes of integrated data processing, are amongst the principal means of affording management this control. In both diagnostic and control activities the emphasis is on the internal operations of the company in the short term.

(c) Intelligence

These are activities directed towards appraising economic and market conditions with the intention of providing information on which company policy can be formulated. Long-term forecasting, the interpretation of market research both home and export, the study of a wide variety of statistical data, the operations of competitors, capital forecasts are the main areas of work and operational research and economics are among the techniques and disciplines used. Much of the intelligence material made available to management might be the product of the firm's own data processing activities but use will be made also of the wide variety of statistical data published by government and by national and international organisations.

(d) Development

Here the activities, concerned chiefly with the future operations of the company with special reference to growth and expansion, include scientific research, the technical development of manufacturing processes, materials and equipment, product formulation, personnel development and training at all levels in the company.

You will note that in the third and fourth categories above, but especially development, Brech's use of the term management services goes far beyond the definition given at the beginning of this section. Brech also suggests that it is not necessarily an attribute of management services that they should all emanate from one department reporting to one manager. The term may therefore be used in two senses, one general, the other specific. Take care to define the sense in which you use the term when you discuss this subject.

The Company Secretary

Each registered company is required by law to appoint a company secretary, one of whose functions is to ensure that the company's activities are in accordance with the memorandum and articles of association (see page 13). When a company is formed, the company's name must be approved by the Registrar of Companies at the Board of Trade. The memorandum sets out the purpose for which the company has been formed and the amount and different classes of share capital; the articles of association represent a contract between the company and its shareholders and therefore set the legal framework of the company (e.g. by specifying the powers of the directors).

The Company Secretary is the official correspondent of the Board of Directors and he is responsible for ensuring that all the legal requirements of the business are met (e.g. by drawing up contracts) and, in addition, he may also assume general supervision over matters of internal administration.

FURTHER READING

Milward, G. E., *Organisation and Methods*, MacMillan.
Laver, F. J. M., *Introducing Computers*, H.M.S.O.
Duckworth, E., *A guide to Operational Research*, Methuen.
Walley, B. H., *A Manual of Office Administration*, Business Publications.
Chandor, A., *Practical Systems Analysis*, Hart-Davis.

QUESTIONS

1. Show that you understand the nature of office work and suggest reasons why an increasing proportion of the working population is engaged in office employment.
2. Describe the main stages of an O & M investigation.
3. Define the term 'Electronic Data Processing'. Identify, and briefly explain the functions of, the principal parts of a computer.
4. What would you expect to find between the covers of a *Systems Specification*?
5. Explain the activities of a Management Services department.

CHAPTER SEVEN

Communications

7.1 THE IMPORTANCE OF COMMUNICATIONS

AN important aspect of the writers of the 'Social Systems' School of Organisation Theory (see page 29) is the attention they give to the special problem of communication. **Information Theory** or **Communication Theory** is a new management science, which has developed from a book published in 1948 by Norbert Wiener. Wiener coined the word **cybernetics**: the science of communication and control in the animal and the machine; the word derives from the Greek word *kybernetes*, a steersman, one who maintains a ship on its correct course.

Information theory is concerned with the problems of defining and analysing information and of examining the stages of communication, which are identified as follows:

(a) Framing a message for transmission
(b) Transmitting the message
(c) Receiving the message
(d) Ensuring that the message has reached its destination
(e) Ensuring that some desired action has been produced as a result of receiving the message which has been communicated

These stages are to be found in communication systems in animal life and also in mechanical devices; the activity of the brain in relation to an upset stomach, which makes you vomit when you have eaten too much, is an example of a communication system, so is the way in which a steam-engine works. Consider the example of a communication in the form of a conversation in the middle of a large crowd at a football match. In speech, the message for transmission is framed in the brain and transmitted by the larynx. The communication is transmitted through a *medium* (in this case, the air) and the *receiver*, which is trying to pick up the signals being transmitted, is the ear of the listener. The presence of any distortion in the medium (such as the roar of the crowd as a goal is scored) makes the message difficult to hear and so it may be misunderstood.

The object of communication is to transmit information. **Information** may be defined as any message which removes prior uncertainty. The receipt of a memorandum from your immediate superior does not yield information if you know in advance exactly what its contents will be and it yields you a great deal of information if the contents cause you any astonishment. One problem in communication is to decide what information must be transmitted in order to produce some desired response; communication theorists use the term , **redundancy** to describe the situation where messages contain more information than is strictly necessary. You will see the relevance of this concept if you think of the example of sending three identical telegrams just to make sure that one gets through; communications that are over-elaborate cost time and money.

In essence, good communication means the transfer of an idea from A's mind to B's, avoiding the expense of 'redundancy' and also avoiding any distortions that may give rise to misunderstanding. In communication theory the term **noise** is a technical term which means any impediment to the transmission of a clear message.

The process of communication involves four main problems;

(a) The technical problem; the task of transmitting information.

(b) The semantic problem; the task of ensuring that messages convey some desired meaning.

(c) The effectiveness problem; the task of ensuring that messages produce some desired response.

(d) The feedback problem; the task of providing for messages to come back through the system to advise the transmitter of the original message of any corrective action that might be required.

You will find it instructive to consider the special problems of communication in relation to the advertisements that you see in newspapers, magazines and on television. Try to evaluate the effectiveness of particular advertisements in relation to:

(a) The copy: is the message clear and unambiguous?

(b) The medium: is the message likely to reach those for whom it is intended? Are there any differences in copy, format, style, illustration between advertisements for products in *Reveille, Tit Bits, Woman,* The *Daily Mirror,* The *Sunday Telegraph,* The *Observer, Management Today?*

In business enterprise, it is of paramount importance to design communication channels with an awareness of the special problems of technique, semantics, effectiveness and feedback, to remove 'redundancy' and to keep 'noise' to a minimum because communications have both an internal impact (as between supervisors and subordinates, between departments and divisions of the company) and also a vital role in relation to individuals and organisations outside the company (share-holders, customers, distribution channels, the general public and the Government).

7.2 METHODS OF COMMUNICATION

Communication channels should be devised to feed specific decision areas in the company and it is necessary for management to spell out precisely what information is required, who is to transmit it and how and when it is to be transmitted.

The two main methods by which ideas may be transmitted are:

(a) By speech (oral communication), as in interviews, telephone calls, lectures, seminars, committee meetings, conferences.

(b) In writing (written communication), as in letters, memoranda, routine reports, special reports, organisation manuals.

Management must be aware of the special skills involved in communication and in large companies specialists provide training in the following key activities:

(a) Framing the message to be transmitted, through courses in making speeches, report writing, computer programming, systems analysis.

(b) Transmitting messages, through training in the evaluation and use of specialised mechanical equipment (telephones, dictating machines, machines for recording telephone messages, typewriters, duplicating machines, data processing equipment).

(c) Receiving messages, through training in special skills and processes, the learning of technical terms peculiar to the company.

In particular, management must ensure that the personnel who work on the main communication channels understand the purpose of communications and realise that the responsibility for clarity lies with the person who is trying to communicate the message. This means that management must design communications systems and also ensure that their subordinates are able to use them. Take, for example, the problem of form design. Consider the problems of a company which recruits clerical labour for the purpose of maintaining records of stock movements. The company may well find that most of its applicants are married women in their early forties, who have returned to work after their children have grown up and who have not used a pen regularly for twenty-five years. The

221

nature of the documents used to record control information will obviously differ considerably from those used for, say, recording experiments made by physicists in a research laboratory, not only because the information to be recorded is different, but because different types of people are filling in the forms and using them. Similarly, when salesmen are sent on tours of their regions to sell soap to retailers, they do not send back reports to the marketing executive in the form of descriptive essays written on blank quarto paper; their reports are routinised and the information required by management is set out on a carefully designed and preprinted form.

Written communications have a special significance in business. They can be retained as legal records and as reference sources and they are usually expressed more carefully than oral communications. Special emphasis is placed on reports of a non-routine nature because they are more likely to contain information on some new aspect of company activity, where there are no set guidelines to guide the communicator.

Consider some of the problems faced by the Government in communicating with such diverse groups as foreign governments, old age pensioners, tax payers, the parties in some serious industrial dispute, the electorate at large. To reach such varied categories of people the Government might use posters, television programmes, advertisements in newspapers; it may communicate directly by mail or by arranging interviews with M.P.s and civil servants. Special problems may be referred to specially constituted committees of inquiry by who, in turn, reports may be published in various styles. The Government publishes 'popular' versions of some reports, written in a simplified style and often illustrated by means of simple diagrams and charts, when it wishes information to reach a wide audience. When an important change in Government policy is thought necessary, first thoughts on reform are usually published in *Green Papers*, which are documents meant to be used as the basis for discussion, further investigation and representation before a decision is made in any particular direction. These publications are usually followed by *White Papers*, which set out Government proposals for action and from these (and from suggestions for amendment made in representations to ministers and to Parliament) bills are prepared to be laid before Parliament. Sometimes 'leaks' of information are arranged as a means of testing possible reactions to new proposals. If information 'leaked' provokes a storm of protest, the 'leak' can always be denied and nobody loses face as a result, so the proposals can be quietly dropped. You will find it a useful exercise to consider how central and local government departments might set about the task of communicating the following types of information:

Nature of information:	*To be communicated to:*
General advice on careers	School leavers
Changes in income tax	Tax payers
Changes in social security benefits for the chronically sick	The chronically sick
The ingredients of a patent medicine have undesirable side effects	Doctors, consumers, manufacturers

Remember that the purpose of a system of communications within a company is to ensure that everyone is aware of what the organisation is setting out to achieve. Communications upwards, downwards and laterally (see page 23) will each have separate requirements as to method, format and frequency. Members of an organisation may receive information by means of interviews, lectures, film shows, posters, notices, memoranda, reports, committee meetings, house magazines and also along 'the grapevine'. Organisations are made up of different groups, for some of whom special methods of communication may have to be devised (as in the case of a group of immigrant workers in a factory, none of whom has a good command of English). Whatever methods are used, they must be related to the goals of the organisation as a whole.

The last section of this chapter is devoted to the special problems of report writing and it is designed to help you to write reports in a business environment and also to write reports under examination conditions, for which the technique is slightly different.

7.3 THE WRITING OF REPORTS

A report is a statement of information required by some superior authority and often records the results of an investigation. In report writing five points must be clarified at the beginning:

1. The purpose of the report.
2. The terms of reference of the report writer(s).
3. The identity of the report writer(s).
4. The identity of the person(s) to whom the report is addressed.
5. Timing: the period to which the report is related and the date of presentation.

These five elements should be incorporated into the heading and introduction to the report (not necessarily in the order given above) as under:

To: Mr Charles Furth,
     Director, George Allen & Unwin Limited.

From: J. A. W. Davies & G. B. L. Johnson,
     Editor and Contributing Author, 'A First Course in Business Organisation'.

SPECIAL REPORT

TITLE: Survey of the market for a new text book for first-year students of Business Studies in the period 1971–74.

TERMS OF REFERENCE:
   To examine the availability of textbooks for first-year students of Business Studies in Technical Colleges in the U.K., 1970–75 and to determine consumer needs in the market for the period 1975–80.

Once the purpose, title, terms of reference and the identities of interested parties have been established, reports should be organised into five main divisions as follows:

1. Method
2. Conclusions
3. Recommendations
4. Discussion
5. Appendices

Method. This is a statement of how the report was compiled and what sources were used.

Conclusions. This section is given first in order to save the reader's time. The main conclusions are given in the form of a summary, in short crisp sentences. It is often helpful to use very short sentences, each identified by a number.

Recommendations. These should follow from the conclusions and should identify what action is required, when and by whom.

Discussion. This is the main body of the report, in which the results of the investigation undertaken by the writer are explained in detail in the form of a narrative. The use of subheadings and numbered paragraphs is useful because it enables information to be passed over in intelligible and self-contained units and it also allows sections of the report to be identified easily for subsequent discussion.

Information must be passed to the reader without the possibility of any misunderstanding, therefore visual aids (graphs, charts, diagrams, photographs) may be used if they help understanding. It may be preferable to relegate statistical material to appendices, especially if there is a danger that the narrative will be impeded by sets of tables.

Appendix. Appendices should contain supplementary material which might impede the flow of information in the discussion. Examples of the sort of information which might go into appendices are:

(a) Lists of organisations or people who have contributed views on the subject of the report.

(b) Complete sets of statistical tables, such as the statistical bases of graphs and charts used in the discussion.

(c) Supporting material outside the direct line of the writer's investigations, but contributing to the conclusions expressed in the report.

(d) Dissenting views. When a report is prepared by a committee, minority opinions on certain issues are sometimes expressed in one of the appendices.

You will find it useful to refer to your public library for copies of the reports of the Prices and Incomes Board. These reports are presented on a wide number of subjects and many of them are models of clarity and organisation. The following are particularly useful:

Report No. 4: Prices of Household and Toilet Soaps, Soap Powders and Soap Flakes, and Soapless Detergents. (Cmnd 2791.)
Report No. 63: Pay of Municipal Busmen. (Cmnd 3625).
Report No. 73: The Prices of Hoover Domestic Appliances (Cmnd 3671.)

Report Writing Under Examination Conditions

The writing of reports under examination conditions presents several special problems, the most important of which is time. Many examinations require candidates to write some answers in report form and this section is devoted to the special problem of writing a report on a given subject without a great deal of background information, in about half an hour.

The principles outlined in the previous section hold good, but it is not possible to use the same format for obvious reasons; detailed statistical information is not available and there is no time to separate

H

out conclusions and recommendations from the discussion. The following guidelines should help you:

1. Set out the purpose, terms of reference, identity of the report writer, identity of the person(s) to whom the report is addressed as given in the previous section. Use the names and titles given in the question and write the report in your own name (unless there is a specific regulation to the contrary); do no waste nervous energy in thinking up elaborate or amusing pseudonymns (they tend to irritate examiners, anyway!).

2. Set out the method according to which you think the report should be prepared.

3. Set out your discussion under subheadings. Here you will have to use your own ingenuity, because part of the exercise is to see how well you can identify the main decision areas that are relevant to the question.

When you have identified the main decision areas and decided what your subheadings are going to be, arrange them in some logical order and write a paragraph or so under each heading. One vitally important point here: *do not make assumptions unless they are explicit in the question.*

4. End your report with some brief recommendations, given in some order of priority and indicate what action is required, *when* and by *whom.*

5. Sign the report with your own name (unless there is a specific regulation to the contrary).

Consider the following question:

The Marketing Director of Universal Soap Limited is required to administer a campaign in which vanity cases are to be offered to purchasers of the Company's product, Gremlin Beauty Soap, when they return five wrappers with 75p. You are a trainee in the Marketing Division and you are asked to make recommendations to the Marketing Director on the administration of the Scheme.

The discussion section of such a report could be divided up as follows. See if you can write a paragraph or two under each of the divisions given:

Internal Organisation

(a) Timing, whether the campaign is to be national or regional.

(b) Allocation of responsibility for the various management activities involved in the campaign, such as, receipt of wrappers and remittances from customers, despatch of cases, stock control.

External Organisation

(a) Purchasing of cases, returns of any surpluses.

(b) Media to be used to communicate the special offer.

Statistical Returns: (a) Frequency and timing of returns of costs and revenue whilst the special offer is open, and (b) What information is to be circulated (and to whom) when the campaign is over.

Of course, this list is not exhaustive, but it is an example of what is manageable in the context of an essay to be written in half an hour under examination conditions.

FURTHER READING

Barry, *The Fundamentals of Management*, Allen & Unwin.

Gowers, *The Complete Plain Words*, Pelican.

Little, *Communications in Business*, Longmans.

O'Shaughnessy, *Business Organisation*, Allen & Unwin.

Sidney, *Business Report Writing*, Business Publications.

QUESTIONS

1. The board of a raincoat manufacturing company, with capital employed of about £250,000, has discussed the possibility of increasing the company sales by entering the export field. You are required to advise the board about the information necessary to enable a decision to be made whether to export or not, and to state the sources from which advisory information for exporters may be obtained (A.C.C.A.).

2. You are the recently appointed production manager of a new factory owned by a large public company. You are requested by the chairman of the company to prepare a report advising him of (a) The main factors to be considered in the selection and training of production control staff, and (b) The duties and responsibilities of the staff of the production section (A.C.C.A.).

3. Your company is planning to acquire a computer. You are required to submit a report to the chairman in which the various stages of a feasibility study are defined and the main considerations which determine the configuration of a computer system are detailed (A.C.C.A.).

4. Why is the subject of communication of such importance in large-scale business and industry? What steps can be taken to improve internal communications at all levels in a business organisation? (A.C.C.A.)

227

5. You have been asked by your managing director to prepare a report on the concept of 'management by objectives'. In your report you are asked not only to define this term but also to set out how the objectives, when decided, are to be transmitted through the organisation so that all levels of management are aware of the current objectives (A.C.C.A.).

CHAPTER EIGHT

Case Studies

A CASE STUDY is an illustration of how a decision is arrived at in a particular context. Case studies may be presented in one of two ways and take the form of either:

(a) A description of how people react, as individuals or as groups, to a particular problem in a given situation.

(b) A description of the main components of a problem in a specific social, commercial or industrial context.

The task of the student in each case is to provide a solution of his own. In the case of (a) this could take the form of an analysis of individual and group reactions after which the student either confirms the actions taken by the role players in the case study, or criticies them and offers an alternative solution; in the case of (b) the student is required to work out his own solutions from scratch. Some case studies are numerical in form, so that it is possible to calculate a correct answer; others involve human problems so that there may be no perfect answer. Case studies are used to teach and they give students the opportunity to show that they can apply principles to a specific problem.

In this chapter we present nine case studies for discussion. Some are numerical and the correct answers are given in the Appendix. The remainder are not amenable to any simple solution and what you must do with them is to try to identify the main components of the problem presented and then decide on a feasible solution. All the case studies in this chapter may be used profitably as subjects for exercises in report writing.

Case Study No 1

The Market Research Department of a manufacturing company has calculated the following relationship between the market price of the company's product and consumer demand.

Retail price (p)	Unit sales (millions)
50	25
100	20
150	15
200	10
250	5

The product is marketed through a chain of retailers and retailers receive a discount of 50 per cent off the retail price (for every article that sells for £1 over the counter, the manufacturer receives 50p).

The Production Department have produced the following figures to show the relationship between quantities produced and unit variable cost at various output levels.

Quantities produced (millions)	Unit variable cost (p)
up to 9	40
up to 15	30
up to 20	25
up to 24	20
25 and over	10

The company has to meet the following Fixed Costs annually:

Factory Overheads	£1,000,000
Administration Overheads	£400,000

QUESTIONS

1. At which of the retail prices given would you sell in order to maximise profit? How much profit would you expect to make?

The Fixed Costs given above include a small sum which is spent on trade advertising. The question of whether to advertise more widely has been raised by top management and, after an examination of the activities of competitors, the Marketing Manager estimates that next year sales could be increased by 10 per cent if a further £500,000 was spent on advertising. This conclusion is represented in the table below:

Retail price (p)	This year	Unit sales Next year, with extra advertising (millions)
50	25	27·5
100	20	22
150	15	16·5
200	10	11
250	5	5·5

2. Should the extra spending on advertising be approved? At what retail price would you sell next year in order to maximise profit? How much profit would you expect to make?

Case Study No 2

The Dreadnought Manufacturing Company is situated on the edge of a large industrial estate in the Midlands and supplies machinery and components for the motor-car industry. The company employs 700 people, 300 of whom are office staff. The company decided to introduce a job evaluation scheme for clerical staff in January this year because it had discovered that the following factors had given rise to a big increase in turnover amongst office staff:

(a) Increases in salaries offered by other firms in the area for similar jobs.

(b) Poor morale in the Accounts Department because of wide differences in rates of pay for similar jobs, these differentials having originated from merit increases awarded in a haphazard fashion in the past.

(c) A lack of incentive for employees to improve performance in their present jobs and to qualify for promotion.

The previous Personnel Manager, Bill Benbow, left the company before Christmas and in February Joe Daniels, a recently qualified university graduate, was appointed in in his place. Joe began the job evaluation programme by sending a memorandum to each employee on the office staff, to which was attached a questionnaire which the employees were required to fill in, giving details of the tasks they performed.

When the questionnaires were returned, Joe called a meeting of managers and supervisors to discuss the replies received. In many cases both managers and supervisors queried the returns made by their subordinates and in some cases it was claimed that the replies to the questionnaires were wholly inaccurate records of the tasks that were actually being performed.

After the meeting, Mike O'Grady, a supervisor in the Accounts Department, challenged two members of his staff, David Wilson and Mary Lofthouse and accused them of claiming to do jobs that they did not do. Both insisted that O'Grady was not aware of what was going on in his own section and were so incensed that they referred the matter to their union representative. The union representative has called on the Accounts Manager and he, in turn, has now sent for Joe Daniels.

231

Joe Daniels now has several problems. He only wanted to find out what was involved in each job, but now he is involved in a dispute on the allocation of work in the Accounts Department as well.

QUESTIONS

1. How should he resolve the dispute in the Accounts Department?
2. How should he try to prevent the same situation from arising in other departments?
3. What should be his next step in installing the job evaluation scheme?

Case Study No 3

James Jones is a senior Local Government official and earns £4,000 per annum. He is due to retire in 5 years' time and he can expect a pension of £2,500 per annum then. If he were to retire now he would receive a pension of £1,500 per annum.

Jones's aunt has died recently and left him £100,000 in her will. A close friend of Jones's, Brian Keers, is a builder, and one evening, when they were discussing the bequest, Keers tried to persuade Jones to invest £50,000 in his business, which is very short of capital. The growth prospects of the business seem to be good because of a great increase in building activity in the area. Jones wishes to make the best possible use of his inheritance and last week he asked his friend for further details.

The accounting year end was just completed and Keers asked his accountant for a provisional Income Statement and a Balance Sheet to show the position at the year end. He has presented this information to Jones and used it to forecast the effect which an additional £50,000 would have on the business.

The provisional accounts are given below:

INCOME STATEMENT

		£
Sales		150,000
Cost of Sales		120,000
		30,000
Less:		
Administration Expenses	15,000	
Selling Expenses	3,000	
		18,000
		12,000
Less Depreciation		2,000
Profit		£10,000

BALANCE SHEET

Capital	100,000	Fixed Assets (at Cost)	110,000	
Add Profits	10,000			
	110,000	*Less* Depreciation to date	15,000	
				95,000
Creditors	10,000			
		Stocks	6,000	
		Debtors	6,000	
		Cash	13,000	
				25,000
	£120,000			£120,000

Keers says that his personal withdrawals for the period are not shown in these statements. He estimates them at £10,000, which would have the effect of reducing total capital to £100,000 and cash to £3,000.

Keers estimates that with additional capital of £50,000 he would be able to expand sales for the coming year to £250,000. Cost of Sales, he estimates, would remain the same percentage of sales as before, Administration and Selling Expenses would increase by £5,000 and £3,000 respectively. Keers offers Jones a part-time partnership by which he would receive a one-fifth share of the profits.

After further discussions, Keers comes to the conclusion that Jones's financial and administrative abilities could be a great asset to the business. Consequently, he asks Jones to consider resigning from his present job in order to join the firm on a full-time basis. Keers reckons that this action would involve an increase in administrative expenses by £3,000 in the coming year. If Jones accepts this proposal, Keers is prepared to offer a one-third share in the profits.

QUESTIONS

Advise Jones. Should he accept the offer of a part-time partnership? Would he be better advised to join Keers on a full-time basis? Are there any other outside factors that should be taken into consideration?

Case Study No 4

Five years ago Machine Tools Limited decided that some action should be taken to obtain a clearer financial picture of the affairs of the business. The company had relied on the audited accounts produced each year but the executives were aware that fluctuations in the fortunes of the business were taking place on a smaller time scale. Accordingly, monthly accounts were prepared as soon as possible after the end of each month and these were broken down into departmental statements for each departmental executive.

Recently, a review was made of the adequacy of the financial information provided to management and an attempt made to assess any possible economies in the provision of information. The transport manager stated that he thought the information given to his department could be discontinued and gave these reasons:

(a) In the main, the statements received told him what he already knew.

(b) Despite the fact that the accountant prepared the statements, he none the less always had to approach the transport manager for explanations of deviations. The transport manager felt that he could identify and cope with deviations in his department without the help from the accountant.

(c) The financial information represented activities in financial terms. Other associated statistics were provided by the transport department. Control had to be maintained by other measures, e.g. miles run per vehicle (loaded and empty), information available in the transport department.

The accountant's reply raised the following questions:

(a) Was the transport manager aware of the deviations from normal before receiving the accounting information?

(b) Could all control information be identified and assembled in non-monetary terms?

QUESTIONS

1. Do you think the statements made by the transport manager regarding his information could be made by other executives regarding the normal financial information received?

2. Should the related statistical information to financial data be prepared outside the accounting department?

3. Do you think the financial information for the transport department should be eliminated?

4. If you think the statements should be provided, what action would you take to ensure that the information is used effectively?

Case Study No 5

XYZ Limited is a large engineering concern with a head office and four factories in the Midlands and South-east, employing some 6,000 people. The Board of Directors have agreed, though with more resignation than enthusiasm, to a computer scheme of production control at one of the factories. It is not proposed to buy a computer at this stage; the intention is to buy 'computer time' at a service bureau belonging to one of the big computer manufacturers. If the scheme is successful a computer may be purchased.

A small team of two systems analysts, both recruited from within the company but based at head office, has been set up, reporting to the company accountant. Programming work will be carried out by staff at the bureau.

From the beginning the two analysts have been in trouble. In the Production Control department itself, resistance is total. Not the least of their difficulties has been the tacit support and sympathy which the factory manager is giving to the head of the Production Control department. It so happens that they are brothers-in-law. Apart from the 'too-busy-to-see-you' excuses and the like which the analysts meet daily, the Production Control department are saying:

(a) That the existing system is working perfectly well—and from their own past experience the analysts know this to be true.

(b) That the computer couldn't cope with the many exceptions there are to the straightforward system.

(c) That the form in which the computer prints out results is quite unacceptable, 'even if the results were correct anyway'.

The accountant at H.Q. is aware of the situation at the factory. He is also conscious of the resentment which the 'works people' feel against head office who in the words of the factory manager himself 'are now trying to start telling us what we have to make'. The accountant therefore asks the analysts to report formally to him about the situation with their recommendations about breaking the deadlock. They are not to be restricted in any way in the scope of their recommendations.

QUESTION

What kind of proposals might the analysts make?

Case Study No 6

In a small engineering works producing transformers, the production

235

planner has the following data available to help him to determine his next production schedule:

Materials	Copper: 600 cwt.
	Cast iron: 1,500 cwt.
Labour	5,000 man hours.

The factory produces three models with the following production costs:

	Copper (£30 per cwt)		Cast iron (£10 per cwt)		Man hours (£1 per hour)		Total cost
	cwt	£	cwt	£	cwt	£	£
Major	4	120	10	100	40	40	260
Minor	3	90	8	80	30	30	200
Minimus	2	60	6	60	20	20	140

Each model sells for a different price, giving the following profit situation:

	COST	PRICE	PROFIT	PROFIT PER MAN HOUR
	£	£	£	£
Major	260	330	70	1·75
Minor	200	245	45	1·5
Minimus	140	180	40	2·0

The sales director has already requested that 50 of each model be made in order to satisfy existing orders. The objective of the firm is to maximise profits.

QUESTIONS

1. What should the production schedule be?
2. What will be the total profit on the production schedule?
3. The **Major** shows the greatest profit per unit. Why should not the planner schedule for this model exclusively, once the sales director's orders have been carried out?

Case Study No 7

Production Control wishes to discover the 'economic lot size' (Q) for a factory which produces 2,000 cars a year (Y) each having a unit cost (U) of £1,000. The 'economic lot size' is the number of cars which the factory can process most economically, i.e. it is the size which will minimise preparation costs and stock-holding costs.

The larger the 'economic lot size' the lower the total preparation costs, for preparation costs come to a total of £5,000 per lot, regardless of the size of the lot.

Stockholding costs are determined by the formula:

$$S = \frac{Q \times U}{4}$$

so that the larger the 'economic lot' the higher total stock-holding costs become. In other words, as one cost increases the other decreases and vice versa.

The task of Production Control is to reconcile these two opposing forces so that combined preparation and stockholding costs are at a minimum.

QUESTIONS

1. The 'economic lot size' may be determined by the formula:

$$Q = \sqrt{\frac{4 \times Y \times P}{U}}$$

where Y is equal to the number of cars produced per annum and P is equal to the preparation costs per lot. Calculate Q.
2. What are the combined costs when producing at 'economic lot size'?
3. Examine combined costs for other lot sizes to prove that Q is the 'economic lot size'.

Case Study No 8

The Research and Development Manager of a group of iron foundries has at his disposal a small laboratory, three qualified scientists and three assistants. From time to time he borrows men and equipment from the production departments to help with his experiments, aimed largely at the improvement of existing products. He is also responsible for quality control and his staff spend about half their time in testing products before they are shipped to customers.

One of the group's major raw materials has trebled in price in the last few months and it looks as if the rise in price is going to continue for some time. The Research and Development Manager has been asked to examine the possibility of substituting different metals for the material that has risen in price.

237

In the past, the R & D Department has not been subject to strict budgetary control. Money has been allocated on an *ad hoc* basis, with the provision that any single item of expenditure greater than £250 must receive prior approval in writing from two members of the Board.

The company has been subject to a very severe credit 'squeeze' over the past few months and the Group Accountant now insists that a budgetary system must be introduced to cover all new projects. The R & D Manager protests that he cannot produce a budget for an activity where neither costs nor benefits can be calculated with any precision and says that he has enough paperwork to cope with already.

QUESTION

You have recently been recruited into the Accounts Department to improve the techniques of planning and budgetary control. Prepare a draft report to the Accounts Manager setting out some principles that might be applied to resolve this problem.

Case Study No 9

Bonzo Manufacturing Limited make pet foods and have recently been required to pay a levy to their Industrial Training Board. Training has previously been the responsibility of the line managers; the Personnel Department is very small and has largely been concerned with co-ordinating the recruitment and selection of staff and with the administration of terminations. Training schemes have been informal, at the discretion of the line manager concerned and mostly in the form of instruction 'on the job'.

The subject of Industrial Training has now come up at Board level and, as a result, Jock McTavish was appointed last month as Training Manager. McTavish's appointment was made at a personal interview with the Managing Director; he was previously employed as a section leader in the Accounts Department, will be 58 next birthday and is due to retire when he is 62.

McTavish has attempted to define training needs in the Accounts Department, but requests to grant time off to members of the department to study for professional qualifications and to attend short courses at the local technical college have been resisted by the Accountant, George Carey, on the grounds that:

(a) It has always been company policy to recruit qualified staff from outside the company in order to save the cost of training.

238

(b) The staff position is so critical that he cannot afford to release staff or else the work output of the department will be seriously affected.

The Personnel Manager, John Blunt, refuses to become involved in this dispute on the grounds that the relationship between himself and McTavish have never been clarified and because McTavish's appointment was made directly by the Managing Director.

QUESTION

How might McTavish proceed to carry out the job he was appointed to do?

FURTHER READING

Haynes and Massie, *Management: Analysis, Concepts and Cases*, Prentice Hall.

CHAPTER NINE

Appendices

9.1 HINTS ON EXAMINATION TECHNIQUE

THE following notes are intended to help you to make the best use of your resources when writing essays under examination conditions:

(a) **Plan your essay in advance.** Never begin an essay until you have worked out the main theme of each paragraph of your answer. This planning stage is the most important of all and may be done in the form of pencilled notes on your answer script, the notes to be crossed out when you have finished. Always begin with a straight definition of any terms of special significance in the question and be careful to define technical terms (if only briefly, perhaps in brackets) as you introduce them later in your essay. In your planning look for some means of classifying the subject-matter of the question. For example, if you are going to write about a management function, jot down the main sub-functions first and consider the application of the question to each in turn; in an essay on an organisational problem, try to classify the *levels* at which the problem may be tackled (for example, departmental/inter-departmental/factory/divisional/company-wide).

(b) **Use diagrams, graphs, charts** to illustrate your answers where possible, because they save time. Always be sure to devote a paragraph to explaining what your diagrams are intended to show.

(c) **Use examples** to illustrate the main points you make. Preferably, these should be taken from your reading and observation (remember your file of press clippings!).

(d) Make sure that the conclusions in your final paragraph are related to the material presented in the essay.

(e) Allow ten minutes at the beginning of an examination for a careful reading of all the questions (especially those that appear at first sight to be impossible) and, in particular, check if any of the questions are compulsory or if some questions carry more marks than others.

(f) Check the time regularly.

9.2 SOLUTIONS TO CASE STUDIES

As we have already explained, some of the case studies are amenable to a numerical solution, others are essentially starting-points for discussions, from which some action should be recommended in some order of priority. Below we give:

(a) Numerical solutions where they apply.

(b) Guidelines for further discussions and action for those case studies where there is no simple and straight-forward solution.

Case Study No 1

1. £2; £5·6 million.
2. Yes; £1.50; £6·35 million.

Case Study No 2

You should have questioned:

(a) The delay in appointing the new Personnel Manager.

(b) The use of the questionnaire.

You might recommend:

(a) The establishment of departmental job evaluation officers, selected from members of supervision in each department, to validate the details of each job with members of staff.

(b) Provision for training in job evaluation for those appointed to serve as evaluation officers.

(c) The setting up of formal machinery for the resolution of disputes.

Case Study No 3

You should have considered:

(a) The accuracy of Keers's forecast.

(b) The satisfaction that Jones might derive from working for himself.

(c) Alternative avenues of investment; the financial pages of the newspapers would be useful for this. We have assumed that current market conditions are likely to yield a safe 12 per cent on his £50,000, which would produce an income of £6,000 a year.

Calculations:

(a) Part-time he would earn £4,000 share in the profits plus £4,000 salary = £8,000 a year.

(b) Full-time he would earn £7,300 share in the profits plus £1,500 pension = £8,800 per year.

(c) Investment outside plus his salary (see the assumption in (c) above) = £10,000 a year.

Case Study No 4

You should have considered:

(a) The objectives of preparing financial data.

(b) How quickly corrective action might be taken under either system.

(c) The costs of providing management information balanced against likely benefits.

Case Study No 5

You should have considered:

(a) The chain of authority that was established.

(b) How company personnel were prepared for changes to come in the future.

(c) How confidence might be re-established in terms of: (i) Organisation. (ii) Communications.

Case Study No 6

1. 50 **Major**; 50 **Minor**; 75 **Minimus**.
2. £8,750.
3. Because profit per man hour is higher in the **Minimus**.

Case Study No 7

1. 200.   2. £50,000, £50,000; £100,000.

Case Study No 8

You might consider:

(a) Charging production departments for time spent on quality control, in order to isolate R & D costs.

(b) Allocating R & D costs to each project by means of the use of job cards.

(c) Providing analyses of costs and benefits on the basis of:

> most optimistic
> most likely.
> most pessimistic

estimates, so that senior management has a guideline against which to allocate further spending.

Case Study No 9

You should have questioned:

(a) The appointment of McTavish in the first place.

(b) Qualities and qualifications you would look for in a training officer.

(c) The lack of definition of formal relationships.

You might recommend:

(a) Publication of an organisation chart and terms of reference.

(b) The development of a policy document on training programmes, preceded perhaps by a meeting of managers attended by representatives of the Industrial Training Boards.

(c) Means of developing cost-benefit analysis to justify specific training programmes, relating to, for example, the cost of the levy, benefits from training programmes, impact on staff turnover, etc.

9.3 FINAL REVISION

We present in the next chapter a collection of questions for you to attempt. Before you do so, see how many of the following terms you can define without reference to the text:

Standard Costing	Administration
Opportunity Cost	'Fixed' Cost
Executive Role	Balance Sheet
Profit/Volume Ratio	Piece Rates
Management By Objectives	'Noise'
Job Enlargement	Batch Production
Operational Research	Liquid Ratio
Market Segment	Skills Analysis
Copy	Merchandising
Cybernetics	Product 'Mix'

Rights Issue
Discounted Cash Flow
Scalar Chain
Line Management
Merit Rating
Bureaucracy
Prime Cost
'Break-Even' Point
Egoistic Needs
O & M

Flow Chart
Test Marketing
Policy
Medium
Brand Image
Factoring
Functional Relationship
Motivation
Theory 'X'
Cost absorption

CHAPTER TEN

Further Examination Questions

1. Identify three organisational principles that you would expect to find in common, between:
   Imperial Chemical Industries Limited
   Manchester United Football Club Limited
   A Day Nursery
   The Ministry of Transport
2. What factors determine the limit to the number of subordinates a manager can manage?
3. Distinguish between 'forecasting' and 'planning'.
4. 'The basic aim of management must be to simplify the process of management.' Discuss this statement and suggest ways in which this aim may be achieved (A.C.C.S.).
5. 'Critical Path Analysis is not just a pretty picture, it pays.' Give a concise outline of this technique and show why it pays (A.C.C.S.).
6. In what ways can good public relations help a company? What practical aid can other sections and activities obtain from the public relations department of their company? (A.C.C.S.).
7. What do you understand by the marketing concept? Explain how the marketing division of a national company marketing consumer durables might be organised.
8. 'The marketing of a product is a complex process involving a number of differentiated activities.' Discuss.
9. Describe the functions of the market research department, and explain its relationship with other marketing departments.
10. 'Investment decisions are among the most difficult in business.' Why is this? Outline the factors which influence such decisions. In your answer distinguish between (i) a decision to establish a plant for a new product, and (ii) a decision to increase the output of an existing product (A.C.C.S.).
11. Describe how you would handle the advertising programme to launch a new non-alcoholic winter beverage, and include a suggested timing schedule.

12. 'Changing from one advertising agency to another is a drastic and often very expensive step for a company to take.' State some of the reasons which would cause a company to make this change and explain how you think it should select a new agency.

13. It has been said that sales promotion is at its best in achieving short-term tactical advantages. Name six methods of sales promotion and briefly illustrate how each may be employed.

14. State the purpose of a staff assessment scheme and outline the stages in the process of conducting a staff assessment (A.C.C.A.).

15. What qualities would you look for in selecting a sales force in the pharmaceutical industry?

16. How would you expect a company's public relations department to assist in achieving a firm's marketing objectives?

17. Consider the influences of equipment availability and consumer demand on product design (A.C.C.A.).

18. Outline the object, functions and membership of typical joint Production Consultation and Advisory Committees. What are the limitations of the functions of such committees? (A.C.C.A.).

19. Discuss the appropriate terms of reference for a Purchasing Officer in a large public company (U.L.C.I.).

20. Production Administration is concerned with:

   (a) Production Engineering
   (b) Production Planning,
   (c) Production Control,
   (d) Operational Research

   Describe briefly the Management responsibilities involved (U.L.C.I.).

21. Set out the steps necessary from the indication of a requirement through the placings of a purchase order to the final payment. What progress and other records would you keep to ensure that the goods are received on time and are, of the required quality and quantity (I.C.W.A.).

22. State what steps you would take to ensure the efficient use of power and fuel supplies in a factory (I.C.W.A.).

23. When laying out a factory what points would you take into consideration in order to ensure maximum production and that the supporting services are conveniently located? (I.C.W.A.).

24. Compare progress chasing with a progress reporting system. Describe the methods used in each (I.C.W.A.).

25. Assuming that the cost of land may be ignored, what economies would be achieved by erecting a single storey rather than a multi-storey building?

26. What are the main points to be considered in deciding upon the site of a factory?

27. Explain the value of an inspection department to an engineering firm which is manufacturing products which are intended to last for a limited period of time only (A.C.C.A.).

28. The following figures apply to a manufacturing company producing a wide range of products which may be classified into three main groups:

Product Group	Annual sales	Variable costs
	£	£
A	3,000,000	1,000,000
B	3,000,000	2,000,000
C	3,500,000	3,000,000

The fixed costs total £2,500,000.

Plot on a graph the contribution lines for the three product groups in alphabetical order to enable you to plot the average contribution line for the total output. What information may be derived from the graph? What conclusions can it be used to illustrate? (I.C.W.A.).

29. The following figures relate to a company manufacturing a varied range of products:

	Total sales	Total costs
	£	£
Year ended 31st Dec. 1968	3,900,000	3,480,000
Year ended 31st Dec. 1969	4,300,000	3,760,000

Assuming stability in prices, with variable costs carefully controlled to reflect predetermined relationships, and an unvarying figure for fixed costs, calculate:

(a) The P/V ratio to reflect the rates of growth for profit and for sales, and:

(b) Any other cost figures to be deduced from the data.

How may the P/V ratio be improved, apart from increasing selling prices or reducing costs? (I.C.W.A.).

30. A small private company, after several years of unprofitable trading, was taken over by a new management on the 31st December. The accounts for the following year were as follows:

247

	£
Direct Materials	78,000
Direct Wages	31,200
Variable Overheads	15,600
Fixed Overheads	30,000
Profit	1,200
Sales	156,000

The balance sheet as at the end of the first twelve months' trading was as follows:

	£		£
Share capital	40,000	Fixed assets	24,000
Creditors	19,500	Stocks	26,000
Bank overdraft	26,500	Debtors	26,000
		Profit & loss account	10,000
	86,000		86,000

The budgeted sales for the second year of trading are as follows:

	£
1st quarter	42,000
2nd quarter	45,000
3rd quarter	48,000
4th quarter	51,000

It is anticipated that the ratios of material consumption, direct wages and variable overheads to sales are unlikely to change, that fixed overheads (invoiced evenly during the year) will remain at £30,000 per annum, and that creditors can be held at three months direct material usage. Both stocks and debtors can be maintained at two months sales.

Bank interest and depreciation, the latter at 10 per cent per annum on fixed assets are included in the overheads. Prepare quarterly budgets for the second year of trading to indicate to management,

(a) Whether the results are likely to be satisfactory, and:
(b) Whether overdraft facilities (which are usually limited to £25,000) are sufficient, or whether further capital must be introduced (I.C.W.A.).

31. Would you advocate the launching of a cost reduction programme as part of the preparatory work of budgeting? Write briefly numbered paragraphs setting out the reasons for your answer (I.C.W.A.).

32. A manufacturing company produces three products, A. B and C. The processes by which they are produced are independent of one another and the sales of any one product are in no way affected by the prices or volume of sales of the other products. The company's budgeted Profit and Loss Statement is as follows:

	TOTAL	A	B	C
	£	£	£	£
Sales	200,000	30,000	20,000	150,000
Variable production cost	120,000	16,000	8,000	96,000
Fixed production cost (apportioned to products)	40,000	2,000	6,000	32,000
	160,000	18,000	14,000	128,000
Gross Profit	40,000	12,000	6,000	22,000
Variable selling and administration cost	16,000	5,400	5,200	5,400
Fixed selling and administration cost (apportioned to products)	4,000	1,400	1,400	1,200
	20,000	6,800	6,600	6,600
	TOTAL	A	B	C
	£	£	£	£
Net Profit	20,000	5,200	—	15,400
Net Loss	—	—	600	—

You may assume that bases of apportionment of fixed cost are acceptable.

In view of the loss shown by product 'B' the company proposes to eliminate that product from its range. You are required:

(a) To redraft the budgeted profit and loss statement to show the profit that would result if product 'B' were eliminated.

(b) To state whether or not you agree with the company's proposals—give your reasons very briefly (I.C.W.A.).

33. A machine purchased new in 1969 for £10,000 is capable of producing at the rate of 25 units per hour. A later model of the same machine is now on the market, costing £15,000 and capable of producing at the rate of 30 units per hour, and your Board

is considering the desirability of replacing the existing machine by the newer model. Describe the various economic factors which may influence the decision and indicate what information you would require in order to assess their importance (I.C.W.A.).

34. An existing accounting system lacks the essential aspects of cost control. List the main matters to be introduced to make good the systems deficiencies (I.C.W.A.).

35. The following budgeted information is available for one period in a factory which produces three products:

	Selling price £	Direct materials	Direct wages	Variable overheads	Production Units	Sales Units
X	3·00	70p	80p	10p	16,000	13,600
Y	2·50	55p	70p	5p	10,000	9,600
Z	2·00	23½p	60p	6½p	8,000	7,200

There is no stock at the beginning of the period. Fixed overhead is absorbed on the basis of direct wages. Budgeted total costs are £70,400 for the period. You are required to:

(a) Prepare a statement having budgeted profit for the period; and:

(b) Show the value of the budgeted stock of each product at the end of the period.

Your answer should show the information required on the basis of marginal and absorption product costing. (I.C.W.A.).

36. An attitude may be defined as a mental readiness or an inclination to act in certain ways. Discuss the factors which determine attitudes and indicate the ways in which attitudes can effect managements' aims.

37. Describe the features which make an incentive acceptable to both employer and employee.

38. What are some of the needs of the employee in terms of work satisfaction and suggest ways in which management can utilize these to benefit both the firm and employee.

39. The planned interview is more effective than a casual meeting between the employer and the person seeking employment. Suggest criteria for structuring a selection interview.

40. The introduction of work study teams often causes conflict. What are the benefits for the worker from work study operations? and how would you attempt to overcome the conflict caused?

41. Why is a recognition of individual differences on the work place

so important to the manager? What are some of the individual differences? Show the need for careful selection of employees.

42. The Industrial Training Act has led to a revolution of attitude towards the responsibilities for training. Discuss this statement and briefly describe the features in a training programme.

43. Rapid technological change in our society brings attendant socio-economic pressure on workers. How might this effect a firm's personnel policy?

44. Assuming that you have been detailed to carry out an organisation and methods review of a purchasing department, prepare a list of the questions which you would ask, in order to ensure that you were able to obtain a reasonably clear picture of the activities and operations of the department (I.C.W.A.).

45. At present, a company permits every department to design and order its own forms. In the belief that it will be more economical and will raise the standard of form design, a senior clerk has been charged with responsibility for this function. Indicate those factors which he should bear in mind when each new form or set of forms comes up for ordering or re-ordering (I.C.W.A.).

46. Draw an organisation chart of a typical computer installation. What are the duties of the different kinds of staff working in a computer installation?

47. A company has for many years been trading as a wholesaler of children's toys.

The company was founded by Mr X who owns 50 per cent of the shares, the balance of which are held equally by his two sons, who have run the company for the last five years. Due to the rapid expansion of the business in the last two years the sons find that they can no longer efficiently organise the detailed functioning of all the departments of the firm.

Outline a scheme for the consideration of the directors of the company (Mr X and his two sons), stating how the company should be organised so that the two sons will retain control over policy and general organisation (A.C.C.A.).

48. Describe the methods you would use to assess the efficiency of the employees in a general office (R.S.A.).

49. What matters would you deal with if you were asked to draft conditions of employment for the staff of a general office? In your answer refer to recent legislation on this subject (R.S.A.).

50. 'Since the determination of advertising appropriation by firms is in most cases irrational, it follows that a large part of annual expenditure on advertising represents a wasteful application of resources' (INSTITUTE OF MARKETING). Discuss.

251

INDEX